PERRY
A DRINKER'S GUIDE

ADAM WELLS

CAMRA
BOOKS

For my parents.
For Caroline (and Nutmeg).
For everyone in *that* WhatsApp group
and perrymakers everywhere.
But most of all, for Greg.

Published by the Campaign for Real Ale Ltd.
230 Hatfield Road, St Albans, Hertfordshire AL1 4LW, United Kingdom
www.camra.org.uk/books

© Campaign for Real Ale Ltd. 2024

ISBN 978-1-85249-388-2

A CIP catalogue record for this book is available from the British Library

Printed and bound in the United Kingdom by Short Run Press, Exeter.

Managing Editor: Alan Murphy
Design/Typography: Dale Tomlinson
Cover Design: David Wardle
Sales & Marketing: Toby Langdon

PHOTOGRAPHY CREDITS

The majority of photos in this book were supplied by
Helen Anne Smith (pages 2, 3, 7, 9, 11, 12, 14, 17, 18, 19,
20, 22, 24, 25, 31, 33, 35, 36, 37, 38, 40, 41, 42, 43, 45, 47,
50, 51, 53, 54, 55, 56, 60, 62, 65, 66, 67, 68, 69, 70, 72, 73,
74, 75, 78, 82, 88, 89, 90, 91, 92, 93, 94, 96, 97, 99, 100,
104, 107, 109, 111, 114, 116, 118, 122, 163, 164, 165, 166,
167, 168, 169, 170, 171, 172, 173, 174, 175, 176, 179, 283,
284) and Lucy Wells (pages 10, 108, 119, 120, 123, 125,
127, 128, 130, 132, 133, 135, 138, 141, 145, 147, 148, 149,
150, 151, 152, 153, 154, 155).

The Publisher would also like to thank all those who
kindly granted permission for their photography
to be used in the book: Showerings Cider; Barry
Masterson; Haritz Rodriguez; Becky Fletcher; Steve
Selin; Billie Charity; Dave Matthews; Anna Gazeley;
Karl Brennan; Matilda Temperley; Martin Harris;
Mathilde de Bazouges; Barney Wilczak; Paul Ligas
Photography; Alex Martin; Paul Ross; Momō Cider
& Distilling Museum; Tom Sloan; Robbie Fleming;
Virginie Thomas; Pacory Gaec des Grimeaux;
Dan Barker Studios; Sascha Walz; Bernadette
Haselberger; Veronika Roosimaa; Louis Laurent
Grandadam; Ben Llewellyn; Lee Reeve; Barry
Walsh; Ap-Art Photography; Alex Simmens; Jonny
Mills; Natalie Waller; Mark Evens; Māris Plūme;
Nashi Orchards; Matt Hickman; The Stock Journal;
Mathias Weis; Dave Carr; Veronique Kolber;
David Nash; Mike Shorland; Adam Davies; Trevor
Fitzjohn; James Fergusson; Arjen Meeuwsen;
Elizabeth Lockhart; Eric Bordelet; Melissa Madden;
Jonathan Gould; Chris Watt Photography.

Contents

ACKNOWLEDGEMENTS

Writing, researching and getting a book published under any circumstances is a massive endeavour. Writing and researching an international subject that has had such minimal historic coverage and then persuading a publisher to take such a niche-within-a-niche subject has seemed, at times, impossible, and indeed, without a large number of extraordinary people it would have been. The book was only made possible by a kickstarter whose contributors blew me away with their generosity. I still can't believe you got it over the line on day one – and I'll never forget it.

But in no particular order, for their additional expertise, advice, insights, assistances and encouragements, my eternal gratitude to: James and Susanna Forbes, Mike Johnson and the team at Ross-on-Wye, Tom Oliver, the team at the Museum of Cider, especially Elisha Mason and Elizabeth Pimblett, Yann Gilles (without whom there would be no meaningful French section), Jérôme Forget, Antoine Marois, Jacques Perritaz, Peter and Bernadette Haselberger, Toni Distelberger, Mostviertel Tourismus (the visit to Austria made this book finally doable), James Crowden, Eleanor Leger, Autumn Stoscheck, Gabe Cook (the Ciderologist and patron saint of cider and perry content), Jim Chapman and Charles Martell, Hanspeter Kreis, Andrew Lea, Phill Palmer, Mike Penney, Gregory Peck, Will Rea (whose help and expertise gave me a chance at a USA section), Lee Reeve, Rita Krawczyk, Nick Geoghegan and Warwick Billings (who made Australia possible). Andrea Bedini and Marco Manfrini (who nipped in late with fantastic information on Italy that would otherwise have passed me by completely). An extra big shout-out to legend of the French cider and perry scene Virginie Thomas who jumped in to save me with photos for the France section as well as to one of my oldest friends, Dave Martin, my Domfrontais travelling companion and kind chauffeur, and, of course, Lucy Wells and our photography day perry-drinking models, Caroline, Diana, Esther, Imogen and Justin. Not forgetting my parents, Graham and Sue, whose support is without limit (and who always have perry in the fridge).

Particular thanks also to those who lobbied at CAMRA for this project and, against all the odds, made a book about perry actually happen. Especially Dick Withecombe, Gillian Hough, Cath Potter, Camilla Weddell, Toby Langdon, Ellie Hudspith, Alex Metcalfe, and my endlessly patient and encouraging editor Alan Murphy.

Without Barry Masterson this book – especially sections on Central Europe and perry history more broadly – would be a husk. There's no more passionate perry advocate, and, my goodness, have I been lucky to know him during this project, as any number of emails and whatsapps can attest.

No one in the world of perry gives me more support than the wonderful, inspiring group of people Caroline calls 'the cider buddies'. Becky, James, Justin and Rachel – your friendship, wisdom, encouragement and tangential asides (alright, that last one's usually me) mean the world, and none of this would be the same without you. Helen, whose gorgeous photography dominates this book and has brought it to life. I'll remember all our expeditions, especially that walk down from May Hill. And Albert, without whom almost nothing that I've done or discovered within cider and perry would have been possible.

Most importantly, to Caroline, who has lived with every moment of this project – every joy and discovery, every gripe and grumble, every time I've convinced myself it wasn't possible, was a terrible idea, was a dreadful piece of writing. For everything you are and do, my thanks and love forever.

And last of all to Nutmeg, for the moments of respite you gave me from having my ankle grabbed or chewed, during which time I just about got the thing written.

Foreword

By **Albert Johnson**
Ross-on-Wye Cider & Perry Company

Perry is to pears what cider is to apples. There. That's it, right? Actually, no.

Adam Wells, celebrated perry and cider advocate, author of more articles on perry than perhaps anyone else in Britain, and definitely the person best suited to write this book for you, is about to take you on a journey around the world, discovering the wonders of one of the most challenging drinks to produce, from its major regions of the Three Counties, Normandy and the Mostviertel, to the small producers the world over who are now celebrating the noble pear.

Perry is a drink on the precipice, turned by commercial endeavour into a 'long' drink and having its soul slowly eroded by marketing. Now, readers like yourself are beginning to see perry in a new light. Aided by the journalism of Adam and others, the authenticity, the provenance, the sustainability of true perrymaking is being showcased, celebrated and sought after once again. The multi-generations-old varieties of pear that have been treasured for so long are being proudly displayed on the front of bottles, as perry enthusiasts in Britain are offered a menu with higher quality and more choice than ever before. The ranks of traditional, small producers who have been making perry and serving it at CAMRA festivals for decades are being augmented by new, even smaller producers, inspired by the opportunity to make a drink that has flavour and character like nothing else.

However, fireblight lurks on the horizon. This bacterial disease is becoming more dangerous and more common as a consequence of climate change, meaning that perry pear trees are under serious threat. On our farm in south Herefordshire, we have had to cut down a third of the pear trees that my father planted 40 years ago, and still we see signs of the disease. The struggle of today is that our varieties of pear were selected before fireblight existed in Europe, and so we have no way to know if the tree has resistance to it or not. Some varieties may die out by the end of the decade. There's not a moment to lose in ordering a glass of perry if you don't want to miss out!

Importantly, though, there is space to hope. A book on perry written for you, the drinker, is a first, and a huge step forward to celebrate this drink. The following pages will make you laugh, gasp, cry out, and most definitely develop a thirst – as Adam masterfully takes you from the orchard to the glass, telling the story of the challenges and delights of perrymaking. And as you read and marvel and imagine, you may find yourself joining in with the producers that make the tapestry of perry so rich. Everyone starts somewhere, so perhaps when you come back to read this book for a second time (and I am sure you will), you might call yourself not just a perry drinker, but a perrymaker too.

Welcome to the club.

INTRODUCTION

I want to tell you about a miracle drink. A drink dating from as far back as ancient Rome – conceivably centuries earlier. A drink that has been, at different times, a sneered-at thirst-quencher for society's poorest and poured for nobility at prices that rivalled French wine. A drink made from fruit whose trees grow taller than houses and can live 300 years or more. A drink that has faced extinction at some point in its life everywhere it is made, but which has hung on, sometimes by a thread, thanks to the grit and care and will and love and sheer bloody-mindedness of people who knew it to be too great a treasure to lose. I want to tell you about perry.

What is perry? In simple terms, it is to pears what wine is to grapes and cider to apples: pressed fruit juice, fermented by yeasts into an alcoholic drink. But to leave things at this rather prosaic definition would be to ignore a drink that is mesmerising in its flavours, textures, characters and complexities. The world of perry is almost entirely overlooked; it has never been fully written about. So, really, what is perry?

Perry is Shy

No other drink so determinedly eschews the limelight. Sometimes it feels as though perry goes out of its way not to be noticed. There are only three countries in the world where enough perry is made for them to be considered 'perry regions', but even in those countries perry generally plays second fiddle to cider. In the Three Counties region of England (Gloucestershire, Herefordshire and Worcestershire), and across the border into Wales, there are almost no producers fermenting more pears than apples. In Normandy in France, cider production is greater in every area except the tiny Domfront appellation. Only in Austria's Mostviertel region, home to the greatest stretch of pear trees in Europe, can perry claim true primacy.

Even in these countries there is often a general misconception of what perry is. You'll find few pubs, bars or restaurants in any of those countries where high-quality 'perry', labelled as such, is served. In the United Kingdom, if drinkers have heard of perry at all, it is usually through industrially produced creations that bear little or no resemblance to full-juice, fruit-driven perry, but which, nevertheless, influence the way it is perceived.

Perry is Hard

Speak to any grower of perry pears or maker of perry and they will give you a long list of reasons not to bother with either. Pear trees are stubborn, barely yielding fruit at all for at least a decade, and not coming into true maturity for far, far longer than that. They need more space than apple trees, are harder work to maintain, and are far less profitable. Their huge size makes them difficult to harvest from, and the pears themselves make life even more painful, whether it be through rotting from the inside while still on the tree, offering a window of ripeness for pressing that sometimes lasts less than a day, or being so small or oddly shaped that mechanical harvesting is rendered out of the question.

Once harvested, the challenges continue: varieties of pear that gum up presses with mulch; uneven fermentations and unfermentable sugars; a tendency to go cloudy or throw unsightly lumps of congealed sediment; susceptibility to every conceivable fault or bacterial infection. Making perry demands absolute concentration and extreme patience.

Legendary perrymaker Mike Johnson takes a bewildered author under his wing

Perry is Confounding

Whenever you feel you have a handle on perry, it throws out something to challenge what you thought you had understood. You think it subtle and delicate, then you taste Flakey Bark or Rock or Butt, all booming heft and tannin. You think it is sweet, then you taste the pristine Birnenmosts of Austria, or dry, mouth-filling marvels of the UK. There are perries that nod in the direction of cider, perries that remind you of fragrant white wines, and, most of all, perries that taste nothing like either, but which are their own spellbinding thing. Some perries even share a relationship with beer (we'll get to those later).

The full, kaleidoscopic picture of perry has never truly been painted, which, perhaps, is why it is so often generalised and over-simplified. The truth is that the sheer scope of perry flavour is larger than anyone has dared to imagine. Whenever you feel you have tasted it all, perry has an unerring tendency to offer up something that makes you think again.

Perry is best shared

Perry is of Nature

It is agricultural produce; a drink of the earth. Not simply in being made from fruit which has grown on trees, but in the way its flavours can reflect the places those trees grew in; the soil, the aspect of the orchard, the hours of sunlight their branches soaked up, the wind that ruffled them and the rain that fell. Locked in every sip is a tangible taste of the land; a unique expression of fruit and place.

Orchard in full fruit

But aside from flavours, pear trees offer a rich and unique strand in the tapestry of biodiversity: they are vital habitats; food and shade for all manner of flora and fauna; complex ecosystems that both enrich the land and nourish the soul. There aren't many more peaceful or beautiful places to while away a quiet hour than in the dappling shadows of a perry pear orchard ... except, perhaps, at harvest time.

Perry is Remarkable

Just think, for a moment, of drinking something from a 60-foot tree planted 300 years ago. Before planes or trains, before the French revolution or American independence.

Then there's the rarity of some varieties of pear: varieties like Flakey Bark, of which only six mature trees are known to exist; or Betty Prosser, so gloriously ripe and tropical, yet down to just a dozen or so trees across the valleys of Monmouthshire; or Coppy, whose perry was rated as exceptional just 60 years ago but which now has only one mature tree left standing.

Most remarkable of all is perry's endurance. Despite its shyness and challenges, despite never getting a real moment in the sun, despite the lack of publicity and its unfair reputational damage, and despite being overshadowed by cider at almost every turn, perry still hangs on, cherished by makers and adored by devotees.

Perry is Ascending

Something astonishing has begun to happen in the last five years or so; an awakening of sorts. In tandem with the meteoric rise in aspirational, full-juice cider, attention has been slowly drawn to its pear-scented cousin.

The size of perry pear trees is astonishing

In perry's ancient heartlands producers are harvesting and pressing more pears than they have for decades. In England, France and Austria the story is the same – awareness of and interest in great perry is growing at unprecedented speed. Ripe, juicy craft perries are appearing in boxes or kegs on the bars of good pubs. Elegant 750ml sharing bottles are starting to grace the lists of restaurants. At home, drinkers are uncovering the delights of this once-hidden drink and are sharing discoveries with a growing online community of enthusiasts.

This resurgence isn't confined to perry's old haunts. Around the world producers are falling in love. In America, where the rise of craft cider has been perhaps more exciting and dynamic than in any other country, perry has found a new audience eager to uncover its flavours, textures and charms. There are perries made across Europe – from Luxembourg to The Netherlands, from Scotland to Ukraine. On the far side of the world, pears, often varieties specific to that country, are being pressed in Australia, Japan, Canada, New Zealand and beyond.

Great Perry is Delicious

This is the nub of it. This is the real reason that great, aspirational, full-juice perry has survived; the reason it is so beloved by those who make it and by those fortunate enough to have discovered it.

'If it didn't make that drink I'd stop tomorrow,' Tom Oliver, one of the world's most celebrated perrymakers once told me. 'But it's that drink, honestly. Cider's great, but if I want to show off to somebody it's usually a perry I go for. What a drink.'

More than the simple fact of its deliciousness, though, it is the dizzying array of flavours perry is capable of producing that takes the breath away: from vivacious green hues with electric bursts of citrus to ripe, tropical, perfumed opulence; from rich, sticky, unctuous, honey-and-marmalade puddingy bliss to the evocative, visceral whispering of rainwater on woodlands and the crunch of earth underfoot; even the spicy baritone of Mostello or mistelle, barrel-aged and fortified with pear spirit.

It is this breathtaking spectrum of flavour that first captivated me. Here was a drink of such mesmerising beauty, yet one that barely anyone seemed to have heard of, let alone know much about. The more I tasted, the more I became desperate to discover. And the more I learned about this drink and the trees, pears and people behind it, the more I wanted to share it with everyone.

The beginnings of perr

Perry deserves far more attention and love than it has been given. It has been confined to solitary chapters in cider books, maligned, misunderstood or ignored. Well, I say no more. To me, and to an increasing body of drinkers worldwide, it is one of the greatest treasures ever poured; not a sidekick to cider or wine, but glorious in its own right, with its own fruits and flavours, its own stories and triumphs and heartbreaks and histories and joys.

There has never been a better time to discover the magic of perry. The greatest perries ever made are certainly sitting on shelves right now. A pear-shaped revolution is spreading across the world, with a chorus of passionate makers, inspiring advocates and curious drinkers. Perry has never truly had 'its time' – the moment in the sun that its quality has so-long deserved – but, just perhaps, that moment could be today.

It is in that hope that this book is written. Welcome to the secret, astonishing and delicious world of perry.

A BRIEF HISTORY OF PERRY

Beginnings

As with most drinks, we will never know exactly when the first perry was made, though, perhaps fittingly, the first time it was recorded it seems to have been aligned with something else. Writing in his *Natural History* of AD 77, Pliny the Elder tells of an excellent pear named 'the Falernian, so called from the drink which it accords'.

Another drink, then? Well, the most famous 'Falernian' of the ancient Roman era, eulogised by Pliny himself, was not perry but sweet white wine. If the pear had come to earn the name Falernian 'for the drink it affords', it seems reasonable to deduce that it was because its flavours reminded Pliny's contemporaries of their favourite wine. And thus begins the long history of perry's 'sidekick' status to wine and cider.

But before we get into how perry became the drinks world's perennial supporting actor, a few words on the fruit itself.

The 20 subspecies and mind-blowing 3,000 varieties of pears in existence today begin their story in what is now Western China, north of the Himalayas. From there, carried initially by the droppings of hungry animals, they spread east and west, with subspecies developing as they went; for example, the Nashi pears of East Asia are entirely distinct from pears in Western Europe.

The ancestry of the modern so-called 'perry pear' is complicated, involving all sorts of crossing and counter-crossing, but our central character is a subspecies called *Pyrus communis*. This subspecies emerged as a natural hybridisation of wilder forebears (*Pyrus pyraster* and *Pyrus caucasica* for any scientifically curious readers who are keeping score). As it headed west through the 'wildwood' of Europe, influenced and hybridised by the other pear subspecies it encountered, it gradually evolved into a feral fruit used by early populations of hunter-gatherers.

Many of these pears would have been distinctly unpleasant to eat, and those varieties would have continued their natural animal-dropping path west. But those which proved especially tasty to the hunters, softer of acidity, less astringent of tannin, would be pulled out of the wildwood and specifically cultivated for food. Evidence suggests that domestication first took place from these varieties in the hillier areas of North Iran and Transcaucasia, in the Fertile Crescent.

Key to this – and perfected by Persians and, later, Greeks and Romans – was grafting. Suddenly pears of specific varieties could be selected, cultivated, spread across orchards and transported across countries. Which is how, courtesy of the Roman Empire, these edible varieties of *Pyrus communis* made their way to Britain.

Tempting as it might be to imagine, especially given Pliny's fondness for Falernian, there's no evidence to prove the Romans made perry in Britannia. Indeed, for the next thousand years written evidence of perry drinking is fragmentary. The best comes from Palladius, in his agricultural work *Opus agriculturae*, where he describes bruising fruit then crushing it under weights or with a press to make a wine.

Palladius notwithstanding, perry seems likely to have been fairly widely made, but not important enough to be written about. Most of the references come from France, particularly the church (often the best place to be a curious medieval drinker). A century after Palladius was writing, Saint Radegonde retired to a convent where she allegedly drank nothing but water and perry. In the eighth century St Ségolène apparently refused all drinks but water and perry throughout Lent – a spirit of sacrifice I could live with. And Lupus Servatus, ninth-century Abbot of Ferrières, invited 'Folchric and Maurus' to 'enjoy with us the pear wine, of which they are especially fond' in one of his communications, lamenting that 'a shortage of fruits leaves us with a meagre supply'.

Probably the first concrete suggestion of perry as a significant concern comes from Charlemagne's *Capitulare de Villis*, a document laying out how the emperor wanted his estates to be run, and which stipulates: 'every steward shall have ... people who know how to make beer, cider (pomatium), perry (piratium) or any other suitable beverage'. With a border more or less on the Mostviertel, Charlemagne's empire, perhaps tellingly, covered everywhere that would become a major perry region on the European mainland.

These pears took a long route to Britain

Five hundred years later perry references still come predominantly from the continent; it was even sung about in poems by 13th-century Austrian and Bavarian bards as it emerged as a cultural staple of rural Central and Western Europe.

In 1529 Joachim Vadian, scholar and mayor of St Gallen in Switzerland, writes: 'in many places in the country, a wonderful drink is made from apples and pears. They call the best Bergbirnenmost, which becomes very stable and sweet when it is boiled, made from a special kind of pear. It is also delivered to other countries, served in taverns like wine.'

In France, *La Maison Rustique*, written in 1564, offers perhaps the earliest account not only of how to make perry but of numerous perry pear varieties. The authors, Charles Stevens and John Liebault, suggest that cultivated pears, likely hard culinary varieties, were ideal, citing a list of varieties that made a pleasant drink with little keeping quality, but noting that 'the best and most excellent Perrie is made of little yellow waxy pears … the Amiot Pear above all the rest'. Wild pears they seem less taken by, remarking that 'there is no cause why you should greatly esteem the Perries that are pressed out of wild pears and all such as are unhusbanded, untamed, of a sharp taste'.

The writers discuss perries both as single varieties and blends and highlight the use of stone mills over a century before such things were deployed for perry in Britain. They mention perry's greater susceptibility to faults and infections compared to cider and even describe perrykin – a drink made by hydrating the pomace of pears already pressed: 'Good house-holds do make a sort of perrie of the draffe of the pears coming from pressing, and that by casting them into some vessel with sufficient quantities of fountain water.'

Despite admitting that cider is more popular in Brittany and Normandy, the writers contend that, like for like, perry is the better drink, suggesting it held medicinal properties, and that it 'relieves and refreshes more'. They even mention one learned doctor who rates the drink ahead of wine – almost heretical in France!

Meanwhile, across the channel, perry was virtually undiscussed. The orchards planted by the Romans had long since been neglected, their trees swallowed up. But it was here that a happy accident occurred. Abandoned *communis* trees, originally cultivated for food, cross-pollinated with indigenous wild pears – those strains of *communis* that the hunter-gatherers rejected for their astringency. Wherever this occurred, new feral trees would rise, each slightly different to its parents; a unique variety of pear. These seedlings were something new to Britain. Acidic, tannic, but with some of the juiciness of the old, cultivated varieties, untended in woods, hedges and the edge of fields, they became what

Jim Chapman wonderfully calls 'a shadow orchard' of varieties we would come to know as 'perry pears'.

Pear growing got a second wind after the Norman conquest, when England came under French influence. But these were culinary pears, far too valuable to turn into perry. Some – early-ripening 'gennets' – were soft, juicy and edible straight away; others – the much firmer 'wardens' – had brilliant keeping quality, could be stored over winter, and were best for cooking. As demand for pears as a source of food grew, the growers of the Home Counties around London dedicated more orchard space to them, removing wild indigenous pear trees.

In the west of the country the shadow orchard of crossbred pears survived, but perry only really existed in a minor way, mainly as a drink of subsistence. 'Pirrie' or 'piriwhit' was made by the poorest in society from whatever sort of wild pears – or more often a mixture of pears and apples – they could get their hands on. As late as 1585 a curate from Malvern, Richard Drake, observed that people in the worst poverty would harvest feral pears from common land and pound them into a drink. Another drink – perhaps the same as drunk in 'penance' by Radegonde and Ségolène – involved steeping slices of fruit in water before allowing the mixture to ferment (known as the depensé method). It wasn't inspiring stuff. Even when 'full juice' perry was made, such as by the monks of Worcester, or in London from surplus dessert fruit, it was thought of as pretty thin gruel and considered a long way below wine.

Perry's Golden Age – A Tale of Many Johns

It was a perfect storm that changed perry's fortunes. Firstly, the end of the medieval warm period, when temperatures dropped and Britain became unsuitable for vines. No longer able to make their own wine, landowners and the church were forced to rely on imports or find an alternative. With England's diminishing territory in France, and constant wars with Europe putting major strain upon the wine trade, finding a 'native wine' became imperative.

Orcharding had expanded and commercialised during the 15th and 16th centuries in any case, and in the 17th century, to a continued backdrop of continental warfare, an age of enlightenment arose in the UK. To address the demand for an indigenous drink, intellectuals began to advocate the making of cider and perry. In 1655 Samuel Hartlib, a German polymath who had settled in England, described two ways of producing perry: 'one by bruising and beating [pears], and then presently to put them in a vessel to ferment or work of themselves. The other way is to boil the juice with some good spices, by which the rawness is taken away.'

Hartlib wasn't alone. A veritable wave of cider and perry interest had swelled up, not least among members of the recently formed Royal Society, a group of Britain's leading thinkers. The Society's very first book was *Sylva, Or a Discourse of Forest Trees*, by scholar and gardener John Evelyn. It carried an appendix, 'Pomona', which not only named and described the best varieties for making perry but advocated their grafting and cultivating.

Centuries-old tree at Hellens Manor, Much Marcle

The identification of particular pears for perry had begun in a smaller way a few decades beforehand, with John Gerard noting that astringent and sharp pears seemed to produce the best perry, citing brilliant names like 'Great Choke' and 'Small Choke'. This was built upon by John Parkinson (there are a lot of Johns in this tale) who wrote of 66 varieties of pear in 1629 and commented: 'The perry made of Choke Peares, notwithstanding the harshnesse and evill taste, both of the fruit when it is greene, as also the juyce when it is new made, doth yet after a few moneths become as milde and pleasant as wine.'

But it was with 'Pomona' that the identification of varieties specifically for perry really comes into its own. It referenced Taynton Squash, a pear that was to become the most historically prized variety in the UK's perry history, and compared to Champagne on more than one occasion (a little erroneously in my opinion). It also cited Barland (bare land), which Samuel Hartlib had heard about from his friend, John Beale, a leading authority on orcharding, who wrote:

> Without hyperbole, I assure you ... That our hungry swine will not bite these peares, & most especially the Bareland peare of Bosbury which makes a liquor That in common houses & with little or no care increaseth strength & excellency for 3 yeares together, & in the second yeare takes a deepe fulvous color, & hath a pungent stroke on the tongue as I have found in well-commended Greeke Wines.

Both Barland and Taynton Squash, astonishingly, are still grown and harvested for perry in the Three Counties today.

There was international communication too. John Pell (yes, another John), political agent to the Swiss Cantons, wrote to Hartlib to describe a particular variety of pear, named only as 'the Turgovian pear'. It was of similar astringency to Barland, and made a truly marvellous drink – so marvellous, in fact, that grafts were brought to England, and a later writer, J. Worlidge (no prizes for guessing what the 'J' stood for) wrote of it as 'the Turgovian-pear that yields that most superlative Perry the world produces'.

Between acclaimed varieties, comparisons to wine, and even the invention of a technique by which cider and perry could be made sparkling – later to be pinched by a certain French wine region and renamed 'the Champagne method' – perry had truly ascended. With the adoption of the stone mill making the process easier – no more need for bruising pears with sticks – and an increase in orcharding across the Three Counties,

Barland has been drunk for over 350 years

perry was being made in unprecedented quantities. Not only was it drunk in serious volumes in London, and frequently described as superior to European wine, but with French imports banned, cider and perry brandies became the high-end spirit of choice, ahead of grape brandy. Bottled Gloucestershire and Herefordshire perry was in such demand that it was shipped from London and Bristol for consumption in the West and East Indies. This was truly a golden age for quality perry's prominence – one that has never been matched since.

End of an Era

It couldn't last. Although relationships with France remained patchy, new alliances were made with Portugal, and grape wines began clawing back market share and prominence, led by a rich and hearty new style called Port. While wine land-grabbed perry's newly established place at the dining table, beer – which, unlike harvest-based cider and perry, could be made all year round and more or less anywhere – remained the dominant force in less expensive drinks for working people, especially in urban areas.

Continental wars had increased the price of wheat, meaning arable land became far more valuable than orchard space. Trees were replaced with cereal, something that only accelerated as the population increased. Though land leases often stipulated a requirement to replant trees in orchards, less care was given to varieties, and any old thing would be carelessly grafted, rather than pears specifically intended for great perry.

But the real killer came in 1763 when, to pay for the vast increase in national debt brought about by the Seven Years' War, the British Prime Minister, Lord Bute, proposed a Cider Bill, introducing a tax of four shillings per hogshead of cider or perry on commercial makers, whether it was intended for sale or for personal consumption. Families that made the drinks exclusively to drink themselves – ubiquitous in rural communities – were still charged five shillings for every member of the household over eight years old.

More than the financial burden, the bill was seen as a violation of the right to privacy within one's own home, since excise collectors were given freedom to enter any house unannounced to uphold the new measures. Protests began across western England before the bill had even been passed, with full-scale riots, burned effigies of Lord Bute, mourning processions and even the printing of slogans such as 'No Cyder Act' or 'Liberty, Property, and No Excise' on household goods like plates and teapots.

Bute's successor, George Grenville, pushed through the bill in 1764, despite opposition motions for appeal and a rousing speech from William Pitt the Elder, who insisted: 'The poorest man may in his cottage bid defiance to all the forces of the Crown. It may be frail; its roof may shake; the wind may blow through it; the storm may enter; the rain may enter; but the King of England cannot enter – all his force dares not cross the threshold of the ruined tenement!'

Public opposition eventually wore the government down, and the bill was repealed in 1766, but it had hammered another nail into perry's coffin. Orchards had been abandoned or torn out, and wine was completely reinstated as the preferred high-end tipple, with beer unassailable as the urban working-class drink of choice.

The problem was exacerbated by 'cidermen' – middlemen merchants who bought excess cider and perry in bulk, often to mislabel it as, or blend it into, cheap knock-off versions of fashionable wines. An 1865 *Journal of the Bath and West of England Society for the Encouragement of Agriculture* mentions much Taynton Squash 'sent to London as perry to be resold as Champagne'.

Fifty years earlier, Pomologist Thomas Knight wrote of perry from the Barland pear: 'many thousand hogsheads are made … it sells well, whilst new, to the merchants, who have, probably, some means of employing it with

Ancient perry pear p[...]

which the public are not acquainted … it may be mingled in considerable quantity with strong new Port without its taste becoming perceptible.'

Though it didn't fall to the same abject status it held before its 17th-century revival, perry was never seen in quite the same glorious light again. It clung on in the west of the country, in part thanks to the longevity of the surviving pear trees themselves. Knight, though seemingly not the greatest lover of perry, made a great study of pear trees and catalogued varieties in his seminal *Pomona Herefordiensis*, featuring published illustrations of perry pears for the first time in the UK. He was also a pioneer of deliberate cross-breeding, creating many new seedlings himself (naming many after his friends).

An even more comprehensive picture of Herefordshire's perry pear orchards was provided in the *Herefordshire Pomona*, by Robert Hogg and H. G. Bull, commissioned by the Woolhope Club between 1876 and 1885. The club was formed by amateur naturalists, dismayed by the neglected state of Herefordshire's orchards and keen to restore the county to former fruit-growing glory. Besides cataloguing an unprecedented number of perry pears and offering opinions on growing and quality, the *Herefordshire Pomona* made extensive recommendations for establishing cider and perry businesses. It also records how the Taynton Squash pear, on the point of extinction, had been saved by a diligent countywide grafting effort.

Despite the best efforts of the Woolhope Club, despite 1963's *Perry Pears* by L. C. Luckwill and A. Pollard – the first British book devoted solely to the subject – and despite the resurgence of cider in the early 20th century – thanks to the emergence of huge companies like Bulmers – full-juice perry continued to dwindle. But in the latter half of the century a couple of brands emerged which took the country by storm, and whose impact would resonate across the category, and in the minds of consumers, to this day.

Sometimes pears need a bit of encouragement to come down

Commercial Brands

Regardless of whether you have ever knowingly drunk perry in your life, I'd wager that if you live in the UK (and probably many other places further afield) there are two perries you've heard of – even if you didn't realise they were perries: Babycham and Lambrini.

Now, it's worth acknowledging that these brands come in for a fair bit of criticism. Partially for the image they have historically projected, with Lambrini in particular coming to be associated with price-to-unit drinking culture.

Within full-juice perry drinking circles, however, the primary objection to big commercial brands is their low juice content. In the United Kingdom 'perry' is legally defined as containing a minimum of 35% pear juice – all of which can come from concentrate. (Other countries such as France and the USA have a higher stipulation of 50%). The remaining 65% can be made up of water, sugars and a long list of additives. The use of concentrates, water and sugar mean that industrial producers can achieve a consistent product and make their perry at any time of year.

While no one has the right to dictate or criticise what anyone else drinks, it's understandable that 'full-juice' producers, using entirely freshly pressed pear juice and only able to make their product once a year, at harvest time, would take umbrage with being taxed and perceived in the same way as industrial producers taking shortcuts in the name of efficiency and revenue.

Irrespective of your thoughts on these two famous brands though, the role they have played in British drinking culture and its portrayal over the last 70 years is monumental: as has been their commercial success. Babycham, at its peak, was filling 30 bottles every second and manufacturing 2.5 million every week, while Lambrini is currently worth over 50% of the British perry market, despite many drinkers not realising it is 'perry' at all.

'The Genuine Champagne Perry'

Let's begin with Babycham, a drink that was ubiquitous in British pubs between the late 1950s and late 1980s, and which, arguably, achieved fame beyond any other perry ever produced. Though its heyday came long before I was even born, it was still the first perry to enter my consciousness.

I remember my younger sister being allowed it at Christmas dinners. And I remember assuming it was something to do with Champagne – which, of course, was just what its inventors wanted.

Babycham was the creation of a Somerset-based company called Showerings. They had previously made cider, brewed beer and even bottled mineral water, but in the 1940s, looking to diversify, they tried their hand at perry. This was unusual for Somerset, where perry pear trees had never historically grown in great numbers.

Francis Showering, a trained chemist, approached the classic perry headaches of troublesome fermentations, cloudiness and sediment by pioneering a new process of sterile filtration. His perry emerged spotlessly bright and clear as natural sparkle was induced in its bottle.

d: I'd love a Babycham
re happiness sparkles Babycham's there!

BABYCHAM·
THE GENUINE
CHAMPAGNE PERRY

'Champagne de la Poire', as it was first known, proved a triumph at agricultural shows, and Showerings began packaging it in two different bottle sizes: the standard 750 ml, and the smaller 200 ml, referred to within the company as the 'baby'. As their creations racked up trophies, Showerings came to call their smaller bottle simply 'Baby Champ'.

By the time of their national launch in 1953, the 'p' had been dropped, along with the larger bottle, the two words compounded, and 'Babycham' was born. From the start its success was phenomenal. By Christmas 1954 it had proven so popular that, unwilling to compromise production methods at that time, Showerings was forced to ration it. In 1957 Babycham became the first alcoholic drink – and, behind Colgate toothpaste, the second product of any sort – advertised on television.

Showerings were selling so much perry that the orchards of Somerset and the Three Counties couldn't keep up with demand. They planted extensively in Somerset and used radical methods in an attempt to shorten the notoriously long time pear trees take to achieve maturity. Luckwill and Pollard's *Perry Pears* describes 'a completely new approach … a modern system of hedgerow planting … in which it is hoped that root competition will help to control tree vigour and induce reasonably early cropping'. As time went by, they also imported concentrate from Switzerland, particularly of the Schweizer Wasserbirne variety, on which Francis Showering was apparently very keen.

Every part of the Babycham brand was laser-targeted at making a specific customer feel a specific way: namely, offering women (seldom directly targeted by alcohol advertising before) the feeling of drinking Champagne. 'The Genuine Champagne Perry', as its tagline ran, was drunk from Champagne coupés by glamorous women in numerous adverts. Since it clearly didn't directly compete with beer, pubs were all too happy to stock it. At one point it was said that only two pubs in the UK didn't: both were, ironically, based in Showerings' local town of Shepton Mallet.

So keen were Showerings to associate their drink with Champagne that they reduced the bottle size to 100 ml, declaring 'the Babycham bottle fills a Champagne glass' in their new advertising. It wasn't long before they had their own glass commissioned, complete with Chinese water deer mascot. Unsurprisingly, it was the exact shape and size of a Champagne coupé.

Other companies took note. Bulmers, already boasting their own Champagne lookalike in the form of apple-based 'Pomagne', had acquired a brand called Golden Godwin, a Champagne method perry, when they bought Godwin's Cider Company in 1948. Reducing their bottle size and hiring actress and singer Diana Dors to front an ad campaign – 'I'd never say no to a Golden Godwin' – Bulmers hoped to compete with Showerings. But the Babycham brand was too strong to stop. 'I'd love a Babycham' was the confident refrain of both the marketing campaign and the British public.

Such obsessively Champagne-centric marketing inevitably ruffled feathers. In 1965 Showerings sued Raymond Postgate, founder of the *Good Food Guide*, for an article in which he cautioned readers not to be taken in by the drink 'which looks like Champagne and is served in Champagne glasses [but] is made of pears'. The jury found in Postgate's favour, and Showerings were forced to pay costs.

It didn't stop their marketing though, and in 1978 Showerings were in court again, this time sued by Champagne producers themselves, led by Bollinger. In this case it was Babycham which triumphed, the judge ruling that consumers wouldn't possibly confuse it with the French sparkling wine.

Despite victory, the brand began to tire as a new generation considered it to be 'what their parents drank', and, ultimately, a bit old-fashioned and uncool. Throughout the 1980s their Somerset pear orchards were largely torn out, and in 1993 the brand was sold to Accolade Wines.

A New Disruptor

It wasn't long before a new perry behemoth hove into view – from a truly unexpected location. In 1994, just a year after Babycham's sale, Liverpool-based Halewood International launched Lambrini.

Like Babycham, this was a perry designed to primarily masquerade as another drink. Though not pretending to be along the same lines

of sophistication and prestige as Champagne, Lambrini's large, curving bottle, along with its very name, evoked a fun and frivolous Italian sparkling wine. This was heightened by the addition of 'Bianco' – Italian for 'white' – to its label; hardly a colour distinguisher required for perry, but one that came with wine-like associations. Considering the name and branding, it's perhaps not surprising that the winemakers of Italy's Lambrusco region brought legal action against Lambrini in 2000, eventually settling out of court.

At a fraction of the price of its competitors, Lambrini proved a huge commercial success, accounting for over 40% of British perry sales within six years of launch, even as its low price and sweet flavour profile brought lingering associations with underage, excessive under age drinking.

Once again drawing from Babycham's playbook, Lambrini focused explicitly on the female market. It wasn't long before the so-called 'Lambrini girl' became not only a feature of their advertising, but a term used in general British discourse. 'Lambrini girls just wanna have fun' remained the brand's strapline until 2015.

Leaning into heavily gendered marketing and the depiction of Lambrini as a fun-loving party tipple continued to be a theme throughout the 2000s, with the brand not afraid to court controversy and provoke the Advertising Standards Agency. In 2004, at the time of the Grand National (another Merseyside institution), they were forced to remove posters from Liverpool train stations featuring bottles alongside quotes like 'I love a man with a powerful beast between his legs', and 'Better be on the jockey who comes last'.

A year later they became the first brand to be found non-compliant with new standards prohibiting links between 'alcohol and seduction, sexual activity or sexual success', via an advert featuring 'Lambrini girls' fishing for a man at a fairground hook-a-duck stand. Astonishingly, the regulator ruled that the man in question was simply 'too attractive' and should be replaced by someone 'unattractive – i.e., overweight, middle-aged, balding, etc'. Perhaps even more remarkably, rather than ditching the advert, Lambrini did indeed replace the model and went ahead as planned.

Despite the stigma that continues to be attached to it, and further advertising controversies including a 2014 accusation of suggesting alcohol contributed to the success of a night out, Lambrini remains far and away the best-selling perry brand in the UK. Intriguingly, in 2021 it was bought by Accolade Wines, the same year in which that company sold Babycham back to the Showering family.

Perry in Disguise

However you spin it, Babycham and Lambrini remain by some distance the most commercially successful perries of all time, despite – or perhaps even because of – leaning away from perry itself in most of their marketing. While many people are unfamiliar with 'perry', there are few in the UK who haven't heard of, tasted, or formed opinions on Babycham or Lambrini.

Whenever perry has been successful or well thought of, right from that first reference by Pliny, it is because it has been directly compared to wine. Seventeenth-century pomologists explicitly saw perry as an alternative to various wine styles, and though I have yet to see any evidence, there is an

abiding claim that Napoleon dubbed perry 'the Champagne of the English'. So perhaps the only difference when it came to Babycham and Lambrini's positioning was that those brands increasingly moved away from using the word 'perry' in their commercial propositions. Both found – and still find – themselves in the remarkable position of being a brand stronger than the category itself. Even today, with full-juice, vintage-based perry growing faster than at any time in recent history, its total market share across Britain is dwarfed by annual sales of Lambrini alone.

In 2006 the so-called 'Magners effect' – an unprecedented boom in cider sales brought about by Magners cider's wildly successful 'over ice' campaign – proved a rising tide that carried all ships. Every cider producer in the country – from the biggest macro producers to the smallest farm-gate makers – saw a spike in their sales. Though few of the craft producers would describe themselves as fans of Magners, I've heard dozens acknowledge the debt they owed to the 'Magners effect'.

The real shame of Babycham and Lambrini is that in their drive to align themselves with – or even disguise themselves as – different drinks, neither of their respective heydays proved a boon to perry more broadly. While they demonstrate perry's potential to achieve cross-category appeal – especially to wine drinkers – they also underscore an anxiety common to perrymakers of all sizes: that 'perry' is too little-known, too niche, to achieve success in and of itself. If this book stands for anything, it is the hope that one day such fears may no longer be founded.

On 'Pear Cider'

Picture the scene. It's 1995. You're a new cider and perry making company, albeit one whose family have, as we'll see, massive clout in the industry. You've wangled a pitch at Glastonbury Festival, but the presence of Burrow Hill's legendary, long-standing, and much-loved cider bus means you're only allowed to sell your perry.

This being Somerset, where cider is close to religion, but perry barely exists (outside of Babycham), most potential customers are greeting you with a confused 'what's that then?' What to do?

The apocryphal answer for Brothers Cider – founded by the grandsons of Babycham's Francis Showering no less – was to reply 'it's like cider but made from pears'. Repeated a few thousand times, the term stuck and soon became a feature on bottles. 'Pear Cider' was born.

Just over a decade later a producer from a small town in central Sweden introduced their product to the UK. Packaged in a distinctive black 500ml bottle that stood out on a shelf and also fitted comfortably into pub fridges, Kopparberg Pear Cider became an overnight phenomenon. In its first year the brand was being stocked in all of the UK's biggest supermarkets as well as the country's biggest pub chains. Within two years the pear cider market had grown from £3.4 million to £46 million and was described by Tesco's beer and cider buyer as 'the biggest success story of the UK drinks industry'.

The same buyer added: 'an important factor in the growth of pear cider is that the drink has been demystified. It used to be known as perry but now it has been remarketed as pear cider and people understand what they're going to get.'

What's the Difference?

You hear and read all sorts of takes on what 'pear cider' – as opposed to 'perry' – is. A common culprit is 'perry is made from perry pears whereas pear cider is made from eating or culinary pears which don't contain tannin'. Not true. You can make perry, legally defined and understood as such, from any sort of pear; just as wine can be made from any sort of grapes and cider from any sort of apples.

A second alleged definition is that 'pear cider' only applies to mass-produced, concentrate-based brands. Not true either. Since it was first used, makers of every size and level of craft have emblazoned their perry's label with 'pear cider' – from the UK to Sweden to Australia.

Let's make something absolutely clear, to avoid confusion: as far as the UK's government – and, most pertinently, tax collectors – are concerned, **there is no difference whatsoever between perry and pear cider**.

What's more, the UK's National Association of Cider Makers (NACM) states explicitly that 'there is no difference between "perry" and "pear cider" in how they are produced or how they are taxed. The industry feels that "pear cider" is the better name to explain to consumers what it is they are drinking.'

Some devotees of full-juice, vintage-based perry would point out that the NACM *would* say that, given the majority of their members come from the country's larger producers. But the fact remains that whether the label reads 'perry' or 'pear cider', the legal definitions are identical. Nothing to do with pear varieties, nothing to do with size, nothing to do with whether concentrate is or isn't used. Simply two different names for the same drink.

Oliver's Perry could legally be renamed 'Oliver's Pear Cider', just as Kopparberg Pear Cider could be swapped to 'Kopparberg Perry'. So long as the drink contains a minimum of 35% pear juice, fresh or otherwise, it can be labelled as either.

So Why is Anyone Bothered?

Perry has been aligned with other drinks for as long as it has been written about. Besides the 2,000-year-old wine comparisons we have seen already, the immense and historic perry cultures of Germany and Austria in Central Europe have long been calling the drink 'Birnenwein' (pear wine) or 'Birnenmost' (pear cider). Varieties like Bayerische Weinbirne and

Oberösterreicher Weinbirne, with their 'wine pear' suffix, underscore the interchangeability of these different drinks in the mind of the European consumer. After all, perry, cider and wine are all made in more or less the same way. What's really in a name – especially if eschewing that name makes it easier to sell the drink?

An avenue of perry pears at Hellens Manor

Identical legal definitions means that any answer to this question is inherently subjective. So, acknowledging that this comes as much from the heart as from the head, I might as well admit that I am firmly in favour of 'perry' over 'pear cider', and will use it as my preferred term throughout this book and advocate for its wider usage.

While 'like cider (or wine) but from pears' is invaluable shorthand for quickly explaining to a new customer what to expect, the name 'perry' stretches back through centuries of tradition and struggles to maintain its identity. To label it 'mystification' is as absurd as claiming that such terms as 'wine', 'lager' or 'cider' are wilfully exclusivist rather than simply long-established names of particular categories.

What's more, 'perry', like its counterpart 'poiré' in France, offers the benefit of clarity. Although 'pear cider' might be legally defined (in the UK) as the same product, it leaves the door open for people to assume that it could be a blend of apple and pear fruit – which is indeed a separate product called 'pider' – or, as it is in certain cideries in the USA, an apple-based drink to which pear juice or flavouring has been added.

'Perry' offers clarity. It can't be anything but that which it has been known to be for centuries: a drink fermented from the juice of pears, particularly, if not solely, specific 'perry pears'. It is a drink and a name that has been hard-fought-for by determined people and saved from the brink of extinction on more than one occasion and in more than one country. It deserves the respect of its own distinct identity.

Speaking of which, there is a twist in the 'pear cider' tale. Just five years after its meteoric success, the category's fortunes had taken a dramatic reversal. By 2014 sales of pear cider had plummeted 29% in just a year, knocking 25% off the value of the market and reducing pear cider to just 6.4% of the cider category, down from its pinnacle of well over 10%. Today it is less than 5%.

What happened? Well, if you can have 'pear cider', why stop there? What about something more exotic – strawberry and lime cider, perhaps? Mixed berries? Dark fruits? The success of pear cider eating into the all-apple category led to big companies in Sweden and the UK expanding their portfolio of flavoured ciders. Suddenly, 'pear cider' seemed pretty boring. As *The Grocer*, a UK-based magazine reporting on food and drink sales, suggested: 'the view is that pear's decline reflects the emergence of more choice from the fruit ciders and that pear is now one of many fruit cider choices'. It is telling that today Kopparberg makes the top two best-selling on-trade ciders in bottle in the UK, yet neither is their pear.

The Grocer went on to remark: 'if the overall category is growing then pear's woes may be nothing to worry about'. Yet pears – perry – had for centuries been an entirely separate category, whose artisanal makers saw sales plummet to around a quarter of what they had been due to the advent of fruit ciders. Only in recent years has it recovered.

This, to me, underscores the importance of perry retaining and proclaiming its own unique identity. If it's linked too closely to wine or cider it loses individuality, ignores its wealth of varieties and styles, and puts itself at the mercy of a fickle consumer who sees 'pear' as just another flavour in the global fruit bowl – and a fairly uninteresting one at that.

As 'perry', it retains all the wonder, flavour, variety, innovation, tradition, depth and breadth that comes from being one's whole self rather than merely subsidiary to another drink. To my mind it would be a tragedy if perry's complexity, fascination, idiosyncrasy and, yes, occasional messiness was homo-genised and lost. So I'll keep on calling it 'perry', and I hope readers of this book do the same.

IN THE ORCHARD

Perry, like virtually every other drink, is ultimately agricultural produce. It is something that grows; a drink of the land, dependent on its tree, on weather conditions, on the fluctuation of the seasons, the quality, depth and makeup of its soil, and a million environmental factors besides. Its flavours are led, first and foremost, by the specific varieties of pears used, and those flavours may be further enhanced by the skill and choices of the maker, but they are influenced and fixed by the tree, the place in which that tree grows, and the slow cycle of the growing year that brings everything together to produce a living drink.

This is, to my mind, the greatest magic of perry: the role that tree and orchard play in the flavours in your glass.

The Glory of Pear Trees

Perhaps no other fruit tree in the world, and certainly no plant that I know of whose produce is used in a drink, is as grand, imposing, ancient and enormous as a perry pear tree.

In certain places in the UK, France and Austria it is possible to stand in front of a pear tree which has been harvested since before American independence. Trees over 60 feet high, with canopies over 50 feet wide and which can yield a ton of fruit apiece are not uncommon; in, fact, they are widespread across the Three Counties, the Domfrontais and the Mostviertel, and have been for centuries. At Gregg's Pit, in Herefordshire, there is a pear tree of the same name, thought to be the original of the variety, and at least 250 years old. Not far away, and even more staggering, is the avenue of perry pear trees lining the driveway of Hellens Manor. Originally planted

Perry pear royalty

to celebrate Queen Anne's coronation, several are still standing and bearing fruit over 300 years later.

With age comes experience. The fruit that grows on older pear trees seems to increase in intensity of flavour compared to fruit from a younger plant. Perhaps, when it comes to a pear tree, that is simply because a larger plant with deeper roots is able to access more food. As with all things perry, there is little funded research on the subject, though the Long Ashton Research Station, now closed, recorded markedly higher specific gravity (sugar), acid and tannin levels in the fruit of old trees.

From my own tasting, the starkest comparison I can remember was between a single variety Thorn made from 30-year-old trees at Ross-on-Wye next to another they had made in the same vintage from neighbouring trees over 140 years old. The younger trees made delicious perry – zesty, bright, packed with citrus and dabs of honey – but the older tree perry was off the scale; a huge, bombastic, full-throttle blast of elderflower and green fruit and cut grass amplified by mouthwatering acidity and the most enormous tannins I can remember from a Thorn pear. Some years later that bottling continues to mature spectacularly and remains a reference point for one of my all-time favourite perry pears.

A well-ordered refordshire orchard

Aside from the marvellous drink for which they are responsible and the wonder they instil, the benefits that perry pear trees offer the environment are indisputable. As huge perennial plants, they are tailor-made for carbon sequestration. Perhaps it's all that blossom and fruit, but it always seems to me, when walking in an orchard, that you can taste the sweet cleanness in the air.

Orchards, particularly old, traditional orchards with tall, venerable trees, allow your soul to breathe too. There is something inherently mystical about them; man-made places sculpted from nature. They are distinct from a wood in ways it takes a few moments to adjust to: lines of trees a little too unnaturally straight, the ground thick with grassy sward rather than the earthy scrub of forest floor; to say nothing of the joy of being surrounded by trees all hanging heavy with gleaming, many-hued fruits. Orchards are the blurry line between wilderness and more obvious agricultural impact. No wonder they have been the stages for myth and religion for millennia; from the Garden of Eden to the Garden of the Hesperides, from the tales of ancient China to the fables of medieval England.

And the wildlife! Teeming, buzzing, thick in the scented air. Pear trees are havens for birds, mammals, reptiles and amphibians, all looking for a

ready-built home packed with its own food sources and nesting materials. Many traditional orchards boast thick, biodiverse carpets of wildflowers and grasses throughout the year, pollinated by insects that, in turn, provide meals for bird and beast. You cannot visit an orchard without feeling a living presence; in the chirrups and tweets, the knocking of woodpeckers, the percussion of crickets and the thrum of buzzing wings.

Their size, grandeur, history and ecological importance make it all the more devastating that so many pear trees are at permanent risk from landowners, developers and the whims of government. In 2020 the 250-year-old Cubbington Pear, the second oldest and largest wild pear tree in Britain, was felled to make way for an HS2 train line that has yet to be built. In the course of writing this chapter, Nottinghamshire maker Blue Barrel has reported that trees in the county's best example of an ancient heritage orchard, from which they have harvested for years, are now marked for destruction so housing development can go ahead. For the time being, any hope for protected status seems forlorn.

This is all the more wasteful because pear trees do not grow back quickly. Where certain apple trees, grown in a particular way, will start offering a decent crop within a few years, perry pears often don't offer a single piece of fruit in their first decade, and can take over 30 years to reach proper maturity. The famous phrase in the Three Counties is 'pears for your heirs'. Planting a perry pear tree is an act of long-term faith.

Establishing Your Orchard

Let's say you take the plunge and decide to plant perry pear trees.
There are many points to consider.

What to plant?

The pear tree is a comparatively hardy creature. Whereas particular
varieties of grape are often quite picky in where they ripen, pear varieties
aren't (generally) so fussy. Visit a perry pear orchard in the UK and you may
find a bewildering spread of varieties covering every conceivable shape,
size, flavour and flowering and ripening time. The perfect conditions might
be cool and temperate, but there are orchards in the cold of Canada and
the fierce heat of Mexico.

For a more commercial grower, considerations might include yield,
earliness of maturity, ease of harvesting and resistance to pests and
diseases. If that grower is also a maker, they might also think about how
easy the varieties are to work with – how quickly they need to be milled
and pressed, for example.

Ray Williams of the Long Ashton Research Station listed 14 recommen-
ded varieties according to these criteria in Luckwill and Pollard's *Perry
Pears*. They were, in rough order of ripening time: Hellens Early, Judge
Amphlett, Moorcroft, Thorn, Blakeney Red, Hendre Huffcap, Newbridge,

Winnal's Longdon, Barnet, Brandy, Brown Bess, Red Pear, Butt and Gin. He further volunteered 12 'supplementary' varieties that made excellent perry but which were in some way challenging to grow or work with.

Handy for the commercial grower perhaps, but sticking strictly to that list feels somewhat limiting given there are over 100 varieties of perry pear in the UK alone. So how about planting purely for flavour? That's what Somerset's Paul Ross did in planning his orchard. Captivated by the taste of the Plant de Blanc of the Domfrontais, and by the single variety Champagner Bratbirne made by Germany's Jörg Geiger, he planted both along with his favourite English varieties, Thorn and Winnal's Longdon. A rare example of international intermingling in a perry pear orchard.

Alternatively, you might be driven to seek out and preserve the rarest, most endangered varieties, or those of special historical significance. That's what's driven Barry Masterson to establish his International Perry Pear Project in Germany, an orchard dedicated to just such pears, including ultra-rare varieties like Flakey Bark, Lullam and Belgium's Colomas Herbstbutterbirne, as well as all sorts of vulnerable treasures from around Europe.

Where to plant?

Fairly hardy and adaptable the pear tree might be, but there are certain things for the grower to consider before they start sticking trees in the ground. The site of the pear tree will be critical to the quality of pears you are able to grow.

A soil's water-retentiveness can be crucial. 'Pears don't like wet feet,' Barry Walsh of Killahora Orchards once told me. Some varieties, such as Barland and Oldfield, are particularly prone to canker, a fungal disease, exacerbated by wetter conditions, that disfigures and 'sinks' the bark of a tree and which can seriously damage its health and productivity.

Being based just east of Cork, exposed to the Atlantic on Ireland's south coast, you'd have thought that Barry's trees knew a thing or two about wet feet, but being planted on a fairly steep slope means water drains away quickly. In a hotter, drier climate the grower might prefer to plant on flatter land so that trees don't suffer the opposite problem of finding themselves too thirsty.

Speaking of slopes, those who plant on hillsides will want to take precautions to make sure their trees aren't overly wind-battered. The taller pear trees grow, the greater the likelihood they'll be blown over in storms; pears

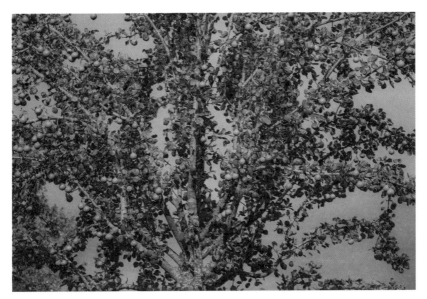

planted at the top of slopes are especially susceptible to wind damage. A barrier of hedges or other sorts of trees can act as a useful windbreak.

Hillsides can also mitigate frost damage, which is a major headache for growers, as late frosts can kill blossom and wipe out a year's crop before it has even really begun. Frosts slip down to the bottom of slopes, so, ideally, you'd want to plant earlier-flowering varieties closer to the top, and later varieties – which are less likely to encounter rogue spring frosts – further down. As trees grow taller, they gain better frost protection, though your tree's height will be dictated principally not by age but by the rootstock to which you graft it.

Aspect – exposure to sunlight – is also an important consideration, particularly in the chillier, greyer climes of England. For maximum exposure, a south-facing slope is the gold standard, or, if you are planting in the southern hemisphere, a north-facing slope that will drink up the sun's rays throughout the day.

Then there's temperature. The pear likes to be a little warmer than the apple on average. Indeed, Luckwill and Pollard suggested that 'the perry pear appears to need more sunshine and warmth than that provided by an average English summer' – which is slightly surprising in one of the world's three great perry making nations. Although my own tasting 60 years later suggests that this theory no longer fully holds, it is depressing to think that an improvement in ripeness owes much to climate breakdown.

Large bodies of water can be crucial in moderating temperatures. Water heats and cools more slowly than land, so trees grown in coastal regions such as Normandy in France, and even areas only comparatively close to the coast such as the Three Counties in the UK, enjoy more consistent growing conditions throughout the year than a more inland region like Austria's Mostviertel, which records warmer summers but far harsher winters. France and the UK also benefit from the effects of the Gulf Stream, the Atlantic current that brings warm water up from the Gulf of Mexico.

While not as effective as an ocean, a large enough lake can play a role in moderating an otherwise cooler region. The glacier-formed Finger Lakes in north New York State, and the far larger Great Lakes to the north-west, for example, reflect sunlight back onto fruit trees as well as offering a certain level of mediated warmth.

Conversely, pears growing in hotter countries benefit from coastal exposure for the opposite reason. Anywhere far inland in Australia would be far too hot to grow pears, but on the island of Tasmania, the west coast south of Perth, or southern areas of Victoria and South Australia, cooling sea breezes moderate the sun's heat, preserving fruit freshness and acidity.

The altitude of planting can have a similar effect. Anyone who's tramped up a decent-sized hill can attest to pulling out bobble hats and jumpers as they ascend. In hot countries, the lower temperatures found at higher altitudes can both mitigate excesses of heat while increasing exposure to sunlight – a win-win situation that packs fruit with intense, gentler-ripening flavour. The valley floor around California's San Diego would be far too hot for pears, but Raging Cider & Mead's Dave Carr harvests beautifully cooled fruit between 3,500 and 5,500 feet.

In truth, while pears in perry's traditional heartlands see comparatively similar growing conditions, as perry becomes increasingly international our idea of the perfect site is likely to keep evolving. The modern orchard can be found in those old, bucolic vales and valleys of the West Midlands and the pastoral landscapes of Normandy and Austria, but they exist in so many other places besides. They creep down the sides of mountains and paddle out towards the sea; they luxuriate in grand gardens and hide in dark forests. They have even made their way into cities, as urban communities celebrate the power of orchards to grow food and drink, clarify air, and bring people together.

As thirst for perry continues to drive plantings, we're likely to discover that it is precisely the range of different climates, geologies and topographies exploited by pear growers around the world that provides the greatest flavour diversity of all.

Traditional perry pear trees can bear a huge amount of fruit

The alternative orchard

Orchards are not the only places you'll find perry pear trees. In some parts of the world it is more common not to see them in orchards at all.

In the Mostviertel the most famous and common planting method is the Neidzeiler system; lines of trees planted along fields as natural 'borders' to stop unscrupulous neighbours widening their boundaries. 'It's easy to remove a cornerstone,' Bernadette Haselberger told me. 'With a tree, not so much!'

Southern Germany and Switzerland operated a similar type of open field system since the medieval period. Groups of fields – *gewanne* – were divided into strips that were farmed individually. Long and thin, meaning fewer turns of the plough, and more often than not divided by rows of apple and pear trees planted in the available space, as well as lining trackways across the landscape.

Even in the UK, pear trees have not always been cultivated in orchards. The Domesday Book of 1086 notes old pear trees used as boundary markers, and in 1100 a monk called William from Malmesbury Abbey wrote that in Gloucestershire 'you may see the high wayes and common lanes clad with apple trees and peare trees, not set nor grafted by the industry of man's

Tree lines were once a common sight in southern Germany

hand but growing naturally of their own accord'. Over 500 years later John Parkinson continued to report perry pears being harvested from 'the woods, forests, fields and hedges'.

'Historically a lot of perry pear trees were planted in really inaccessible places,' Tom Oliver tells me. 'Slopes, spare bits of ground – they were used to fill space that nothing else was appropriate for. Sometimes the location of the great old trees is bloody ridiculous.'

Pear trees had a reputation for being able to grow on heavier or poorer soil than apple trees. In 1789 William Marshall wrote, 'I have observed a pear tree flourish on the side of a cold blue clay swell where the soil is so infertile that scarcely any herbage, except the wood fescue, will grow upon it; and where the native crab evidently starves for want of nourishment.'

What's more, it seems pear tree lines also served an important purpose in British agriculture – less as field markers, more as the protectors of apple orchards. As 1754's *The Compleat Cyderman* puts it: 'the best of all other [trees] for a large, high, strong and most profitable fence is the perry pear trees, for either wet or dry, high or low grounds, for keeping them warm and securing them in the most rigorous cold season from the nipping North and East winds.'

Pear trees were often used as field boundary markers

Frustrating as the locations of these historic plantings might be to busy makers at harvest time, there is an indescribable grandeur to these ancient landscapes; the solemn lines of field markers in Central Europe and majestic lone rangers studding the Three Counties. They are a living chapter in a rural history book. Fragments of the past still yielding treasure centuries after they were planted.

How to plant ... and why it mostly isn't just 'planting'

It's time to share something that blew my mind when I first learned it, and which has continued to be one of my favourite facts about drinks ever since: if you plant a pip, it will not grow into a fruit of the same variety as that from which the pip was taken.

This holds true irrespective of the fruit. A Chardonnay pip will not yield a Chardonnay vine. Nor a Bramley pip a Bramley tree. Pears are no different. You will certainly get something by planting pips – all wild pear trees have been propagated this way, via animal droppings, fallen fruit or simply humans throwing seeds about. But you can't guarantee what that pip will grow into.

Think about it. You and I may share much in common with our parents, both in terms of genetics and personality, but we are not the same people. We have our own traits, our wayward streaks and unexpected interests, our extra half-foot of height and our funny-shaped noses. The same goes for trees. Just because you plant a Thorn pip, don't expect those characteristics of pronounced acidity, green fruit and medium tannin to appear. The majority of randomly grown trees, however interesting, are unlikely to create especially high-quality perry.

So how do we pass genetic material down without a random rolling of the biological dice? The answer is grafting.

Grafting is the practice of binding living material from one tree to the root system of another so the upper part of the plant bears fruit of the desired variety. This can be achieved with as little material as a bud but is mainly done with small wood cuttings called scions.

To achieve a graft, the grower will cut a particular shape into the host rootstock before binding the scion to it, forming a union. In a short space of time the cambium – a layer of cells beneath the bark of each piece of wood which is responsible for the tree's growth – will fuse together. The scion's growth will be influenced by its new roots, but the fruit it bears will be the same as it would have done had it remained on its original tree.

It's astonishing to think about. Every pear of the same variety is the result of someone having taken a piece off the original tree and then attached it to the roots of another. All trace their ancestry back to one plant that first grew hundreds of years ago. Grafting has been practised for millennia, and it is the way that varieties have been preserved.

It is even possible to graft several varieties – even types of fruit – to a single tree. A horticulturalist near Chichester in England has managed to graft 250 varieties of apple to just one tree, while another tree in Australia boasts plums, apricots, almonds, peaches and cherries. Generally, though, if you're growing trees for perry, sticking to just one is best.

The difference between grafted tree and rootstock here is huge

It doesn't always work. Grafts don't always take, so it's common for makers to graft several scions of the same type to one rootstock. The practised eye can always spot a graft mark, and on some trees it's more obvious than others. Thorn, for instance, seems to rage against the rootstock to which it is grafted, and its telltale mushroom billowing over the graft mark is a good way to spot it in an orchard.

If you visit Gregg's Pit, in Herefordshire, you can see the original Gregg's Pit mother tree, towering over its children. Despite their own ancient age, those grafted offspring are neither as large, nor as productive. An inevitable consequence of grafting – or perhaps that age-old long shadow cast by a formidable parent?

Roots

Just as crucial as the choice of variety to graft is the selection of the rootstock to which it is grafted. Their biggest impact will be on the speed of a tree's growth, its vigour in producing fruit, and the ultimate height it will achieve. For instance, a more commercially minded orchard would likely use so-called dwarf rootstock, restricting how tall the plant will ultimately grow but encouraging it to put more energy into growing larger crops earlier in its life. Those growers looking to encourage a traditional, tall tree would choose accordingly.

Rootstocks provide other characteristics too, with pest and disease resistance being a particular priority. The world of wine was decimated in the 19th century when a louse called *phylloxera* attacked the roots of Europe's vineyards. It was only by grafting vines onto rootstocks resistant to *phylloxera* that Europe's wine industry was able to stagger back to its feet. With perry pear trees facing a seemingly ever-increasing tide of pests and diseases, continued research into appropriate rootstocks is certain to prove an essential tool for the budding orchardist.

A word on terroir

Whether you plant your pear trees in an orchard, in a row along a field, or as a mighty standalone, the quality and character of the pears – and thus the perry – that they produce will be affected, not only by their variety but by the specific conditions in which they grow.

The type of soil, for instance. Free-draining gravel or squelchy, water-retentive clay? How deep is it, and what is the nutrient availability? Are your trees on a slope, and, if so, how steep, and in what direction does it face? How protected is it from the wind and how many hours of sunlight does it get? Are they in the rain shadow of mountains, or close to the sea and regularly drenched? All of these factors, and hundreds besides, make up a pear tree's natural situation. They are the determiner of precisely how it will be able to ripen a crop.

There is no single word in English that quite sums up this phenomenon, but in winemaking it is called 'terroir'. Terroir is a concept farmers and gardeners understand intrinsically – even if they don't call it that. It is why they might choose to plant a rosebush in the corner of the garden that gets the most light, rather than the corner overshadowed by a pine tree. It is why the part of the field that runs into bog is the part they don't bother sowing in.

From perry's perspective, it is why trees on one side of a valley result in different flavours than the same trees planted at the same time on the other. It is why pears might taste different from a particular soil type or a higher altitude. Each environmental factor will directly affect ripening: for example, to impede it, so that the resultant juice is lower in sugar and higher in astringency, or to offer such favourable conditions that perfect levels of each can be achieved.

Terroir has been remarked upon in perry for centuries. In his *Opus agriculturae,* Palladius relates that 'a stony pear will change its flavour if it is grafted into generous land'. Over a thousand years later, in 1664 in Britain, Dr John Beale wrote: 'He that would treat exactly of Cider and Perry, must lay his foundation so deep as to begin with the Soyl… neither will the Cider of Bromyard and Ledbury equal that of Ham lacy, and Kings-Capell, in the same small County of Hereford.'

More recently, the Blakeney Red pear, now the most planted perry pear in the UK, offers a striking example of terroir's impact. In the late 19th century pomologists Hogg and Bull rather rudely described it as 'abominable trash'. Yet, 80 years later, Luckwill and Pollard suggested this assessment was the result of pear trees planted in the wrong place. Writing in *Perry Pears*, they remark: 'When grown on the flood lands bordering the Severn this variety yields a perry of poor quality … yet on higher ground in the Forest of Dean the same variety can give an excellent perry.'

A brilliant modern study in terroir can be found in the orchards of Eve's Cidery, near the Finger Lakes in New York State. Cider and perrymaker Autumn Stoscheck is obsessed with the question, 'Can you taste a place?', and has devoted huge effort and energy to understanding the terroirs she works with.

'One of the things that I think is fun and interesting is that we have an orchard down in glacial material in the valley where it's dry, deep, very well-drained, gravelly soil,' Autumn says, 'and another on the hillside, where it's basically in silt that's the native rock material. It's shale that has weathered for millions of years.'

Autumn is still uncovering precisely what that means for her drinks. The orchard on the valley floor seems to produce bigger, riper flavours, while the one on the hillside heightens acidity, elegance, and minerality. What's certain is that even drinks made from the same varieties and in exactly the same way taste different across the two orchards. That's the terroir effect.

While the exact correlation of individual terroirs to the flavours they produce is generally under-researched in cider and perry, there is little doubt that those flavours and influences are there, to those interested in looking. From Eve's in the Finger Lakes to Eric Bordelet in France, from Little Pomona in Herefordshire to Haselberger in the Mostviertel, many of the world's greatest makers are putting terroir at the centre of what they do.

The Vintage Effect

The joy – and, sometimes, frustration – of great perry is that it is inherently inconsistent in its flavours year on year. This is the vintage effect.

The word 'vintage' is worth a quick note. Occasionally within cider and perry you will see it used to mean an apple or pear of exceptional characteristics. 'A vintage quality pear', for example.

Perhaps it's my former wine industry bias, but I find this unnecessarily confusing. To my mind, 'vintage' refers to the specific year within which a perry's fruit grew and was harvested. 'A 2020 vintage perry,' for example. This is the definition I will use throughout this book.

The vintage effect is why perry made from one single tree might taste radically different to perry made from exactly the same tree but in a different year. Fundamentally, it all comes down to weather.

A late spring frost, for example, might kill most of a tree's blossom, reducing a crop disastrously. But perhaps that tree will be able to offer greater concentrations of energy and nutrients to those pears that remain, resulting in a smaller but riper harvest. Too much rain and not enough

Some pear trees literally buckle under their fruit weight

sunshine in late summer and pears, particularly those earlier ripening, might seem weak, diluted and perhaps astringent, blazing heat throughout and sugar levels might fly off the charts.

In a country like the UK, where weather can be so fickle, this effect can be particularly significant. Think of 2018 and 2022, for instance, when baking hot summers resulted in huge, ripe perries. The summer of 2019 was colder and wetter; a more challenging vintage all round.

Perry lovers celebrate this natural inconsistency. There is a special joy to lining up similar perries from different years and imagining the little fluctuations of weather that bred those differences, subtle or significant, in what we're drinking.

Naturally, this constant weather-watching is far less attractive to the beleaguered perry maker at the mercy of the elements, praying against September thunderstorms, August deluges and April frosts. A challenging vintage marks out the greatest makers – those who most painstakingly reject underripe fruit and press only the juiciest, ripest pears.

The vintage effect is something the largest, perhaps more industrial makers deliberately look to avoid. To consumers who want to only drink their favourite brand exactly as they know and love it, the inconsistencies of flavour induced by vintage could be undesirable. It is this fear of vintage that generally leads to the use of concentrates, dilution, chaptalisation, and artificial sweetening. A conscious rebellion against the elements.

To my mind, the vintage effect is yet another magical arrow in perry's quiver. No drink is ever the same twice, and there is an infinity of flavours to explore. Alongside terroir and variety, it forms a natural, unrepeatable expression of time, place and fruit. As difficult and as frustrating as their vagaries might be to a maker, it is this combination that I find most soulful of all.

The Vintage Cycle

Beginnings
January–late February (Northern Hemisphere);
August–September (Southern Hemisphere)

This is the deep breath in. The pear trees have a deathly look; bare, wooden, skeletal hands grasping upwards from the frosted earth. But they're merely sleeping; recharging after last year's growth.

Bobble-hatted orchardists scurry from tree to tree with saws and secateurs. They are laying the ground for the year ahead, giving themselves the best chance of a good crop. Branches are pruned to allow even access to sunlight across the whole tree, to reduce the size of a crop but increase the individual energy and ripeness that each pear will achieve, and to remove any dead or diseased branches.

It is also at this time that scions will be snipped for grafting. The grafting won't take place now, though; it's best done when the weather warms and the wood becomes softer and more pliable.

Budding

Late February–mid March (Northern Hemisphere);
Late September–mid October (Southern Hemisphere)

Viewed from a distance, nothing seems to have changed. But step closer and you'll see, speckling the branches, tiny green buds tightly coiled against the last of the winter's cold. This is the first emergence of life, fuelled by carbohydrate reserves built up by the plant over its winter dormancy.

Flowering and fruit set

Late March–early April (Northern Hemisphere);
October–November (Southern Hemisphere)

An eruption of green, white and delicate pink as shoots and leaves unfurl and blossom bursts forth, transforming the orchard with a glorious floral colour-wash. Traditionally, this is a double celebration – not only the most beautiful and tangible sign of the vintage to come, but around the time that last vintage's perry starts to be ready to drink.

So, it's no surprise that the arrival of blossom is marked by festivities across the perrymaking world: from Herefordshire's Blossomtime celebrations to the Mostviertel's Tag des Mostes, it's when makers come together for a party, breaking open the new stuff and comparing notes.

At the same time, this is a nerve-wracking point for any grower, when trees are most vulnerable to the impact of late frosts that could wreck a vintage before it has really begun. Those most at risk are the earliest blossoming pears – Hendre and Yellow Huffcaps and Judge Amphlett in the UK, for instance.

It won't be until the flowers have 'set' into tiny fruits that orchardists can start to relax. There's still a long road left to run in the vintage, but the end of blossoming is when there'll be a first idea of how much fruit there will be.

Ripening
April–September (Northern Hemisphere);
November–March (Southern Hemisphere)

This is the stage I find most fascinating. In just a few months the pear tree has ripened tiny green nodules into full-sized, occasionally fist-sized, pieces of fruit. Sometimes, in the biggest trees, it can amount to a ton's worth.

Sun-blushed perry pear

The pears swell, filling with water and taking in sugars that the leaves have created. Warmth and sunlight are crucial, and, for best results, a mild amount of what's called 'water stress'. In simple terms, if a pear tree has more than enough water to drink, it will concentrate its energy into putting out leaves. If water levels are a little lower – though not so much as to cause drought – the tree will put effort into growing fruit, the means by which it could theoretically reproduce.

Ripening occurs in two stages: sugar ripening, where sugar levels rise and acid drops; and physiological ripening, the development of phenolics – flavours, tannins and colour. These two processes do not occur completely in parallel. The greatest vintages are those that offer the best balance between the two; when sugars have not raced away in the heat to such an extent that the pears lack refreshing acidity, and when the complex phenolics have had time to fully develop.

Harvest

Late August–early December (Northern Hemisphere);
March–June (Southern Hemisphere)

Action stations! When pears are fully ripe, they'll start falling from the trees of their own accord. There's significant variance in the point at which different varieties ripen, but the earliest – Thorn, Moorcroft and Judge Amphlett in the UK, Speckbirne and Stieglbirne in Austria, Petit Blot and Gaubert in the Domfrontais, for instance – will be falling by the end of August or early September.

The perry pear harvest is a long business. Growers will still be picking from the same orchard as late as the end of November, and, in extreme cases, with varieties like Butt and Rock, even early December.

Depending on the grower and the orchard, harvesting can take place by hand – hours scrabbling on hands and knees, digging around in the cold, wet grass, or pushing along small harvesters that look like garden lawnmowers – or they can be harvested by machines that strip the trees and hoover up pears from the orchard floor. The machines are far quicker than hand-harvesting but are only suitable for smaller trees in bush-trained orchards. Machine harvesting is also less gentle on the fruit, so is completely unsuitable for certain pears, and demands careful sorting before the fruit is pressed, as everything will be picked up regardless of quality. In the Domfrontais, only pears that have fallen of their own accord may be used in perries that bear the appellation on their labels.

Pears don't always make it easy. Blakeney Red, for instance, ripens unevenly: harvesters will need to make several trips to the same trees throughout October if they are to bring all their Blakeneys in at optimum ripeness.

Critically, unlike many cider apples, certain varieties of pear need milling and pressing as soon as they're off the tree. Varieties like Thorn, Taynton Squash and Moorcroft won't hang around – in some cases offering only a 48-hour ripeness window before rotting.

Most sadistic of all are varieties that refuse to drop their full fruit load, and, nightmarishly, even rot from the inside when still on the tree. Yellow Huffcap is particularly devious in this respect: the watchful grower needs to gauge the optimum time to go out to the tree with a long panking pole and rattle the branches to bring down the remaining fruit.

Winter dormancy

December–late February (Northern Hemisphere);
June–late August (Southern Hemisphere)

The orchard once again stands bare, carpeted with silvery frost. As the weather cools, the trees slip into dormancy, their new growth of the year hardening into wood; their roots beginning to store carbohydrate for the next vintage.

Frustratingly, certain varieties are inherently biennial, meaning that they only produce a crop every other year – occasionally even less than that. This problem is exacerbated as the tree gets older and larger and has a heavier crop to ripen. The six Flakey Bark trees on May Hill demanded two years off between 2017 and 2020, for instance, and Brandy, Butt and Gin – to name but three – all show varying biennialism.

Dormancy is crucial and requires a certain number of 'cold hours' over winter if the tree is to properly shut down and take in fuel reserves. Without those cold hours the tree may believe that spring has sprung again and attempt to begin the cycle too early.

Not only does this mean that the plant attempts to ripen a crop without having gathered energy, but it runs the risk of blossom emerging at a time when frosts are likeliest. As the planet is warmed by climate breakdown, regions which reliably offered year-on-year winter dormancy are seeing their 'cold hours' tumble. Of all the threats to perry pear trees in their traditional heartlands, it is possible that this will prove the greatest.

Orchard Threats

Wildlife

To naive tourists like me, not responsible for an orchard, the sight of rabbits scampering between trees, or deer stepping through long, wet grass invites coos of wonder. But I wouldn't be half as happy if I were the grower. Wildlife can be a nightmare for orchardists if care isn't taken. All new trees in the Finger Lakes region, for example, have to be protected by deer fences. Animals love to nibble bark, buds and shoots, and soft young trees are particularly vulnerable. Wire wraps around the trees can deter smaller creatures, but you'll have to follow the example of the Finger Lakes makers to keep out the bigger ones. There are some creatures that orchardists are only too happy to see, though. The likes of pheasants and birds of prey can handle pest control free of charge.

Pear midge

One of the best perrymakers in Herefordshire, Martin Harris of Butford Organics, barely made any perry for a few years thanks to this horrible fly. Their larvae develop within pear fruitlets, causing them to turn black and drop off the tree in summer. They can be responsible for the loss of a huge quantity of a crop. While they can be controlled with pesticides, that's not much help to an organic producer. Introducing natural predators such as hedgehogs and ground beetles can help, as can monitoring fruit at the very earliest stage of its development and removing any infected pearlings.

Pear decline

A vicious disease transmitted by insects called pear psylla. Decline can be slow, over years, or as quick as a matter of weeks. The disease kills phloem cells at the graft union of particular combinations of rootstock and scion, stopping the tree from transporting sugar to its roots. Initially turning what to an untrained eye might look like a pleasant shade of early-autumn red, the tree then wilts and dies, in the case of quick decline, or gradually becomes less and less productive over a few years. There isn't a cure for pear decline – prevention involves careful selection of particular rootstocks at grafting and planting.

Fireblight

I know makers in Herefordshire who, without hyperbole, have expressed concern that fireblight could bring an end to certain varieties, if not perry pears full stop. This bacteria, discovered in New York State around 1780, attacks all members of the pome fruit family, but has a particular fondness for pears. It invades through natural openings in the tree and can infect all parts of it. Overwintering in cankers in the tree, the bacteria multiply as the weather warms, causing an ooze of sticky droplets that drip onto blossom or are carried there by insects or other animals.

As the tree becomes infected, the blight gives leaves, fruits and even whole branches a dark, shrivelled, morbid appearance, as though scorched.

From America it has spread around the world. It flared up in the 1980s in the Three Counties, and in the last few years has become devastatingly aggressive, exacerbated by climate breakdown. There is no cure for fireblight; it can only be cut out of the tree.

Certain varieties seem more or less susceptible. Tom Oliver mentions Blakeney Red as especially vulnerable, while the Johnsons at Ross-on-Wye recently had to cut down all of their Gin Pear trees – their favourite variety and responsible for some of the best and most idiosyncratic perries I ever tasted. Fireblight is particularly dangerous in younger, smaller trees, so care has to be taken with new plantings. During the course of writing this book, I was told that new grafts taken from the one mature Coppy tree have been infected – a huge blow to that variety's chances of long-term survival.

While there are a few varieties that appear to be resistant and might offer hope – were someone to begin a breeding programme – there is, for the time being, little interest in breeding new perry pear varieties. Hopefully, as aspirational perry gains traction, investigation into such varieties will increase.

VARIETIES OF PEAR

This is the engine room of perry making. Flavour can be built upon by additional factors, from terroir to age of tree, character of vintage, ripeness at harvesting and pressing, and the skill and stylistic choices of the maker, but the big factor when it comes to making perry is the variety – or varieties – of pear.

One of the joys of walking around an orchard as opposed to a vineyard or grain field is the range of shapes, sizes and colours that different pears assume. Unless you really know your stuff, you'll struggle to tell grape varieties apart, other than one being red and another being white. You can look at two contiguous fields of different barley varieties without noticing an obvious distinction.

But a perry pear orchard is different. It is a feast for the eyes. No two trees, or pears, are even remotely alike. You'll see tiny orbs of gleaming, electric emerald, clustered like bunches of grapes; huge, ugly, lumpen, potato-shaped monsters, all russet-brown parchment to touch; perfect, pyriform beauties, glossy-skinned and blushing red, next to weird, alien, oblate things you might never recognise as a pear if someone wasn't there to tell you; yellow skins with brown freckles; rich, bulbous, claret-robed characters; and shabby, brown pears looking sorry for themselves (but which might make the best perry of the lot).

Their flavours are even starker and more bewildering in their infinite variety. A burst of puckering, lime-drenched citrus here; a ripe, juicy mouthful of tropical decadence there. Soft, near-mushy texture on one tree beside chiselled, crystalline firmness on the next. Tannins as grippy as a cat's tongue, which you can barely chew, then acidity that rasps like a blade. Pears that taste of Christmas and pears that simply taste of pears. I have followed any number of orchardists around their trees in the past, and each experience has left my mouth almost pummelled into submission by a riot of fulsome fruit, tumultuous tannin and perry potential.

To walk an orchard is to appreciate in vivid technicolour the breadth of perry's flavour spectrum. Remarkably, there are over 100 known varieties of perry pear in the Three Counties region alone, not including varieties found across the rest of the UK. In Austria's Mostviertel there are over 300, although only 30 or so are used much in perry. In France, though one variety – Plant de Blanc – reigns supreme, it is backed up by a supporting cast of dozens. Not to mention the probable hundreds

Identifying pear varieties can be extremely tricky

of pear trees that have sprung up as wildings from a stray pip, which have yet to be named and catalogued, but which may well have found their way into perries nonetheless. Pears can also be notoriously hard to identify. Even perrymakers and pomologists are often uncertain what they are looking at, never mind luckless drinks writers trying to caption photos. When it comes to the flavour map of international perry we are all sailing in largely uncharted waters. How exciting is that?

Most fascinating of all, there is very little cross-pollination of varieties across these three regions. Unlike the world of wine, where a handful of mostly French grapes have come to account for the overwhelming majority of the international press, when it comes to perry every country speaks with its own accents. The German-speaking regions of Central Europe probably saw the most cross-border migration of pear varieties in the past, with Swiss and Austrian varieties especially found across southern Germany. But all three still make perry predominantly from their own indigenous pears.

There has been very little written on the flavours of perry pears. While wine lovers can recite flavour lists of their favourite grapes, and beer lovers rattle off preferred hops by the handful, perry pears, historically, have barely had a mention. Going back hundreds of years you'd find them occasionally compared to various wines – mostly at times when, due to wars on the continent, those wines were unavailable to UK drinkers – but rarely described in terms of their own flavours.

In the 20th century the Long Ashton Research Station discussed perry pears in terms of their acidity and tannin, an unquestionably crucial element of the drinking experience. But, once again, nothing when it came to actual *flavours*. These days, when drinks writers talk about perry pear varieties, it is often simply to comment on how funny their names are, which, whether fair or not, isn't much help to the drinker scanning the shelf.

So, this section stands for the modern drinker's attitude towards perry's remarkable flavour spectrum. A tribute to that dazzling library of pears found growing across the UK, France, Central Europe and beyond. If perry, like wine and cider, derives its flavours from the fruit from which it is pressed, isn't it time we talked about what that fruit tastes like?

Clearly, there are far too many perry pear varieties to describe in detail in these pages, even if we stuck solely to those that have thus far been identified. But since it is through learning varietal characteristics that we can best understand the flavours of our perries, I have chosen a selection that you might find in the UK, France or Central Europe today, which are of particular significance in those countries, or which I simply love myself. I hope they help to guide you towards the flavours you enjoy most. If I've left out a particular favourite of yours, I can only apologise.

'Perry pears' vs 'dessert and culinary pears'

Just as the majority of wine is made from grapes you wouldn't eat, so most traditional 'perry pears' are a long way from the sorts of fruit you might find in your childhood lunchbox, canned in syrup or baked into desserts. So-called 'perry pears' – pears cultivated for the sole purpose of making perry – are often loaded with tannin and acidity. These properties add structure, mouthfeel, intensity of flavour and ageworthiness, but you certainly wouldn't want to eat them. Biting into a Flakey Bark pear is a hideous experience; trust me, I've been there. Barry Masterson alleges Germany's Grüne Jagdbirne to be even worse.

Making great perry with either 'dessert' pears such as Conference, Concorde and Commice – pears that are just as happy being eaten as a piece of fresh fruit – or 'culinary' pears traditionally cooked into pastries and puddings – is even tougher than working with varieties grown specifically for perry. It's a fact that most of the world's great perries use the more acidic, tannic fruits known as perry pears. But as perry moves beyond its historic borders into countries and regions where perry pears don't exist and where dessert pears are abundant, skilled producers are making virtues of their different properties; their lighter body, crisp, delicate fruit and floral aromatics. I've certainly tried enough excellent dessert and culinary pear perry from makers like Kent's Nightingale, Cornwall's Vagrant and The Netherlands' Elegast to know better than to write it off.

In a nutshell: not all pears might be classified as 'perry pears', but all pears can be used to make perry.

Flavour Camps

With so many varieties to wrap your head round, each boasting a different flavour, simply listing pears in isolation could result in information overload.

Smell and taste are, furthermore, intensely personal, informed by our own unique experiences of the world as well as the broader cultural and geographical surroundings in which we grew up. Who is to say, for instance, that if I describe Thorn as reminiscent of limes and gooseberries, you wouldn't taste it and be reminded of kiwi fruit and cut grass? My heather and bogmyrtle, gleaned from childhood holidays in the Scottish Highlands, might be your autumn leaves and forest floor. To say nothing of the foods and landscapes in those parts of the world I've not been lucky enough to visit and whose scents and flavours are as alien to me as those of the perry pears described here might be to you.

With that in mind, I have grouped all the pears in this chapter into four broad flavour camps. I undertake this with no small trepidation, bracing myself for the cries of 'what are you on about?' that will no doubt be heard from incensed perrymakers around the world. But, speaking very generally, all perry pears that I have tasted to date reach out and touch one of these flavour camps. Certain varieties could make an argument for belonging to more than one – perry pears are nothing if not complex – and in those cases I have made an authorial decision on which camp to file them into, for which, once again, I ask indulgence!

Each pear listed is described in fuller detail, but these broad-stroke bands should help the curious drinker to navigate this complex drink with a little more ease.

Green, citrusy, zesty

A style to set your mouth watering and your pulse racing with bright, zingy fruit. The kind of bright-eyed, tangfastic perries that demand large, cold glasses to quench your thirst under a summer sun and which cut through dishes like seafood, salads or even chicken with bursts of lime, kiwi, gooseberry and elderflower. These are the perries that fans of wines like Sauvignon Blanc, Grüner Veltliner, Txakoli or Riesling need in their lives; racy, full-throttle, electric. Varieties like Thorn, Yellow Huffcap, Champagner Bratbirne and Grüne Pichelbirne are standouts.

Green Horse

Floral and softly fruited

Possibly the biggest of the four camps, and the style many think of automatically when they have perry in mind. I'm talking about soft, juicy, gentle flavours, pillowy textures and beguiling aromatics of blossoms, honeydew melon, orchard fruits; these are the perries that taste most of pear. They are perries you can confidently pour for anyone – perries that exist to make you happy and put you at your ease. A glass on their own to while away a lazy afternoon? Nothing better. Yet, perhaps surprisingly, with their plump, easy-going character, low alcohol and frequent touch of sweetness, they make a wonderful foil for many a spicy dish. Your friends here are the likes of Speckbirne, Stieglbirne, Blakeney Red, Hendre Huffcap, and many culinary varieties. Fossey (also Fausset) is a wonder in this camp, but, sadly, exceptionally rare as a single variety.

Super-fruity, tropical

Head this way for a mouth-filling burst of luscious, deep mangoes, melons, apricots and tropical fruits galore. These aren't perries that whisper their flavours, they're varieties that bellow their personalities from the glass in aromatic clouds of heady perfume. Full-on fruit salads; joyful, full-bodied riots of flavour to stop the heart of anyone enamoured of wines like Albariño or the aromatic whites of Alsace. They include characters like the legendary Taynton Squash, celebrated in the UK for centuries. Winnal's Longdon is a favourite too, as is France's poster child, Plant de Blanc. Betty Prosser, perhaps, another – if you can find it.

Blakeney Red

Earthy, minerally, countryside

The rarest and hardest of all categories to pin down, yet home to some of the most beguiling, enigmatic and characterful pears. The flavours and aromas here put me outdoors. They aren't, necessarily, intensely fruity per se; their charms are more ineffable and elusive. These are perries that make me think of woodland walks and mountain hikes; of the roughness of pear skin and tree bark; of peering into salt-washed rockpools; of the rising scent of petrichor after a burst of rain. I find these perries haunting and evocative. They are like few other drinks I know. Butt, Flakey Bark and Oldfield are three classics of this style.

Hellens Green

British Pears

Thorn

Green, citrusy, zesty

Ask me my favourite perry pear varieties and Thorn will certainly be part of the conversation. A thrilling, vibrant pulse of green fruit – gooseberries, limes, cut grass, kiwi – always with pronounced elderflower. With its racy, mouthwatering acidity, grippy but not excessive tannin, and intense flavour profile, this has what some perrymakers call 'the holy trinity'. An early-ripening pear that demands to be pressed as soon as it hits that ripeness. Its qualities of flavour and structure make it supremely versatile, whether still, bottle-conditioned, pét nat or even traditional (Champagne) method. This is a perry pear capable of magnificence.

Gin

Green, citrusy, zesty

There's no drink in the world like Gin pear perry. Though I've put it in 'green, citrusy, zesty', and though it certainly has a little nibble of lime-skin, lemony acidity, it is a versatile creature indeed. With its distinct pine needle, herbal, juniper notes (hence the name) and a frequent petrichor minerality, it could easily have slipped into 'earthy, minerally, countryside', and sometimes I taste examples with distinct juicy pear fruit and floral tones too. What's certain is that this is at once the most detailed and delicate of perries, yet capable of billowing aromatics. A pear that is often

Gin

about subtlety and complex nuance yet can pack a blast of flavour and a rasp of tannin. Utterly idiosyncratic, endlessly spellbinding, and exemplifies perry's enigmatic, confounding nature.

Butt

Earthy, minerally, countryside

For years I struggled to get a handle on my understanding of Butt's flavour. I knew it was a big-bodied, brawny pear boasting wonderful juicy fruit, pronounced tannins, a deep pear-skin earthiness and the evocative soul of a bracing autumn walk. But what was that flavour, always on the tip of my tongue but just beyond my grasp? Then one day my *Cider Review* co-editor James Finch remarked 'natural gas', and there it was. Distinctive, immediate, there in every Butt perry I tried. Sounds bizarre and a little off-putting, I know, but so many great drinks evoke something that doesn't sound brilliant to drink. Just think of the best Rieslings, with their classic note of petrol, or the resiny tones of West Coast IPA! All I know for sure is that this reliable, late-harvesting, good-keeping pear is one of perry's true greats.

Early Taynton Squash

Super-fruity, tropical

Britain's most legendary pear. Historically lauded as the country's greatest perry pear – a status it seemed to hold by common consent from the 17th century to at least the end of the 19th – it is probably the pear which, throughout history, has most frequently been cited as a Champagne alternative. This baffles me. Taynton Squash is nothing like Champagne. It is *huge*. Massive-bodied, groaning beneath its own weight of fleshy tropical fruit, pineapples, apricots, even mangoes in extremely ripe examples. Indeed, I often think it could do with a bit of Champagne's acidity. Nonetheless, a phenomenal pear, though be careful, as 'Early Taynton Squash' and 'Late Taynton Squash' are distinct varieties. 'Early' is the one with the historic reputation.

Oldfield

Earthy, minerally, countryside

Nobody puts Oldfield in a corner. It is the ultimate shapeshifter. Just when you think you've grasped its unique, evocative swathe of herbal, floral, woodland foliage, it shimmers and melds into something mineral and sea-green, all petrichor and slate. And if that sounds austere, Oldfield has a perfume of flowers to go with it, and a ripe, full-bodied mouthful of pear and lime-leaf, moving into honeys, pear syrups and citrus jelly in riper, sweeter examples. Its complexity makes it a stellar all-rounder, doing beautifully across the spectrum of sweetness, with just enough tannin and acidity to offer structure without support from any other pears, yet not so much as to be aggressive. Tom Oliver has called this his 'desert island pear'. An endlessly beguiling advertisement for the determined 'otherness' of perry pears.

Blakeney Red
Floral and softly fruited
Blakeney Red just wants to get along. No sharpness, no grating tannin; just a plump, juicy, charming, pillowy-soft mouthful of ripe pear, honeydew melon and a touch of floral honeysuckle. This is the most common of all perry pears in the UK; a lovely, easy-going drink in its own right, yet perfect for adding that ripe, fruity middle to a blend. Intriguingly, not only has this pear been used for perry, but it has long been rated as a good pear for pickling and stewing and, most unusually, was used by the dye industry for the production of khaki during the First World War.

Hendre Huffcap
Floral and softly fruited
Apricots: that's what I think about when I taste Hendre Huffcap. Fresh, juicy apricots, and maybe a little peachiness and nectarine. Stone fruit, in short; all fresh, alluring perfume garlanded with bunches of flowers. No meaningful tannin, and pretty low acidity, but undoubtedly one of the most charming and fragrant of perries. A case could be made for putting it into the 'super-fruity, tropical' category, but Hendre Huffcap's charms are more high-toned and floral than that, for my money. An elegant delight, and one of my favourite drinks when eating a fresher style of spicy food.

Yellow Huffcap
Green, citrusy, zesty
Sometimes the clue's in the name. Yellow Huffcap is a gorgeous, nippy, zippy variety, full of lemony zest and spring blooms. That tingly acidity nudges it into our citrusy camp; it's more vivacious and lilting than softly fruited, adding lift and life to a blend, or starring as a mouthwatering solo act. Long praised as a variety by makers and pomologists, it can be deliciously fresh unoaked but has more than enough force of personality to stand up

Red Pear

Thorn

to barrel ageing. One of the best I ever tasted had been aged in a cask which formerly held peaty Islay whisky. 'It has a reputation, especially for bottle-conditioned, that is second to none,' Tom Oliver says. I'm not arguing.

Moorcroft

Super-fruity, tropical

Also known as Stinking Bishop (the cheese of the same name is washed in this perry) or Malvern Hills, Moorcroft is another with a foot firmly in two camps, as it has all the requisite citrusy tang to be a contender for 'green, citrusy, zesty'. But its bold-as-brass tropical fruits, all pineapple and passion fruit riding atop that citrus, has pushed me into this flavour camp. You don't find too many single variety Moorcrofts, as they ripen unevenly and need pressing within 48 hours of ripeness, if not sooner, but good Moorcroft will make your heart sing. I once had a 2001 Champagne-method Moorcroft from Kevin Minchew, aged over two decades by the time I opened it, and only two or three other perries I've ever tasted would rival it for the title of my all-time favourite.

Red Pear

Floral and softly fruited

Sometimes referred to as Aylton Red, and more rarely as Red Horse, this is a gorgeous variety, which I feel is heavily underrated. Although I've put it in the floral and softly fruited camp, it is more robust than some of its compatriots, with big, juicy pear, white peach and blossom flavours and a full-bodied, lightly tannic heft. More often than not I have found it to carry many of the earthy, minerally characteristics I love so much as well; that brusqueness of pear skin, of petrichor, of woodland. Most single variety Red Pear I have drunk has also carried a light signature nuttiness; more hazel and almond skin than anything deeper. One of the great all-rounders of the perry world and almost my archetypal idea of the flavours of Three Counties perry.

Green Horse

Green, citrusy, zesty

Leaves and nettles and cut grass and hedgerow: if any perry pear makes me think of a walk through fields in early spring, just as blossom emerges, it's Green Horse. Yet underpinning all that woodland greenery is a zingy, zesty streak of lime. In wine lover's terms, if Thorn nods towards the full-throttle intensity of a New Zealand Sauvignon Blanc (albeit one with tannins),

Green Horse is a pear for lovers of the likes of the Loire Valley's Sancerre and Pouilly-Fumé; less an explosion of fruit than an elegant, slatey-mineral celebration of ripe greenness and the countryside after rainfall.

Winnal's Longdon

Super-fruity, tropical

This was the last thing I wrote into the first draft of the book. Why? Because although I'd had excellent perries in which Winnal's Longdon played a role, I'd had too few single varieties to offer a proper tasting note. And then I had the Ross-on-Wye Winnal's keg-conditioned 2022 and I instantly knew the book wouldn't be complete without it. On its own it does what many of my favourite pears have to come together to achieve. It has citrus – but in a ripe, marmaladey sense –lime marmalade and lemon curd; it has voluptuousness and body; it has delicious acidity without seeming lean or tart; it has tropical fruit without bordering on flabby. In short, it is exceptional. A truly complete pear. As it's never too late to discover.

Fallen Winnal's Long ready for harvest

Central European Pears

Bayerische Weinbirne

Floral and softly fruited

This, to my mind, sits somewhere between the two English Huffcaps – Hendre and Yellow. It has the juicy, fulsome, blooming stone and tropical fruits of the former, buttressed by some of the structural properties of the latter; that nippy-zippy tingle of acidity, and cat's tongue lick of tannin. In fact, it has a little more tannin than either of them, making it a marvellously versatile match for a wide array of food. I'd call it a very good all-rounder, if that doesn't sound like I'm damning with faint praise. The sort of variety any maker wants in good supply.

Gelbmöstler

Green, citrusy, zesty

A striking lemon-yellow with an orange blush, these pears, originally from Switzerland, spread all over southern Germany and Austria at the end of the 18th century. They ripen fairly early in the season and need to be worked fast, as they blett quickly. What's remarkable about them is how true the flavour of the perry remains to the pear itself. There's an almost spicy quality: cinnamon and raisins in apfelstrudel, with a light, citric zing that keeps you coming back for more, soft tannins adding a drying structure to the finish. Those comforting, warming appley-spicy notes perhaps lean into the super-fruity, tropical camp, but the thoroughly pleasant zing edges it slightly more towards green, citrusy and zesty. (Note by Barry Masterson.)

Grüne Pichelbirne

Green, citrusy, zesty

A glorious pear, and pride (one of several) of Austria's Mostviertel region, where it seems almost a rite of passage for producers to make a single variety. Indeed, such is the quality and importance of this pear that every farmhouse used to graft a Grüne Pichelbirne nearby. This was partially for the late-ripening variety's handy party trick of clearing up a perry that had begun to go cloudy (I know many a producer in the UK who wishes they had access to such a fruit). But, most important of all, is the sheer character of this pear. Full-bodied, with beautiful fresh acidity and more tannin than the average Austrian variety, it is Austria's answer to Thorn, boasting lime juice, electric-green pear, fresh herbs, and pronounced slatey minerality bordering on gunflint. The best examples can age superlatively.

Hendre Huffcap

Landlbirne

Green, citrusy, zesty

The Landlbirne, to me, feels like a bridge between the two dominant styles of Austrian perry pear – the floral, aromatic charms of Speckbirne and Stiglbirne, with the sinewy body, vivid rasp of acidity and brush of tannin of Grüne Pichelbirne or Dorschbirne. That streak of acidity has dictated its flavour camp for me – rhubarb and gooseberry, almost 'English countryside' in its character – yet the aromas and flavours overall tend to head in a rose petal, blossom, fizzy sweets and loveheart candy direction, augmented by a little spice. Rather rare to find, but it is the favourite variety of brilliant perrymaker Peter Haselberger and so would be an immediate recommendation by dint of that alone.

Speckbirne

Floral and softly fruited

If Grüne Pichelbirne is Austria's counterpart to Thorn, Speckbirne – literally 'bacon-fat pear', for the speck-like sheen of its skin – is a cousin to the likes of Blakeney Red; all blossom petals, icing sugar, sherbet, and soft, juicy apple-and-pear fruit. A gentle perry from early-ripening fruit that reminds me, when I drink it, of nothing more than springtime. Low in acid and tannin but high in floral aromatics and sheer drinkability (a word for which I offer no apologies), this partners beautifully with a traditional Mostviertel cold platter, perhaps spritzed with sparkling mineral water, as perry is often served there.

Stieglbirne

Floral and softly fruited

Often found in the Mostviertel as a happy blending partner with Speckbirne, as it ripens at a similar time. It's actually relatively similar in character, though Stieglbirne perhaps leans more heavily towards the fruit, where Speckbirne brings more of the florals. Especially ripe examples lean into juicy red berries and watermelon, but all share a honeyed pear character, perhaps with a little nibble of citrusy, lemon and yuzu acidity, though, like Speckbirne, this is generally low to medium in acidity and without tannin. Another perry with which to cheerfully while away a long afternoon … if you can resist emptying your glass too quickly.

French Pears

(Fewer are included here, since Plant de Blanc's dominance in French perry, particularly AOP Domfront, is such that single varieties of other pears are extremely rare. I have listed some favourites in the hope that producers will showcase more in future.)

Plant de Blanc
Super-fruity, tropical
If you love French perry then you love Plant de Blanc. In the Domfrontais, the epicentre of production in France, perries must contain a minimum 40% of this pear to bear the label 'AOP Domfront'. Most contain far more, and single varieties are not uncommon. Taste one and you can see why: a swathe of pineapple, tangerine citrus, apricot and golden, honeyed pears. One of the most aromatic of all, low in tannin, with just enough acidity for freshness and exuberant in expression of its generous fruit. An ace-in-the-hole pear, arguably responsible for more of the world's greatest perries than any other individual variety.

Fossey
Floral and softly fruited
The emphasis here is firmly on floral. Indeed, so headily intense in its rose petal fragrance is Fossey (also Fausset) that it's almost surprising the aromatics don't take a turn for the soapy. That they don't is owed to a seam of refreshing acidity that cuts through all that perfume and elevates every-thing to an intoxicating miasma of high-toned springtime joy. A favourite of Jérôme Forget, in the Domfrontais, who makes a delicious example.

Vinot
Green, citrusy, zesty
Speaking of Jérôme, you simply must try his Vinot while you're at it. It's seldom seen on its own, and makes you wonder why when you actually get a chance to try its lemon and lime, electric, crunchy green-pear brilliance. Somewhere between Thorn and Yellow Huffcap, both in flavour and the intensity of its cheek-puckering zest, there aren't many varieties so refreshing on a hot day under the shade of a pear tree.

De Fer

Super-fruity, tropical

Honestly, France! For all that I adore your poiré, how I wish more of your superlative varieties were given greater limelight. Mind you, I can see why De Fer wouldn't be top of most producers' to-do lists: miniscule pears that fall right at the cold, wet, winter-bitten end of harvest season. Most folk leave them where they are. Jérôme's own team call it '*de l'enfer*' – 'of hell' – and yet what fulsome heaven can be unlocked in its pressing: huge, full-bodied, golden, grapey flavours awash with sultanas, deep melon and even dabs of caramel. As is so often the case, life's great challenges yield the richest rewards.

Rare Pears

One of the most remarkable things about drinking perry is the opportunity to taste a variety whose remaining mature trees you could count on your fingers.

In some cases, this is simply a matter of unidentified wildings, created by the one-off dropping of pips. Many won't be noticed, or make perry of particularly high quality, but sometimes a tree will grow into something special, possibly to be named and grafted.

In other cases, varieties are critically rare simply as a matter of neglect, of perry falling out of fashion, and of a complete lack of protected status. Most maddeningly of all, to those of us who love perry, who know of its capabilities and who would like to see the drink appreciated as much as it deserves, amongst these rare pears are varieties whose perry is known to be exceptional.

As recently as 1963, Coppy was described in Luckwill and Pollard's *Perry Pears* as 'of very good quality', a distinction they didn't offer lightly. They noted that it was already rare, but that Hogg, writing 80 years earlier, had reported many Coppy trees growing in Worcestershire.

As of 20 years ago, just one single Coppy tree remained, harvested by Tom Oliver for a perry rated by many as his best single variety of all. It has since been grafted and it is now possible to taste perry from the young trees. Being less mature, their fruit isn't quite as intense or as rich as that of their parent tree, but it is, nonetheless, recognisable as Coppy, and delicious.

Fortunately, today there are several people engaged in the often-thankless work of rescuing and propagating rare pears. From Jim Chapman,

Charles Martell, Chris Atkins and the team at the UK's National Perry Pear Centre in Hartpury, Gloucestershire, to Barry Masterson's International Perry Pear Project in Germany's Schefflenz, true perry champions are working to preserve these critically endangered fruits and ensure that we can all continue to drink the gorgeous perries for which they are responsible.

When you drink perry from one of these pears, not only will you enjoy something delicious – and rarer than even the most coveted and expensive wines – but you will personally be helping save something that could otherwise be lost.

Flakey Bark

Earthy, minerally, countryside

Thought to be extinct until Charles Martell happened to spot six trees on the slope of May Hill as he passed by in a horse and cart (honestly). Those six remain the only mature Flakey Barks in existence, all well over 100 years old. It is harvested by Rob Castle of Castle Wood Press, and by the Johnsons of Ross-on-Wye, whose single variety Flakey Bark is one of my favourite perries. It completely blows away the notion that perry is inherently a delicate, floral drink; this is an earthy, big-boned, hugely tannic bruiser whose flavours and aromas bellow of the land; a textural, visceral medley of petrichor, warm earth, pear skin, dried leaves, lanolin and smokiness, richened by dried pear fruit and peach pits. Once tasted, never forgotten – an iconic, idiosyncratic original which I love with all my heart.

Coppy

Super-fruity, tropical

When I ask Tom Oliver about the taste of Coppy he tells me that it always reminds him of confectionary. He cites yellow fruit and perhaps a little melon, but it is the sweet, sherbety, confectionary character that he asserts most definitely. My own tastings from the grafted younglings offered golden pear, lychee and zingy gooseberry and citrus character (arguably, Coppy could fall into each one of our flavour camps) Tragically, though, many of the young grafts are now suffering from incurable fireblight. The mission to save Coppy is far from complete and may yet end in failure, such is the very real plight of even the most potentially brilliant of perry pears.

Betty Prosser

Super-fruity, tropical

Thought to be down to just a dozen trees in Gloucestershire, more have since been unearthed in Monmouthshire, from which this variety is thought to have originated (the identity of the original Betty herself remains shrouded in mystery). The single varieties I've tried suggest a pear particularly sensitive to vintage. In a generous year it creates a first-rate perry of incredible richness and juiciness; a slathering of red fruits, honeys, exotic flowers and stone fruit. Even in less fulsome vintages it has an always-appealing ripeness, though the flavours in those vintages tend to be more about florals and orchard fruits character, without that riper blush.

Brinarl

Green, citrusy, zesty

Almost the yin to Moorcroft's yang, in straddling the line between citrusy and tropical, but falling (to this author's palate) just on the zestier, more citrusy side. Only two rows of this old Herefordshire pear are known to exist, and the orchardist who picked them told me it was historically considered of average quality. Which is hard to believe after tasting the Pét Nat Perry 2020 made by Little Pomona – my only Brinarl to date. A veritable explosion of crisp yuzu, star fruit, super-ripe lime and quince, with racy acidity and the lightest brush of tannin. A pear that underscores just how little we still know about these fruits and their potential for greatness.

Traditional pressing at Hollow Ash, Herefordshire

MAKING PERRY

Washing, Sorting, Milling and Maceration

The first rule of perrymaking is that cleanliness is next to godliness. Before a drop is pressed it is absolutely imperative that all equipment and fruit be squeaky clean, to remove any chance of spoilage or bacterial infection. This means sterilising the equipment – a process the maker will have to repeat on a daily basis through the pressing season – and washing the fruit.

Washing pears can present a problem, as, unlike apples, pears sink, meaning they can't simply be floated along to the mill. It is especially imperative for pears that have been harvested mechanically, as these will have picked up more dirt and orchard detritus than those harvested by hand. What's more, certain varieties can be especially soft at the milling stage and easily damaged either in transportation or cleaning.

Ross-on-Wye's Becky Fletcher shows author the ropes

Just as important is good sorting. This is the laborious process that takes place before milling and pressing; the removal of any badly damaged, rotten or unripe fruit. It's an occasionally overlooked and certainly under-discussed element of perrymaking, and the most thorough sorting can only be done by teams working with the most favourable ratio of people to pears to time. I would argue that it is here, in the sorting process, in the selection of perfectly ripe fruit for the press, that the truly world-class perries are separated from the very good.

Sorting is critical

Milling is the only stage of perrymaking that differs meaningfully from the making of wine. Unlike grapes, which are soft enough to press directly, pears (and apples) require a bit of what can only really be described as mashing up first. Historically, this would have been done in large stone vats by people armed with heavy wooden clubs. In more recent history, fruit would have been placed in a shallow circular groove around which a heavy millstone would have been dragged by humans or animals. Today, a mechanical 'scratter', which effectively shreds the fruit into tiny pieces, is the standard piece of equipment for perrymakers.

Pomace left in press after juice extraction

A final, optional, step before pressing – one certainly not taken by the majority of makers – is maceration. The milled pear pulp is left for a short time, no more than a day, ideally spread across a shallow surface area. This process allows a small level of micro-oxidation and begins to break down the cell walls and long-chain molecules within the pear flesh and juice. This is particularly useful for softening tannins within the pear (more on those later), resulting in a more rounded mouthfeel and reducing the likelihood of those tannins later binding into clumpy, unattractive sediment (more on that later too). Certain varieties, generally those with higher levels of tannins, such as Butt and Rock, benefit particularly from maceration.

Pears go into the mill for scratting

Pressing

This is just what it says on the tin. Pressure is applied to the scratted pears in a way that separates the juice from the pulp. This can be achieved in a number of ways. The ancient Romans used large, expensive olive presses that operated on a screw mechanism; a solid wooden disk gradually drilled down onto the pulp. Their modern counterparts are concertina 'basket presses', popular for very small-batch perries.

The traditional press in the UK, still used by many small makers today, involves the building of what's called a 'cheese'. Pear pulp is wrapped – in straw, horsehair, or, more commonly these days, cloth – into thin, square parcels called 'hairs', which are stacked on top of each other to form the cheese. Pressure is applied from the top and juice flows out of the hairs and into a receptacle beneath. Modern 'rack and cloth' pressing involves placing a hard wooden rack in between each hair to aid extraction.

Larger makers might choose instead to use a so-called 'belt press'. These involve spreading pulp onto a moving belt which guides it beneath rolling cylinders. Besides being more efficient and requiring far less physical labour than is involved in the building of a cheese, the belt press allows more even pressure to be applied to the pulp.

Rack and cloth press above, belt press left

The gentlest ways of pressing are with a hydropress or pneumatic press. These both work by putting pulp into a container with a deflated bladder. As the bladder is filled – with water in the case of the hydropress, or air in the case of pneumatic – it expands to put pressure on the pulp and the juice runs out of the press through thin slats in the bottom or sides.

Pneumatic presses are expensive and more commonly found in the wine world, but the control they offer in the firmness of the press makes them attractive to some perrymakers, despite their cost.

The level of pressure makes a difference to the quality of juice as well as its basic quantity. The weight of the pulp itself inside the press will release a certain amount of juice even before additional pressure is applied. This is known as 'free run' and considered the purest juice of all. The more pressure applied, the more juice will be extracted, but the more significant the impact of stalks, pips and skins on final flavour is likely to be.

It wouldn't be perry if there wasn't an extra complication. Besides the urgency with which some pears need to be milled and pressed once ripe, certain varieties, thanks to softness and physical makeup, are particularly prone to clogging. Tom Oliver cites some early season pears like Blakeney Red and, especially, Judge Amphlett as particular culprits: 'Pressing goes downhill rapidly, because the juice has no way of escaping,' he tells me. 'So it always requires a lot more cleaning of the belts on a belt press, a lot more cleaning of the cloths on a rack and cloth press, and in a hydropress or a concertina press pears are a nightmare!'

Nightmarish it may be, but now, with pears pressed, and juice racked into containers, it's time for the fun stuff to start.

This labour-intensive style of press is centuries old

A Word on Bletting

You cut the pear in half and it looks ruined. Where you expect pure, crisp, pale flesh, there is instead a brown, bruised-looking centre. It looks as though the pear has rotted from the inside. But this isn't rot ... or rather, it isn't 'the bad' sort of rot. It is bletting.

Depending on the variety, bletting can take place on the tree itself or after the pears have been harvested. Within the unbroken skin of the pear, cell walls have begun to break down, reducing the firmness of tannins and the sharpness of acidity, and increasing the levels of sugar in the pear. It is a sort of internal fermentation – an 'ultra-ripening of fruit'.

Bletted pears taste different to the same varieties that are unbletted: they are riper, juicier, sweeter. Citrusy flavours deepen and tropical flavours are heightened. To a perrymaker, bletting is very much something to be desired – with the right varieties.

Not rotten – in fact, perfectly bletted

Not every pear is suitable. You wouldn't want to allow bletting in the faster-ripening varieties for instance; it's best kept for the more tannic, later varieties that can ripen off the tree a while. What's more, allow too great a degree of bletting and the pressing becomes a mulchy, clogging hell that looks far too much like a dirty protest for comfort.

But with the right varieties, and given the right time, bletting is a very special card in the maker's pack. It is invisible magic within the pear; the acceptable face of decay.

Fermentation

Where would we be without yeasts? Whatever your drink, be it perry, wine, beer, whisky, rum, mezcal or any other alcoholic potation, you have these magnificent little creatures to thank. Not to mention the sterling service they also perform in your yoghurts, dried fruits, sauces and all manner of delicious baked treats.

Very simply, drinks fermentation is the transformation, by yeasts, of a sugar source into alcohol. If we were making beer or whisky this would require the additional process of brewing to convert the starch in grains into soluble sugars, but pear juice, already rich in glucose, fructose and sucrose, does not require this. Perry is made, not brewed: it simply ferments. (There are certainly a few makers who wouldn't forgive you for using 'the b-word' within earshot!)

Spontaneous

Yeasts are so abundant in nature that, left to its own devices, freshly pressed pear juice will begin to ferment of its own accord. Indeed, many makers prefer to allow their pear juice to do exactly this. They want their perry to reflect the local ambient cultures of yeast, and they believe that the multifarious cultures of yeast that are found in the orchard and the barn itself will imbue their perry with greater complexity. This is known as 'wild', 'ambient' or 'spontaneous' fermentation.

Kloeckera, so-called 'apiculate yeasts', live on the very skins of the pears themselves, and play a role in the beginning of fermentation – from the moment the skins of the pears have split (whether or not they have reached the perry barn by that point). They can't survive at high levels of alcohol, though, so the majority of spontaneous fermentation will be the work of the *Saccharomyces* strains present within the perry barn.

Since spontaneous fermentation is less 'controlled', by its very nature, it tends to be rather slow, often taking a matter of months. I've tasted perries that have still been fermenting over a year after the juice was pressed. These fermentations are also more likely to become 'stuck' – a term for when yeasts simply stop converting sugars to alcohols, either through cold temperatures, lack of nutrients in the perry, or insufficient numbers of yeasts. What's more, perrymakers choosing spontaneous fermentation must be even more scrupulous in their attention to hygiene, since the risk of a long, wild fermentation spoiling or becoming infected is

Washing pears in the background before milling

all the greater. Nonetheless, many makers believe that the potential flavours found through spontaneous fermentation justify the risks.

Pick-your-own

The alternative approach is for the perrymaker to inoculate their pear juice with a particular strain of yeast they have selected themselves – a so-called 'cultured yeast'. First, they need to kill off the wild yeasts, as well as any bacteria that may be on the fruit. This can be achieved either with a dose of sulphites or by pasteurisation. Their chosen yeast strain will then be added to the juice.

There are several reasons a maker might choose to 'pitch' a yeast rather than leaving the job of fermentation up to nature. The first is control. Fermentation can be unpredictable, and it's hardly surprising that many makers would prefer it to take place under the quicker and more manageable conditions that selected yeast strains afford.

An argument sometimes put forward against 'pitched yeast' perries is that their profile, influenced by only one strain of yeast and over a short period, may be less complex than a wild fermentation that has been subject to many yeasts and for much longer. But the term 'pitched yeast' covers a broad church of yeast strains that may be used for different reasons or to promote particular flavour profiles.

'Champagne yeast', for instance – *Saccharomyces bayanus*, sometimes called 'ec118' – plays a very specific role. Despite the name (which can certainly be weaponised for marketing purposes, given its glitzy connotations), its job is nothing to do with making something taste like champagne.

Juice running off the press for collection

'Champagne yeast is a unique strain that does a specific job, which is it starts fermenting in a liquid that already has alcohol in it,' maker Eleanor Leger of Eden, in Vermont, tells me. 'Which is hard to do with regular *Saccharomyces cerevisiae*. But *Saccharomyces bayanus* can get going from a standstill in a liquid that already has alcohol in it for a secondary fermentation. That's why you use Champagne yeast.'

From a flavour perspective, Kveik yeast, most famous as a farmhouse beer yeast from Norway, now much-loved by craft brewers around the world, acts very fast and at high temperatures, but can promote an especially tropical flavour profile. There are other yeast strains designed to heighten the characteristics of particular varieties.

'Pitched equals boring is definitely wrong,' says Barry Masterson, who has explored both spontaneous and pitched fermentations. 'There is such an incredible range of yeasts selected for certain properties.'

Certainly, some perrymakers, wanting to keep the finnicky business of fermentation as straightforward as possible, will choose a yeast that simply gets the job done cleanly and quickly, and will use this same yeast for all their perries. But, as with so many things, the question of whether spontaneous or pitched fermentation is 'better' when it comes to flavour is far too binary to answer with any certainty. The creativity of perrymakers, and the infinitely colourful world of yeasts, makes sure of that.

Managing fermentation

Temperature is enormously important to fermentation. Too cold and the yeasts become sluggish and inactive, too hot and the more delicate flavours and aromas in the juice can be spoiled. While there's no hard and fast rule – that complex world of yeasts and varieties again – by and large temperatures of around 20°C are ideal. (For many if not most farmhouse makers it comes down to whatever the barn temperature is!)

Fermentation generates heat, so, especially in hotter countries, monitoring and controlling temperatures can be important, particularly if working with a faster acting yeast. Conversely, in colder climates, and particularly with slow, wild fermentations, it's not uncommon for the yeast to stop working altogether until the weather warms up again.

Occasionally, a spontaneous fermentation might simply stop of its own accord, even if the temperature seems to be perfectly fine. This can be because there aren't enough nutrients in the juice to keep the yeasts happy. These 'stuck' fermentations can be managed either by simply deploying a 'wait and see' approach, increasing the temperature a little to try and liven up the yeasts, or, as a last resort, adding a culture of more voracious yeasts to finish the job.

The danger of ignoring stuck fermentations can be twofold. In the first instance, yeasts stressed by lack of nutrients start producing hydrogen sulphide, which, left unchecked, can move into various disulphides, producing a spectrum of flavours and aromas running from rotten eggs to mouldy cabbage and even sewage. More dangerously, if a perry that seems to have stopped fermenting is packaged before fermentation is complete, fermentation may restart within the container itself. Since another byproduct of fermentation is carbon dioxide, this can build huge pressure inside the container, leading to potentially explosive consequences at worst.

There's another danger when it comes to fermenting perry that isn't a feature of cider or wine. In both of these latter drinks, a process can often take place called 'malolactic fermentation'. This involves malolactic bacteria converting sharp malic acid (think zesty green apple flavours) into softer lactic acid (think buttery tones). Indeed, in most red wines, certain whites (especially Chardonnay) and a number of richer bittersweet ciders, this effect can be very desirable.

However, unlike grapes or apples, pears contain significant quantities of citric acid. Whereas malolactic bacteria will metabolise malic acid into lactic acid, when they meet with citric acid they will metabolise it into a

very different acid – acetic. Acetic is the acid associated with vinegar, and if malolactic fermentation is allowed to take place in perry, that's precisely what you'll end up with. Tasty on chips, but not something you want to drink!

Depending on the quantities they are fermenting and the flavour profile they are looking to achieve, makers may choose to ferment in inert plastic or stainless-steel containers, or in wooden casks (more on those when we talk about maturation). Fermentation is completed when all fermentable sugars in the perry have been converted to alcohol, when there are no yeasts remaining, or when the perrymaker has decided to end the process safely and early by pasteurising the liquid to kill the remaining yeasts. Depending on the variety, the season, and the climate in which the pears have grown, a fully-fermented dry perry should reach around 5.5–8.5 per cent ABV, though certain regions and pears have the potential to go even higher.

A word on sorbitol

Yet another in perry's endless list of potentially frustrating quirks for the maker is that it contains a reasonable amount of a sugar-alcohol carbohydrate called sorbitol, of which grapes usually have none and apples only a trace.

Sorbitol is unfermentable. Once the yeasts have finished their work on the sugars in the pear juice, the sorbitol will remain, and the perry will retain a touch of sweetness. In the vast majority of fully fermented perries this will present as very slight. To most palates, an entirely fermented Thorn or Butt or Grüne Pichelbirne, for instance, will seem completely dry, just as a cider or wine would, perhaps with the perception of a slightly heightened fruitiness.

Sorbitol's real bad rep comes from the fact that in significant doses it has laxative properties. This has given rise to all sorts of comments on the alleged purgative properties of perry – hardly the best advertisement for a drink! Indeed, this has been remarked upon historically for so long that it is referenced in the nicknames of certain varieties of pear. Holmer, for instance, a very old Herefordshire pear variety, had such a fearsome reputation that some referred to it as 'Startlecock', which I don't think we need to elaborate on.

However, it bears repetition that the quantity of sorbitol in the majority of perry pears is small. Greater than in apples, sure, but small, nonetheless. While those more sensitive to sorbitol might not want to open that second bottle in an evening, the vast majority of us will see no ill effect besides that which we'd expect from drinking excessive amounts of any alcohol. Having spent many an evening drinking perry with friends and makers, I speak from experience on this point.

Ray Williams, one of the greatest ever authorities on perry pears, suggested that the historically off-putting claims about the laxative properties of some varieties were not down to the effects of sorbitol at all, but rather to an overuse of fruit that had been left too long before harvesting and milling. 'It is the effects of drinking perry made from rotten fruit that has given Holmer its bad name. Similarly, the milling of rotten fruit is the probable reason for the bad reputation of Blakeney Red,' was his assessment.

Bottom line: unless you are particularly sensitive to sorbitol, perry from a good maker may be drunk without fear of anything but a hangover.

Maturation

During fermentation, particles made up of pear solids and dead yeast cells will form larger solids and begin to settle in the bottom of the vessel. These are known as 'gross lees' (as in 'big', rather than 'horrible'). Nonetheless, if the fermented perry is left on too large a quantity for too long, those lees can begin to live up to the latter definition and induce 'stinky' flavours in the perry.

It is therefore important for the maker to rack the perry – draw it off the gross lees and into a fresh container. There it will continue to throw 'fine lees', far smaller solid particles, usually mostly dead yeast cells. But rather than being damaging to the perry's flavours, these fine lees will provide a double bill of benefits – acting both as an antioxidant, preventing oxygen damage to the perry, and adding textural body and richness. These effects can be further stimulated by stirring the lees from time to time, a process known as bâtonnage.

Oak casks remain a popular maturation choice

Not every perry is destined for lengthy maturation after fermentation is complete. Indeed, the vast majority will be packaged, and intended for drinking more or less then and there. These are the bright, light, crisp, floral and fruity perries; the charmers intended to delight you with touches of zingy refreshment, plump orchard fruits and dabbles of lip-smacking citrus. Don't stash these away. When it comes to this style of perry, sooner always beats later. In fact, further ageing, far from benefitting these perries, may well be detrimental to the freshness of their flavours. Get those bottles open!

But some of the very best perries, made from the greatest varieties – those with more pronounced tannins, the highest levels of acidity and the greatest concentrations of flavours – have the potential to develop further, and indeed may not reach their pinnacle of complex greatness without extended maturation. Acidity and tannins are preservatives, meaning that the freshness of these perries will not be compromised by time.

Resting in their new vessels, these perries will gradually see their sharpness and coarser astringency soften; their fine lees add body and complexity, and their larger flavour compounds break down, becoming less concentrated and 'opening up' their flavours in the process. If they are ageing in wooden casks, this process will be aided by micro-oxidation, and the perry may also take on varying degrees of flavour from the wood itself.

Perry is a living thing; it continues to develop and, ultimately, decay, not only once fermentation has finished but even after it has been bottled. Many of the greatest perries I have ever been lucky enough to try are those that have continued to mature for years in bottle as their flavours continue to develop and broaden. Their tannins and acidity soften and integrate more harmoniously with the liquid. While not all perries have the capacity to mature – and judging the precise likely lifespan of a perry is not an exact science – tasting something like a 2001 Malvern Hills from Kevin Minchew, an aged Thorn or Flakey Bark from Ross-on-Wye, a 2005 Mostello from Distillerie Farthofer, or a venerable Poiré Granit from Eric Bordelet is about as profound an experience as perry affords.

Inevitably, the more perry that is put aside for extended maturation, the more space is taken up in the barn and the less packaged perry there is available to sell. So, longer-aged perries are likely to fetch a premium. Many makers will not have the space to mature perries themselves for as long as they would like and will bottle them before their true optimum drinking time. By learning which varieties and styles benefit most from

further ageing, the perry drinker can discern which bottles to crack open for drinking today, and which to stash away for special occasions yet to come.

A word on casks

I should admit a bias (yes, another one): I love casks. I think they're magical. These bulbous wooden containers so perfectly designed for the job they do, holding large amounts of liquid and exerting particular effects on that liquid while being surprisingly manoeuvrable. So perfect, in fact, that they have remained more or less unchanged for thousands of years and are still in use today.

As a perry lover who is also a cider writer who worked for almost a decade in the wine industry, and currently covers whisky and rum for a living, casks play a role in every drink that matters to me. But what is that role?

Well, first of all, not every perry is suitable for cask ageing. The most delicate of flavour and light of body run the risk of their flavours being overwhelmed. Indeed, many perrymakers eschew casks altogether, preferring to ferment and mature perry entirely in inert vessels of plastic and stainless steel so that the only flavours present in the drink are those

Little Pomona's cask portfolio is one of the UK's best

derived from the pears themselves and the act of fermentation. I once memorably heard a maker describe the cask-ageing of perry as 'an act of vandalism'. Many of the best perries I have ever tasted were aged in inert vessels, and I have tasted more than a few that barely tasted of perry at all, so strong was the influence of the wood.

But writing off casks altogether? No chance. There is a special alchemy to the perfectly judged marriage of cask and perry; a development, or embellishment of flavours achieved by nothing else. I think of the likes of Tom Oliver's Barrel Room Series, the Haselbergers' Pyrus, the mistelles of Normandy and the wine barrel-aged perries of Little Pomona and my palate purrs.

Casks may be made of any sort of wood, but the most common, and – by reasonably broad consensus – the best, is oak. It's robust enough to withstand fairly rough handling, tight-grained enough that it doesn't suffer the same leakage issues as many other woods, and capable of imparting delicious flavours.

By far the most common oak casks are made of American or French oak. These, importantly, are two different species. American, *Quercus alba*, is particularly high in vanillins and aromatic lactones, compounds that give flavours of vanilla, coconut, caramel and sweet spice. Meanwhile, French oak, *Quercus robur* or *Quercus petraea*, offers toast, clove and richer spices.

As it rests in a cask, perry will take on some of the flavours of the oak. However, it is very rare for perry to be aged in a brand-new cask.

Far more common is for perry to be aged in casks that have been used, and then emptied, at least once before – more often several times. Think of a cask like a teabag: the more times it is used, the less flavour will be left in the staves of the wood to leach out into the liquid. Once we reach a third, fourth or fifth use, the cask will barely be exerting flavour at all.

Since new casks are so impactful, and since they are also very expensive, it is common to find perrymakers choosing casks that have previously held another sort of drink, such as whisky, rum or wine. In addition to the flavours of the wood itself, perries aged in these casks will take on some of the flavours of those former inhabitants. Some makers swear by the effects of white wine and sweet wine barriques, while Tom Oliver has offered particularly high praise for former rum barrels. I have even had perry that was aged in casks that formerly held peated Islay whisky or tequila. And you know what? I loved them all.

Doris Farthofer extracting years-old Mostello from cask

But casks perform another function too. Since oak, unlike plastic and stainless steel, is porous, microscopic quantities of oxygen are allowed through the staves. Not enough to damage the liquid, so long as lees are present and the cask is full, but enough to contribute to the softening of tannins and the 'rounding' of body and mouthfeel. This is often the preference of perrymakers who choose to use oak casks: the benefits of micro-oxidation without too much impact of wood flavour.

Blending

While many perries are packaged as single varieties, for all sorts of reasons it is more common to find perry presented as a blend. Some varieties of pear, drunk on their own, might not offer huge amounts of individual character. Others might be extreme in one aspect – tannins, acidity, body – but low in others, and therefore seemingly unbalanced to some drinkers. In each case, these perries might be better suited to a harmonious marriage with other varieties rich in the qualities they themselves lack. In the words of Albert Johnson, one purpose of a blend 'is to showcase qualities of varieties and hide deficiencies'.

The very largest makers, those whose customers demand a familiar product time and time again, and who are perhaps less interested in the idiosyncrasies of pear varieties and the inconsistencies of vintage, also need to blend to ensure a consistent product.

But blending can also be a platform for artistic licence; a chance for the maker to create something unique to them; a blank canvas for expression of flavour. Not simply bringing different varieties together, but possibly perries that have aged in different vessels – a splash of barrel-aged, perhaps, adding depth and richness to the leaner crispness and freshness of something aged in plastic or stainless steel. How about blending perries of different ages, or varying levels of sweetness? Heretical as it may be to some makers, how about introducing different fruits, spices or herbs, as has been done to various perries for various reasons and in various countries for hundreds – possibly thousands – of years? With endless different directions to take depending on the preferences and palate of the maker, the sky's the limit.

Blending can take place at a couple of different stages. Different varieties can be mingled at pressing, creating a juice comprising several different pears. This requires the varieties to either share a window of ripeness or to be suitable for keeping off the tree before pressing.

So, it is common to see in-press blends of 'early season' or 'late season' pears. In Austria, for instance, Speckbirne and Stieglbirne often share a September press, with Dorschbirne and Grüne Pichelbirne combining at a later stage of harvest.

Perry may also be blended after pressing has taken place but before fermentation has begun. This often happens for logistical reasons; for example, a maker may not have enough of a particular variety to fill a container, so must top up that container with the juice of a different pear to avoid oxygen getting into excess headspace.

Finally, perry might be blended after varieties have fully fermented. This allows makers a clear view of precisely what flavours and textures they have to play with, rather than working on the assumed knowledge of an in-press blend. However, perry's ever-mischievous nature may come into play once again here. The complex tannin structure of certain pears means that some perries might be crystal clear in their own container, but on contact with another seemingly bright-as-day perry transform into a liquid as opaque and dense-looking as the haziest of New England IPAs. While this doesn't affect flavour, such appearances can be off-putting to some consumers. As a result, there are certain pear varieties which some makers wouldn't dream of trying to blend post-fermentation. For example, Tom Oliver cites Rock as a pear he would only ever bottle as a single variety.

Many of the greatest perries are blends

Because of the scope for individual expression it affords, blending is often the most romanticised stage of the perrymaking process, conjuring images of the maker with a nose-in-a-million concocting their alchemy amongst slumbering barrels in a dimly lit cellar. And occasionally that is indeed the case.

More often, though, especially for producers with a larger output, the true skill of blending lies in holding a three-dimensional mental image of all their maturing stock, balancing what they need to sell with what they have available and what they want to make with what their particular market seems to call for. It is the makers who are able, at scale, to create a balanced, diverse and high-quality range of perries within these parameters for whom I have the highest respect.

A word on sediment – don't fear the flakes!

Honestly! Sometimes it seems perry just doesn't want to behave itself.

All drinks made of fruit, be they perry, cider or wine, throw a bit of sediment during fermentation and maturation. We've talked about lees already. They're simply the natural result of large particles in the liquid, be they from the pears themselves, or the yeasts that have acted upon them, falling out of suspension and settling at the bottom of the container. The maker gets rid of most of them by racking, and can remove most, if not all of the rest, if they choose, by fining or filtration during the packaging process.

Sediment isn't the least bit harmful. If anything, it's a sign that the drink hasn't been over-filtered. Often it is part of an exceptional package: think of the flakes left in a bottle of old Bordeaux or vintage Port after it has been decanted. But people buy and drink with their eyes, and sediment doesn't look particularly attractive in your drink, which is why many makers, especially at big commercial enterprises, try to avoid it altogether.

When it comes to perry, things get more complicated. Perry pears, especially the more tannic varieties, contain an especially high concentration of a compound called procyanidin. This compound loves to bind itself together in all manner of visible ways; from hazes in the liquid that range from a light mist to a full-blown milkshake, to large flakes of sediment that give bottles the look of a snowglobe when upended, and, most

Natural sediment is often part of great perry

unsightly of all, heavy precipitates that look like – there's no other way of putting this – the brains of alien creatures.

Maddeningly, makers can filter a perry to remove this sediment, only to see it reform in the bottle of its own accord. Maceration before pressing can reduce the problem by absorption of tannin on the pulp, and certain extremely tannic perries can be used as clarification agents in perries that have thrown a haze, but the only absolute guarantees for sediment-free perry are the tightest of filters or the use of pasteurisation, which may have negative effects upon the quality and flavour of the liquid itself.

My message, therefore, to lovers of the greatest and tastiest drinks: don't fear the flakes. Rather than the sign of something that has gone wrong, the deposits in a perry bottle may well be the sign of a drink that will taste oh-so-right.

While sediment won't affect your drinking experience – personally I barely notice it any more – you can avoid pouring any into your glass by standing a bottle upright for a little while after opening, allowing all sediment to settle in the bottom before pouring it into your glass. Pouring the perry gently into a decanter (a jug is absolutely fine) will also ensure sediment-free drinking, and if you pour it through something like a tea-strainer (sometimes the only solution for removing larger sediment from a sparkling perry) you'll have a crystal-clear drink every time.

Faults

Sometimes perry goes bad. Pear juice is so delicate and so finnicky that preventing it from going bad takes special care from the maker – more so than apple or grape juice. Improvements in hygiene and professionalism mean faulty perry is less common than it was even a few years ago, but faults still exist, and it is worth being aware of the most common.

There are still too many perries available on shop shelves and the back bars of pubs that show at least one of the faults listed below, and sadly not all retailers or publicans are even aware of them as 'faults'. There have been several occasions when I have been told that an overtly faulty perry was 'just what traditional perry is supposed to taste like'. Utter nonsense – and reputationally dangerous for the category to boot. Just as we aren't afraid to send back a bottle of wine that is corked, and just as beer drinkers are aware when a cask has been poorly kept, so the perry drinker deserves to be able to return something that simply isn't good enough.

Acetic acid

Left entirely unchecked, the ambition of all fruit juice is to turn itself into vinegar. This ambition can be thwarted by distilling or fortifying it so that it is protected by sheer level of alcohol, or at least significantly slowed down by either the use of preservatives or by fermenting it and protecting it from the influence of oxygen.

Oxygen in significant quantities is the greatest enemy of the perrymaker. It will give a drink a stale 'sherried' flavour and will allow ambient bacteria called acetobacter to turn a drink to vinegar in no time. Think of the dregs of drinks glasses you might smell before washing up the next morning. Once oxygen is in the drink there's no way back. The best ways to safeguard your perry are the careful, moderate use of sulphites and ensuring the perry is kept in sealed, full containers at all times.

Acetic acid is the most common perry fault. In fact, it has historically been so endemic, particularly in British farmhouse perry, that some makers and drinkers actually prefer their perry to showcase a little of it. This is the fault you are most likely to be told 'is supposed to be there'. To those of us who don't enjoy it, or are sensitive to it, this can be intensely frustrating.

Mouse

A particularly unpleasant fault resulting from lactic bacteria produced by particular compounds. They tend to appear in perries with higher pH – so lower levels of acidity – especially when that perry has not had sulphites added around pressing.

A fortunate 40% of drinkers are unable to detect mouse. To the rest of us it presents as a horrendous mustiness which appears retronasally a few moments after swallowing or spitting. Once experienced, never forgotten, it gets its name from tasting – allegedly – like the bottom of a mouse's cage.

Ethyl acetate

A natural ester and byproduct of normal alcoholic fermentation but which in high concentrations, usually accelerated by acetic acid bacteria when exposed to oxygen, gives off an unpleasant smell of intense pear drop or nail varnish remover. As with acetic acid, attention to airtight conditions is the maker's friend here.

TCA (trichloroanisole)

Wine lovers might know this one as 'cork taint', but although it can come from a cork, it can also be produced through the storage conditions (especially wooden casks) in the perry barn. TCA is created when a particular fungus interacts with certain chlorine-based products. Sensitivity levels vary from person to person, but a corked perry will smell and taste of anything from wet dog to cardboard. Send it back – just as you would a corked wine.

Sulphides

Not to be confused with *sulphites*! (More on those shortly). Hydrogen Sulphide (H_2S) is produced in excessive quantities when the yeasts become stressed through lack of nutrients (specifically nitrogen). This can be a particular problem in keeved perries, in pears from particularly old trees, or if the tired wild yeasts are asked to perform a further fermentation of sugars in bottle-conditioned perries. It can be a particular issue if the weather is cold and the yeasts are less active. Stressed yeasts really let rip, giving off smells of rotten eggs and cabbages … and even sewage. Keep those yeasts happy!

Brettanomyces

This is controversial. *Brettanomyces* ('brett') is, in certain quantities, and certain drinks, not really a fault at all. It's a feature of many of the best Belgian beers, for instance, and more than a few celebrated wines, and it pops up in some good ciders too.

Brett is a naturally occurring and extremely voracious strain of yeast. When it gets into a drink it can produce flavours ranging from spices and clove to leather, barnyard, sweaty animal and even dung. At a less-dominant level, and providing they stay away from the naughty-step end of those characteristics, a little brett can, to some palates, add complexity to a drink.

But just as most makers of white wine would shudder at the thought of it, so any more than the lightest brush of brett would overwhelm and clash with the flavours of virtually any perry. On the whole – admittedly very much in my opinion – it's something best avoided in perries. Though I'm always open to an exception that might prove the rule.

A word on sulphites

Sulphites get far worse press than they deserve. Far from criticism, they deserve celebrating as having protected our favourite drinks from infection for literally thousands of years.

Sulphites are chemical compounds (Sulphur Dioxide – SO_2) that in tiny doses occur naturally in all types of fermented fruit drinks as byproducts of the yeasts' activities. However, most makers also choose to add an additional dose of sulphites as a preservative against oxygen and against most of the nasties we have just discussed.

This is nothing new. At a fundamental level, sulphur was used as a preservative as far back as the ancient Greeks and Romans. Pliny the Elder mentions the burning of sulphur candles in amphorae for just this purpose.

More recently, sulphites have started to come in for a great deal more criticism. That's probably in part down to the name. 'Sulphites' sound chemical, mostly because that's precisely what they are, and people would probably rather not think of such things over a glass of perry.

It's also true that some people are allergic to sulphites, which is the main reason why anything containing over 10ppm (parts per million) of SO_2 is required to state 'contains sulphites' on the label. However, the number of people who are allergic to sulphites – fewer than one in a hundred – is significantly lower than the number who claim that their rough morning after was sulphite-induced.

In truth, perry – like wine – is far lower in sulphites than such foodstuffs as dried fruit, even at the maximum permitted levels (which most sulphited perries don't begin to approach). Sulphites don't cause headaches unless you happen to be allergic to them, nor are they to the detriment of the perry, except at the highest levels, which good makers are invariably a long way beneath. Perry, being lower in alcohol than wine, is more delicate and susceptible to infection, making it all the harder to create a stable, fault-free product without the application of sulphites. Perry is even more fragile than cider, and many's the natural maker I know who won't sulphite their apple juice, but will always add a small trace to their pears. Very sensible, in my book.

Where sulphites can be excessive is where they are used in large doses to sterilise perry after fermentation is complete. This is where natural aromas can be suppressed, and the character of excessive sulphites begins to show through. Typically, these perries would be from bigger, industrial makers – again in in the name of ensuring consistency.

It is marvellous and inspiring that many makers are attempting to reduce or remove sulphites in their perry. But it is important to acknowledge that this approach requires the highest level of care and can sometimes result in infection even when that care is taken. It is equally important not to

Sulphites are often added to protect fresh-pressed juice

indulge mistruths and over-generalisations about sulphites and their application.

Many of the best perries I have ever tasted took a zero-sulphite approach, but just as many had been dosed with an appropriate level at the appropriate time. As with all things perry, it isn't a black and white issue, but a matter of balance, care and preference.

Stabilisation

The choices continue. The point of stabilisation is twofold. In the first instance, it is to remove any remaining yeasts and possible microorganisms in the perry which might spoil it after packaging. It can also be a cosmetic choice, particularly for a larger-scale producer, to ensure no sediment or haze remains, and that the perry has the absolute brightness that the majority of the market demands.

This is generally achieved via pasteurisation – heating to a high temperature to kill off microorganisms – or passing the perry through a very tight microfilter. Most producers aiming at the higher end of perry choose to avoid these methods, as both can result in damage to the texture and delicate flavours of the liquid.

The other reason a producer might pasteurise or microfilter is if they want to either retain natural sweetness, or have added any sugar to their perry after fermentation is complete. If any live yeasts are left in a liquid containing sugar they will continue to ferment after that liquid has been packaged. Sometimes this is specifically desired, but for the most part producers are looking for what they package to be a finished product, and, especially if the perry is intended to be still, will want to preserve it as is.

Continued fermentation in container, if not done under controlled conditions and in specific, toughened, Champagne-style bottles, can be genuinely dangerous, since the carbon dioxide produced by fermentation will put pressure on the container, and, in the most extreme cases, cause it to explode. If this happens in a bag-in-box, the worst that will happen is a horrible sticky mess to clear up, but in metal cans or glass bottles the effects can be seriously unpleasant.

Many producers, especially those taking a minimal intervention approach, will opt not to pasteurise or filter, but will simply rack perry off its lees and into the container.

Packaging

What the producer opts to package their perry in will be dictated in no small part by local traditions and by how they intend their perry to be served.

Globally, the most common format is the 750ml bottle, which dominates perry packaging in France and is extremely common in Austria. This is influenced by the significant wine culture in both countries and reflects the way perry tends to be served there: with food and in stemmed wine glasses. In Austria, where a vast quantity of perry is still, bottles often take a straight-sided table-wine shape. In France, where perry is almost invariably sparkling, expect a more curved, Champagne-style bottle complete with cork and cage.

England and Wales buck the trend. Here, where 'real' perry is served, it is often in the format of pints or half pints, generally directly from the perry farm or on draught in a pub. This has popularised so-called bag-in-boxes; inflatable pouches inside cardboard boxes which might hold anything from five to 20l, and which, providing they are kept in consistently cool conditions, can keep the perry relatively fresh for a month or two.

In the last few years, however, as a result of the reappraisal of cider and perry and the rise of a higher-end sector, it has been increasingly common to find British perry packaged in a 750ml format. Unlike France or Austria, there is no traditionally established shape for these bottles, though most tend to be of the curved Champagne or Burgundy style, often reinforced to cope with high-pressure sparkling methods. It is equally common to find perry in the UK bottled in 500ml or even 330ml bottles. These are usually perries intended to be drunk more casually.

Cans are rare in perry, though the American market has led the way in beginning to explore the format and one or two English producers have followed suit. Generally speaking, these are intended for the same casual drinking as smaller bottles, and are usually pasteurised, filtered and force-carbonated.

STYLES OF PERRY

If varieties of pear and choice of yeast are the starting points of flavour, style is where those flavours continue to be shaped.

At their most simplistic, styles of perry boil down to how sweet or dry a producer intends their perry to be, whether they want it still or sparkling, whether they wish it to be fortified, whether they want to introduce additional flavours, and the ways in which all of the above are achieved.

Though generally less important than varieties of pears in establishing how perry will taste, styles are full of nuance, and crucial to the drinking experience. Distinctions and decisions made here separate, say, a dry Champagne-method perry from a fortified, barrel-aged mostello or a sweetened, force-carbonated bulk brand.

A word on transparency

Part of the importance of delineating styles is that it offers the perry drinker clarification as to what they're drinking, which is another reason why it's also important to list varieties where known and possible.

This fits into a wider, much-needed conversation around transparency when it comes to perry. As we've seen, perry – or pear cider – can be made perfectly legally in the UK with as little as 35% pear juice, all of which can come from concentrate. The upshot, of course, being that a bottle that is around 65% water and 35% concentrate – which can be made at any time of year and at very low cost – can sit on the shelves beside a full-juice, sensitively made product that can only be made once a year and features far more expensive ingredients – to say nothing of the additional costs incurred by the producer when it comes to ageing times, stock storage and so on – and both can be labelled as the same thing.

Inevitably, the industrially produced perry made with cheaper ingredients will be priced more competitively, meaning that the consumer is likely to vote with their wallets against the full-juice option, unaware of differences in ingredients and quality. While everyone is entitled to their own preferences, and should be allowed to peacefully drink whatever they want, this is a system that clearly works against both the unsuspecting consumer and the artisanal maker.

Author looks for more detailed labels...

What's more, since most industrially produced perries are also not using 'perry pears', and since their juice content is, in any case, markedly lower than that of the full-juice perrymaker, this situation is plainly to the detriment of the endangered, priceless and ecologically important perry pear trees; a natural resource that would be a devastating loss were they to be pushed out of existence.

I would, ultimately, love to see a world where 'full juice' is the accepted standard, though I realise, sadly, that this is wishful thinking at present. In the short term, raising the minimum required juice content to at least 50% – as it is in countries such as France and the United States – would be a major first step, increasing the juice content of some industrial creations by almost half as much again. Even better if that juice was required to be fresh-pressed rather than from concentrate.

Additionally, I would like to see labelling standards improve. Even though this isn't mandated at a governmental level for the time being, if producers making high-juice-content perries showed their working on labels – explaining to the consumer what they have done, with what fruit and the difference it makes – those consumers would at least be able to make educated decisions for themselves. A transparent, clearly defined and explained world of perry is ultimately better for makers, better for drinkers, and better for the trees themselves.

Every perry fits into one of five base categories:
Still 'table'
Sparkling
Sweet/dessert
Fortified
Flavoured

Still 'Table' Perry

Simply, a perry to which nothing has been done to introduce bubbles. To distinguish it from the later dessert and fortified styles, which are also usually still, I have included the term 'table', borrowed from the world of wine.

These perries are around 5–8% ABV, and may, theoretically, be served from any format – bottle, can or bag-in-box. Depending on such elements as fruit selection, bulk, rarity and maturity, they range from the cheapest to some of the most premium in price. Because of its seeming simplicity, this can be a style that garners less excitement. But it is arguably the most important and certainly the original, fundamental style of perry, and includes many of the greatest perries ever or currently made.

Sparkling Perry

Bubbles are fun. They lift the spirits and the mood of the room. Celebrations are marked by the popping of corks; they symbolise the full spectrum of conviviality, from shared moments of joy to decadence and excess.

Importantly, they have a significant impact on how we experience a drink. Think of flat cola vs freshly opened, or of the first sip when you move from, say, Champagne to still wine. Bubbles add mouthfeel, structure and vibrancy to a drink. Most perries in the world currently feature them in one way or another.

But there are bubbles and then there are bubbles. The way in which carbonation is introduced will not only impact the feel of the fizz but can shape the flavours of the perry as a whole.

Force carbonated

This is the most straightforward method and very much what it says on the tin. Carbon dioxide is bubbled directly from a gas canister through the perry, imbuing bubbles without involving any of the more laborious processes below. Think Coca Cola.

This method is favoured by producers interested in consistency: not only can the precise level of carbonation be easily controlled, but other than a textural change, the actual flavours of the perry will not be significantly affected. All larger brand sparkling perries are likely to have undergone this technique, but it is also used in the majority of 500ml or 330ml bottles, even from smaller-scale producers.

A word on Verre Anglais

The story of the true origin of the method for making Champagne has become perhaps the favourite tale of the English cider or perry writer, and since it is relevant to everything in the remainder of our sparkling section, I won't let the side down today.

Really though, it is less a tale of how the English 'invented the Champagne method' than a tale of how a new and particular sort of glass was devised. You see, bubbles had been around in wine for some time beforehand. Firstly, possibly, via the pétillant naturel method, also known as the méthode ancestrale, which allegedly dates back to the monks at St-Hilare in southern France's Limoux region in 1531 (although this is questioned by some sparkling wine experts).

Secondly, unwanted bubbles would frequently occur, particularly in colder regions like Champagne, simply through poor understanding of fermentation. As we've seen, yeasts don't like the cold, so when winter bit in northern France they would simply shut down. The winemakers (usually monks) would believe fermentation to have completed and might bottle the wine, but when the weather warmed and the yeasts woke up, fermentation would start again, produce carbon dioxide, and hey presto, unwanted bubbles.

The real problem was that ordinary glass isn't designed to withstand the effects of much carbon dioxide. The pressure in a bottle of Champagne is as much as six atmospheres – the same level as that of a fully inflated HGV truck tyre. Put that much pressure into normal glass and you're in trouble. Bottle explosions, even a couple of centuries ago, were common in Champagne's cellars.

So how to toughen the glass?
As with so many great discoveries,
the answer arrived almost by accident.

In 1615, concerned by the rate at
which oak forests were disappearing,
and keen to ring-fence what was left
for the building of warships, King
James I banned the use of any sort of
timber as fuel for glass kilns. As a result,
glassmakers were forced to turn to
coal instead. Coal burns much hotter
than wood, offers a slower annealing
process during longer cooling, and
contains impurities that contributed
to a notably dark colour of glass –
almost black – that was also thicker
and stronger by far than conventional.
While other makers contested it, the
invention of this bottle was eventually
credited to one Sir Kenelm Digby, poet,
privateer, constant tinkerer and son of an executed Gunpowder Plotter.

Digby may have invented the bottle, but he was nothing to do with
making its contents fizz. However, the kilns in which his bottles were fired
stood in the Forest of Dean, in the heart of the Three Counties, where a
drinks renaissance was taking place.

It was at this time that, in search of 'native wines', cider and perry had
achieved prominence. It is striking, when you read sources from that time,
how often perry is directly compared either to wine generally, or of a
particular variety or region. As John Beale wrote in 1656, 'the wild apple &
the pear which chokes the biter … yields strong Rhenish, Backrac, yea
pleasant Canary'.

Since it was known that further fermentation of bottled wine or cider
would produce carbon dioxide, intellectuals concluded that fizz could be
induced in a more controlled way. In 1657 a man named Ralph Austen
recommended cidermakers 'put into each bottle a lump or two of hard
sugar, or sugar bruised'. Why? To provide yeasts still present in the bottled
cider a source of sugar for the creation of additional alcohol, and, crucially,
deliberate bubbles.

Thanks to the research of James Crowden in his excellent *Cider Country*, we learn that John Beale, in the same year, states: 'We will rather drinke pure water, than the water of rottenes, as we call all drinke that does not mantle vigorously … our Cider, if it bee brisky, will dance in the cup some good while.'

'Mantle', as Crowden explains, is used as a verb, meaning 'to form a head, to cream'. These people were describing the addition of sugar for the deliberate inducing of bubbles to cider, in a not dissimilar way to that deployed today in the making of Champagne, though Beale and Austen are writing over 70 years before the founding of the first Champagne house.

Strictly speaking, the Champenois might argue that what Beale is talking about is not quite the méthode traditionnelle, since that requires the addition of liqueur de tirage, a mixture of wine, sugar and yeast, rather than simply sugar, as well as a subsequent process of disgorgement. What Beale and Austin are describing is arguably closer to what is known as 'bottle conditioning', a method still practised by some perrymakers.

Nonetheless, today all sparkling wines, ciders and perries whose bubbles are not created through force carbonation rely on what the French came to term 'verre anglais' – English glass. And although Beale's letters refer to cider, it is this writer's suspicion that another liquid protagonist was also sparkling before Champagne.

While John Beale clearly preferred cider, his writings leave no doubt that he acknowledged perry to be a potentially outstanding drink. 'The harsher sort of Peares, & wilde Peares, may bee soe ordered as to produce a rich winy Liquor that may be compared with some of the richer sort of Wines that procced from the Grape.'

It seems highly improbable, at a time when perry was reaching prominence, and in exactly the same place as cider was being deliberately fizzed for the first time, that perry would not have received the same treatment in the same all-important Verre Anglais.

Pétillant naturel

Pétillant Naturel ('pét nat'), translates as 'naturally sparkling', and is distinct from the methods below because it only requires one fermentation, and doesn't involve anything else being added to the perry. This has made it popular with makers of drinks who wish to take a minimal intervention approach.

The pét nat method (sometimes 'méthode ancestrale') involves bottling a perry before it has completed fermentation. The yeasts continue to work on the remaining sugars in the liquid while in the bottle, and once fermentation is complete the perry will have taken on a natural sparkle.

Generally speaking, pét nat perries are designed to show off fresh primary fruit characteristics, rather than augment them with the biscuity influence of lees, as is sought by practitioners of the traditional method.

Though it has gained significant popularity with the rise of natural wine in the last 15 years, the production of pét nat perry comes with some risk. The maker must know exactly the point at which to bottle the fermenting liquid; too late and there may not be enough sugar left to offer more than the lightest sparkle, too early and the pressure in the bottle may become so great that half of its contents gush out on opening.

This latter risk can be exacerbated by makers who allow too much unfiltered sediment into the bottle. These large particles can act as 'nucleation points', which further disturb the carbon dioxide in the drink, and combined with the pressure, can result in dripping kitchen surfaces – even ceilings! – and rather a lot of swearing.

Perry being perry, prone to throwing excess sediment even after bottling, the risk of nucleation is even greater. What's more, since a variety's unfermentable sorbitol level can vary year on year, judging the level of fermentable sugars remaining in a liquid pre-bottling can be a far trickier business than with wine or cider. Too many pét nat perries turn into sticky volcanoes without proper chilling and care. Nonetheless, pét nats include some of the most delicious and downright *fun* perries I've tasted – as well as virtually every French perry full stop.

Since 'pét nat' is a term borrowed from the French wine industry and only recently adopted by English perrymakers, it is still common, confusingly, to find pét nat perries labelled as 'bottle-conditioned'. However, since 'bottle conditioning' is also used to describe another distinct process, I have chosen to go with the globally understood 'pét nat' to describe this method.

Bottle conditioning

In some ways this is the closest spiritual descendant of the technique first described by Ralph Austen and John Beale, in that it involves the bottling of a fully fermented perry with the addition of a touch of sugar and a tiny bit of the most recently fermented juice to induce a sparkle.

However, bottle conditioning is not aiming for what you would describe as a fully sparkling liquid. Rather, the addition of sugar in bottle conditioning is around 5g per litre – about a fifth of that used in traditional method. Some makers who prefer not to add sugar look to achieve the same result by adding a little sugar-rich ice perry.

The aim of bottle conditioning is to have merely a brisk little brush of fizz. A mild lift of bubbles to augment texture without distracting from the character of the fruit itself. Lees from this minor secondary fermentation remain in the bottle, offering a degree of protection from oxygen, and thus greater ageing potential, but they are insufficient in quantity to have a major impact on the flavour of the perry, as traditional method lees do.

A risk of this method is that without adding additional yeast cultures and sufficient nutrients, the yeasts remaining in the fermented perry, already exhausted and dying out after the primary fermentation, can become stressed during conditioning and produce hydrogen sulphide, with eggy, sulphury aromas. This risk is exacerbated if conditioning takes place in cold weather.

Nonetheless, in careful hands this method results in perries that revel in the individual characters of their fruits, enlivened by a gentle spritz.

Traditional method

(Also Méthode Traditionnelle, Méthode Champenois)
This is the technique behind the world's most famous fizz, immortalised as a creamy stream of the finest golden bubbles, frothy jets of pristine white foam, and the trail of misty smoke that lingers around the bottle-neck after the popping of a cork. It's come a long way since those first experiments in Herefordshire and Gloucestershire 370 years ago.

The traditional method, as it now exists, and as it has been refined over centuries by its most famous practitioners, the winemakers of Champagne, involves a secondary fermentation inside the bottle. This is achieved by bottling fully fermented perry with a so-called liqueur de tirage, a mixture of perry, yeast and sugar (around 25g per litre).

However, secondary fermentation achieves more than simple carbonation. Once the added yeast cells have finished their work, they die and sink to the bottom of the bottle as lees. Left in contact with the perry, these dead yeast cells begin to break down in a process known as 'autolysis', creating a fuller, creamier mouthfeel and producing flavours of pastry, biscuit, even brioche.

The longer the perry remains 'on its lees', the more pronounced their effect. I once tasted a traditional method perry left on its lees for a whopping 18 years; 18 months or even less is far more common. Producers who want more primary fruit character will lees-age for a shorter time, while those seeking more richness and complexity will go longer.

Most people don't want Champagne – or traditional method perry – to be cloudy, so those lees need to be removed once they have sufficiently impacted the flavours and textures of the drink. This is done by a process known as disgorgement.

Bottles will slowly and gradually be inverted over a long period – either by hand or machine – so that the yeast cells gradually sink into the neck of the bottle. The necks are then cooled so the cells freeze into a solid lump, the bottle is opened and the pressure in the liquid fires out the small frozen puck before a new closure – typically a cork fastened with a cage – is put in place.

Interestingly, though it wasn't described as such, and was far more rudimentary, an agriculturalist named John Worlidge described a similar process being applied to cider in 1676, 140 years before it was introduced to champagne. Once again, I'm indebted to James Crowden, who finds

Worlidge writing: 'Some place their bottles on a frame with their noses downwards for that end. Which is not to be so well approved of, by reason that if there be any least settling in the Bottle you are sure to have it in the first glass.' Not quite as sophisticated as proper disgorgement, certainly, but an understanding of how to at least remove sediment from the second glass onwards. And if this was applied to cider, you can stick a fiver on it also having been used on its pear-shaped orchard mate.

Following disgorgement and before the bottle is resealed, the wine can be topped up with a liquid known as liqueur d'expedition. The amount – *'dosage'* – of sugar in this determines the sweetness of the finished perry; some producers will choose to add none whatsoever. Fun fact: the foil traditionally wrapped a long way down the necks of champagne bottles was originally to hide how much liquid had been lost in disgorgement before the introduction of liqueur d'expedition.

Due to the labour involved in this method – and, if the perry is lees-aged for a long while, the time it takes – traditional method perries, like tradition-al method wines, are almost invariably positioned and priced as premium products. The good news for perry drinkers though is that a really top-end traditional method perry is still likely to be far cheaper than an equivalent-quality Champagne.

Charmat method

I have only knowingly come across a tiny handful of producers using this method. Tony Lovering, founder of Halfpenny Green, Patrick and Wendy at Germany's 1785, and a few makers in Italy. (If you know of others, let me know!)

The Charmat method is best known as the technique used for prosecco (hence the popularity with Italian perrymakers!). Rather than a second fermentation taking place in bottle, it is induced in a larger pressurised tank from which the perry is then bottled directly.

The idea here is that by increasing the volume of liquid being fermented a second time, the dead yeast cells will have less impact on flavour, the aim being to create a bright, fruit-forward drink without the biscuity notes of autolysis. Equipment is large and costly – likely the main reason perry-makers aren't often found using this method (Tony built his tank himself) – but the soft, fruity nature of many perry pear varieties would seem to lend themselves to it. Certainly, the results I've tasted back this contention, and I hope in future that more perrymakers will be able to give it a go.

Sweet/Dessert Perry

It's a popular generalisation that perry is always sweet, which certainly isn't true. There might always be a trace of sorbitol, but in the majority of varieties you'd likely not notice it in an otherwise fully fermented perry. Dry perries do exist – and I'm tremendously grateful for it.

But some perries *are* sweet. In fact, some perries are really, really sweet, and what marvellous things they are. The pure, radiant, starlit juice of a great keeve is a thing of surpassing wonder. I'll take a fresh glass of something cold-racked any time you want to hand it to me – and would recommend it to anyone who loves the great demi-sec Chenin Blancs of the Loire, or the Spätlese and Auslese Rieslings of Germany. As for the luscious, honeyed nectar that is ice perry: just try to stop me.

Sweet drinks, properly balanced by depth of flavour, and, crucially, refreshing acidity to cut through the sugar and stop things getting cloying, can offer some of the greatest perries of all.

But just as 'sparkling' is far too simple a term to cover the breadth of fizz that perry has to offer, so 'sweet' doesn't begin to scratch the surface of the ways in which international perrymakers have gone about crafting their wares. So, with a merry wave to the dentist, let's dive in.

Added sucralose or arrested fermentation

Alright, sometimes sweetening methods feel a bit prosaic. Simply adding sugar or sweetener to a perry and then pasteurising to prevent yeasts from fermenting further sounds a little unnatural to some drinkers and producers.

There's a reason for this approach. The flavours of fully fermented perry are different to those of one only partially fermented. Adding sugar post-fermentation allows the producer to achieve fully fermented flavour while still offering a level of sweetness that might be deemed more commercial or closer to the producer's own taste.

This approach wouldn't be taken by the most aspirational perries, since pasteurisation will affect taste and texture while also being unattractive to producers looking to present perry more naturally.

Pasteurisation doesn't just kill off bacteria. If a producer wants to capture a particular moment mid-fermentation, they can bring the process to a halt by pasteurising the liquid, thereby killing off yeasts. Although this will slightly impact the flavours of the perry, it can be a useful 'click of the camera' to catch that perry at precisely the preferred flavour profile.

Keeving

As far as I'm aware, keeving is unique to cider and perry. Common in English ciders and perries of the 18th and 19th centuries – and now being revived – its true modern home is France, where cider and perrymakers have perfected the art.

Keeving is a way of starving yeasts of nutrients such that they are unable to complete fermentation, leaving naturally sweet liquid. And it's possible because of something called pectin.

Pectin is the glue that holds the cell walls of fruit together. If pears are left to macerate after milling, more pectin will leach into the juice. This pectin, combined with an enzyme, binds with calcium to form a gel-like substance that rises to the top of the juice as a 'cap', taking nutrients with it. By racking juice from underneath and into a new container, the perrymaker is left with low-nutrient liquid that yeasts will be unable to ferment to full dryness.

Since both calcium and the necessary enzymes are present in certain quantities in pear juice, it is possible to achieve a wholly natural keeve. However, makers can also add enzymes and calcium carbonate directly. Although pears have less pectin than apples, their particular make-up – the physical properties that can make them such awful cloggers at pressing – lends itself to forming a gel-like cap so much that many makers report instances of 'auto-keeving' whether that was the plan or not.

A successful keeve requires a good spell of cold weather to prevent fermentation from running away before the 'cap' has formed. The most ideal fruits are therefore later harvested pears, naturally lower in nutrients, and more common in pears from old, traditional trees.

To taste great keeved perry is to experience a Dom Perignon-esque 'come quickly, I'm tasting the stars' moment.

Cold racking

This is how most natural perrymakers prefer to achieve sweetness.
Racking is the process of removing a perry from gross lees, something
producers need to do in any case. But the more often a producer racks,
the fewer yeasts are left to continue fermentation.

By racking several times, ideally in the depths of winter when the
yeasts are sluggish, largely settled in the bottom of the container and
easiest to separate from the liquid, producers can achieve naturally sweet
perry without artificial additions or pasteurisation. This is very skilled
work, however; the yeasts must be successfully separated or fermentation
may continue after the perry has been packaged.

Great cold-racked perries are perfect for drinkers who love German
Rieslings, demi-sec Vouvray or the aromatic white wines of Alsace.
Not as unctuous or sweet as dessert perry, they are stunning matches
for richer seafood or even poultry. Blooming with ripe, indulgent fruit,
and heightened by that touch of sweetness, glasses often disappear at a
fiendish rate.

Ice perry

Ice perry is where I exhaust my superlatives. These are true dessert
perries – drinks that rival the likes of Tokaji or Sauternes in richness,
depth and sweetness, and in some ways resemble them in flavour.

Great ice perry is simply one of the most intensely gorgeous drinks
that humankind ever fermented. A derivation of the ice ciders first
invented in Canada in 1990, ice perry is rarer still. But make no mistake,
these are drinks to seek out with relish.

There are three ways of making ice perry and, as the name suggests,
coldness is crucial to each one.

Cryo-extracted This method is only suitable for certain pears – those
which hang longest on the tree – and only in the regions where cold bites
hardest. (I am only aware of it being utilised in Canada but would love to
hear otherwise.) If these conditions are met, pears can freeze whole while
still on the tree, the force of the cold desiccating the flesh within the pear.

Once harvested and thawed (frozen pears would break a mill) ice
crystals within the pear can be separated from the juice, resulting in
liquid that has not only been rendered far sweeter than ordinary pear
juice, but has had its very flavours altered by the freezing process.

Yeasts can only operate so far in such extreme sweetness. So, once they have gorged as much as they can – to around 9–11% ABV, still higher than an ordinary perry – they die off, leaving a liquid still lusciously sweet in natural sugars.

Cryo-concentrated (natural cold) This is a more common method of producing ice perry. It can be deployed with a greater range of varieties, though it still requires an intensely cold climate.

Rather than freezing on the branch, pears are harvested and pressed, and their juice is left in large containers outside, where the extremities of the weather gradually freeze it. Since ice floats, the juice itself, along with its sugars and acids, gradually moves towards the bottom. As the weather warms and the block starts to thaw, the juice drips away from the ice to be collected.

Eleanor Leger of Eden Ciders in Vermont explained to me the role that natural cold plays in this process: 'the temperature fluctuation that you get with natural cold weather really helps separate water from sugars and flavours and acids … it's not just the sugars, it's the acids and everything else'.

Removed from the water, the maker is left with a highly concentrated juice which, like cryo-extracted juice, is too sweet to be fully fermented by normal yeast, yielding an intensely naturally sweet perry of similar strength. The key difference will be in flavour. Where cryo-extracted perries are affected by that pre-pressing dessication, cryo-concentrated perries should taste intensely of the specific flavours of the variety or varieties from which they are made.

Cryo-concentrated (artificial cold) If you want to make an ice perry, but local conditions are insufficiently cold, you can achieve a similar effect by freezing the juice yourself. The same process will follow – ice rises and juice drips to the bottom.

This method might sound less romantic, and as Eleanor notes, the faster, more even process of freezing the juice and allowing it to thaw, rather than subjecting it to longer, random fluctuations of the elements, is likely to result in some of the acids and flavours being left in the ice.

That said, I have tasted delicious ice perries made through this method, and as such, I feel it would be a mistake to dismiss it. Perhaps the best solution would be for regulations to be put in place requiring ice perries to be specific about their methods. Given it is such a niche concern though, I won't hold my breath.

Fortifieds

Perry isn't just a drink for heady summer days of lounging outside with a cold glass. Of course, it is for that *as well*, and performs the role superlatively, but it has more strings to its bow. Between big, earthy styles perfect for autumn walks, full-bodied, tannic bruisers, and refined classics for the dinner table, there truly is a perry for all seasons.

But no perry does winter better than a fortified. These are the big, bold, booming styles to which a righteous helping of distilled pear spirit has been added; a lick of warming fire to set the pear ablaze and wrap you in a bear hug of comforting flavour. I have always been a lover of fortified drinks, perhaps the most underrated of all categories, and the fortified pear deserves a place in the glass of any lover of sherry, Madeira or Port.

Mistelle

Strictly speaking, this is not a fortified perry, as it involves the addition of pear spirit to unfermented pear juice, rather than to something which already contains alcohol. Mistelles are gorgeous, mouth-coating treats, the natural sweetness of juice tempered by the spirit's power.

They are usually fortified to around 17% ABV and can be matured in oak, or bottled young, fresh and unaged as a pure expression of pear.

The true home of the mistelle, so far as pears are concerned, is France, where the makers of Normandy, Brittany and Maine are frequently distillers as much as they are cider and perrymakers.

Other pear-based mistelles can be found from aspirational producers dotted around the perrymaking world. Look out particularly for 'Poireau', made by Charles Martell in Gloucestershire, as well as the long-aged mistelles of Quebec's Domaine des Salamandres.

Fortified perry

There are few drinks with which I fell in love as quickly and comprehensively as the mostellos of the Mostviertel's Destillerie Farthofer – to date the only examples I have tasted of true fortified perry.

Taking inspiration from both sherry and Port, while simultaneously treading a path entirely their own, organic farmers and distillers Josef and Doris Farthofer make their mostello in two distinct ways. The süss (sweet), like Port, is fortified with their pear spirit to around 19% ABV shortly after fermentation has begun, to capture remaining natural sugars in the perry, whilst their trocken (dry) is fortified after fermentation has completed.

In each case they then age most of the fortified perry in oak, both inside and outside the distillery, for a whopping four years before bottling. The results are wildly complex, deep and instantly compelling drinks revelling in caramels, dried apricots and chopped hazelnuts in the case of the süss, and walnuts, soy and dark dried fruit in the case of the trocken. They also make small quantities of unaged mostello, a pure encapsulation of fermented and distilled pear.

All have an astonishing capacity to mature. When I was lucky enough to try the 2005 süss I found it coursing with vigour and life, surely capable of continuing to improve for at least another decade.

Flavourings/Additions

The flavours of good perry should be driven by the pear. Otherwise, why go through the heartache of producing this troublesome drink in the first place? But throughout history producers have embellished perry's flavours both through use of wood, or the addition of herbs, spices and other fruits and flavours. The ancient Romans were certainly at it, and although early flavourings and fruit additions may partially have been in the name of disguising questionable liquids, they were undoubtedly also added as a qualitative choice.

Writing to Samuel Hartlib in 1658, John Beale extolled the virtues of blending crabapples with perry, writing that 'it brings the worst sort of peares to bee an excellent liquor'. A year earlier, he commented, intriguingly: 'I am promis'd by a Lady a rare secrete of altering all kinds of Cider, perry, french wines & sacke, into a most cordiall & gustfull liqvor, by a secrete way of infusing clovegelliflowers [gilliflowers].' Who this lady was, and whether she shared her secret, is a mystery.

Today, flavoured perries often get a bad rep. They are either associated with mass-produced drinks that have barely had a sniff of a pear, or seen as somehow sullying the sanctity of the pear fruit itself. Drinks like these often come in for a bit of a kicking from purists.

But anyone who has tasted a good, full-juice example knows that when the flavours of the perry itself are allowed to harmonise with carefully chosen flavourings, wonderful things can be achieved.

Whatever your take, this is unquestionably a significant category within perry and has been for hundreds of years. Ignore it at the risk of missing out on some intriguing and delicious creations.

Wood

Already covered in our chapter on 'making', wood should only really be considered a flavouring if the cask is still 'active' – as opposed to casks which have been reused so often that all flavour has been leached away, leaving them more or less neutral.

Flavours come both from the wood itself, or from the liquid that was held in the casks beforehand; other perry or pear brandy, even rum, whisky or wine.

Since casks are expensive, producers might choose to use wood 'flavouring', either through adding oak chippings or inserting wooden staves into otherwise neutral vessels. These can be variable in quality, and will not offer the additional micro-oxidative properties, but is a useful and cost-efficient alternative for achieving some similar flavours.

Adjuncts

The sky's the limit! If you can think of a fruit, spice or herb, it's likely to have been added to a perry at some point. As we've seen, adjuncts were deliberately included in historic fermentations across Europe for centuries.

While perries with adjuncts can now be found all over the world, it is arguably among American producers that they find most enthusiasm. Many of these producers have limited access to perry pears compared to the UK, France or Central Europe, so adding various fruits or spices to their fermented perry can offer a way to quickly diversify their range.

American consumers, like those in the UK, are also increasingly fond of flavoured ciders, and cideries are now releasing combinations that truly boggle the mind. Guava and chilli flavour, anyone? Smoked blueberry? How about peanut butter? While some might be a bit extreme for my taste (though I'll try anything once), it's easy to see why many perrymakers are catching on to it, not least because the perrymakers are often the same people making the cider.

One key distinction always worth looking out for is between producers who are using fresh ingredients – be they fruits, herbs, hops, spices – compared to those using artificial flavourings and syrups. The former is always likely to be better-balanced, fresher and more sensitive to the flavours of the perry itself.

Perrykin

This is an 'addition' insofar as it involves the addition of water, but, unlike some perries that are fully fermented and then diluted, perrykin is made by 'rehydrating' and then re-pressing the pomace –skins and dried flesh – left over from the initial pressing. This coaxes out remaining sugars, creating liquid that can be fermented to only a very low strength.

As we've seen, this method has been written about since at least 1534 in France. Perrykins (and ciderkins) were also a staple thirst-quencher for farm labourers in the Three Counties and Central Europe for centuries thereafter.

Today, mainly for tax reasons, few ciderkins, and even fewer perrykins are still made. But some makers still produce them, often fermented with additional fruits and hops, and magnificently refreshing things they are too.

Co-fermentations

To my mind, co-fermentations are distinct from adjuncts, since, rather than fruits or flavours being added at the end of the process, they feature the combined fermentation of pear juice with something else – typically apples or grapes. It was common practice, historically, in both Germany and England to either soften acidic ciders with the addition of pear juice – or conversely to add a spine of acidity to a perry through the use of sharp apples.

Since fermented cider and wine tastes very different to the juices from which they originate, the overall effect of a co-ferment is wholly removed from the taste of a finished perry to which other fruit has been added. Co-fermentations have become increasingly common in modern perry as more and more cider and winemakers turn their attention to the fermented pear.

Apples and grapes are far from the only fruits that can be co-fermented with pears though. As with added fruits, the only real limits are the producer's imagination. I have come across creations that featured quinces, various sorts of berry, and even, in the case of France's Côme Isambert, a 50:50 co-ferment of perry and carrot!

Grafs

Strictly speaking, many grafs are also co-fermentations, but I have kept them as a separate section, because they specifically refer to the marriage of cider – or, in this case, perry – with beer.

Beer and perry might seem unusual bedfellows, but in the right hands they can be induced to sing unique, arresting and mouthwatering tunes. They can be created by fermenting beer wort with pear juice, by blending finished beer and perry, or by fermenting a beer on a perry's spent lees or pomace.

Some of the best perry grafs I have tasted were made by Gloucestershire's Jonny Mills in collaboration with Tom Oliver. A robust Pilsner wort was brought together with a classic blend of Three Counties perry pears and wild-fermented in barrels (including one that had previously held Islay whisky) for three months before bottling. Wonderful. Wilderness Brewery, in Mid-Wales, also made a beautiful example.

APPRECIATING PERRY

First thing's first; if the way you most enjoy perry is from a plastic sippy-cup or mixed with ice and pink lemonade as a slushy then you do you and don't let anybody instruct you otherwise. (Actually, that second one sounds amazing, to be honest).

The way we appreciate our drinks often comes with an off-putting and frequently problematic helping of handed-down and societally enforced ritual. Much of this comes from a good, or at least reasonable, place; glassware, serving sizes and temperatures designed over generations to enable a drink to express itself fullest; shared language of tasting experience that has evolved, at least in part, through group discussion and interest. At their best, many of these rituals and traditions can unlock a broader world of drinks and allow new drinkers to get the most out of what's in their glass.

Step one: assemble a group of friends...

However, it would be wrong to pretend that much of this ritualised and strictly guarded behaviour is not gatekeeping. Take wine, for instance. For all that it is a fine and fascinating drink, without which I would not love or understand perry half as deeply, it can so often be rife with snobbery and stricture.

This environment – and, especially, the looking down upon those who do not already understand or observe it – not only creates firm barriers to entry but sends out clear implications as to who these drinks are 'for', and, conversely, who they are not.

Not only is this not something I wouldn't wish within the world of perry, it is an attitude perry cannot afford. Perry's availability is so sparse compared to wine's, and its need for broader audience so great, that any perceived snobbishness around it could be ruinous. Returning to my opening point: please drink your perry exactly the way you want and describe it in the language that works best for you.

That said, just as the sections on varietal flavour and perry styles offer what I hope are some useful guidelines for navigating this world for yourself, a long, practical experience of drinking various perries in various ways has, through trial and error, left me with a few thoughts on how I most enjoy serving and drinking them.

It is those thoughts that are shared in the following chapter, in the hope that they will prove useful first steps towards discovering how you most appreciate perries for yourself.

Where to buy?

Honestly, perry can be difficult to find. Even in the countries that produce it, perry is almost invariably a single shelf or two in a cider shop (and there aren't even all that many of those). You're most likely to find a bottle, perhaps a couple of bottles, squirrelled away in a bottom corner of a wine or beer store, especially if it is based in or around the Three Counties, the Mostviertel or Normandy. I can think of only two shops I've visited where perry was the primary concern, both in museums dedicated to perry: MostBirnHaus in The Mostviertel and Musée du Poiré in Normandy.

While many producers have their own small shops, your best bet for trying a range is the internet. In the UK over the last couple of years, driven especially by the lockdowns of COVID-19, there has been a rise in online cider and perry merchants. While one or two existed before, the selection of makers and bottlings now available through online retailers such as The Cat in the Glass, The Cider Vault, Aeble and The Fine Cider Company has never been more exciting.

It is particularly useful when retailers have divided perry from cider within their ranges, saving you the trouble of sifting through a far larger cider collection. Retailers, to my mind, are the ultimate arbiters of quality and education, and dividing perry from cider – establishing it as its own distinct drink – is key to this.

Good retailers will always be happy to offer advice should you contact them. They will bear your preferences in mind when making recommendations, and never come across as supercilious when guiding you through an unfamiliar world.

How to store?

For most perries, today is best. Don't worry about storing. Get them open, get them drunk, and enjoy them in the full vivacity of their fruit-filled youth.

If your perry is intended for longer maturation, consistency of light and temperature is your greatest friend. In a perfect world we would all have a barn or cellar in which our bottles could enjoy dark and cool slumber. But if, as it is for me, the idea of a cellar is likely to forever remain a daydream, there are plenty of options that will serve you almost as well.

The classic is the cupboard under the stairs, though any dark cupboard will do, so long as temperature is consistent. For those of us whose cupboards, both under the stairs and elsewhere, are deployed in less hedonistic service (hoover, paint, tools and camping gear, since you're asking, though a bottle or two might have snuck in as well) the best bet is to simply find a cooler, shadier area of the house. As long as bottles are out of direct sunlight and not too close to a heat source, they should be ok.

Why are temperature changes and sunlight so damaging? Well, higher temperatures risk damaging the more fragile and delicate compounds involved in a perry's flavour. Think of it as a very slow 'cook'. When you open the bottle, it will feel 'flatter' on the palate. This is a known and well-documented phenomenon in wine which, don't forget, has around twice the preservative alcohol level of most perries. Particularly high temperatures also risk increasing the pressure in sparkling bottles, causing leakage and, at worst, bottle explosions (though the latter are exceedingly rare).

Sunlight, of course, often comes with its own serving of heat, but more than this the ultraviolet rays themselves can degrade a perry, particularly one lower in tannins, and can even cause chemical reactions resulting in stinky, gone-off-cabbage-like aromas.

The classic bottle shape of Austrian most

Most perries, particularly from the UK and Austria, are bottled under crown cap or screwcap. Being made of inert materials that are unlikely to change in shape, bottles featuring these closures can be stored upright.

If your perry features a cork – like most traditional method perries and the majority of French poiré – make sure to store it on its side if you are keeping it for longer than a few months. When not kept in contact with liquid a cork will dry out and shrink, becoming a less effective closure and potentially allowing oxygen in.

Very little is known about the ageing potential of perry, though it has certainly been observed for centuries in some styles and varieties, with John Beale remarking in 1658 that some of the more intense varieties didn't even become pleasant to drink until they had aged at least two or three years. More research into this subject is needed before any definite conclusions can be drawn, but in general, pears with higher tannin and acidity allow longer ageing, as will intensely naturally sweet styles, fortified styles and traditional methods.

That said, I once had a still, dry, single variety Schweizer Wasserbirne, a pear with little tannin or acidity, that was 31 years old and still drinking with not far off the freshness I would have expected of something 25 years younger. So really, if anyone tells you they know all about the maturation potential of perry, treat them with healthy scepticism. Like so many things perry, this is a map in which very little space has been filled. That's part of the fun.

Serving Temperatures

Quite often the default with perry is to bung it straight in the fridge and serve it well-chilled. For some styles this is just the ticket: young ice perries or Domfrontais Poiré, other sweeter styles and low-tannin English and Central European varieties are perfect served this way. Cold glasses, pure refreshment, a cool shiver that accentuates their crisp freshness, and, in sweeter cases, joins the acidity in lending balance to sugars. Beautiful.

But one size doesn't fit all. Large molecules like tannins aren't fond of cold; literally 'clenching', becoming less expressive and more astringent. Over-chilling perry can be detrimental to your drinking experience.

One size doesn't fit all when it comes to serving perry

As a rough guide, this is how I would serve certain perries myself:

Well-chilled
Big brand, lower juice-content perry
Charmat method
Cold-racked, lower tannin perries
Perrykin
Young AOP Domfront (though I might give this one half an hour out of the fridge first)
Younger ice perry
Younger traditional method

Lightly chilled
Cold-racked, higher-tannin perry
Dry varieties high in acid and low-medium in tannin
Dry varieties low in acid and tannin
English keeves
Older AOP Domfront
Older ice perry
Other French perry
Older traditional method perry
Young or unoaked fortifieds

Room (or cellar) temperature
Dry varieties higher in tannin
Older or longer-oaked fortifieds

Glassware

I adore glassware. I am fascinated by how it is made, captivated by how it looks, and besotted with how it feels (and, more crucially, how it makes me feel). Open almost any cupboard in my kitchen without due caution and something weird-shaped and designed for holding liquid is liable to fall out.

Sadly, as with so many things, there can be an awful lot of snobbery around glassware ('You're drinking out of that? Really?') Returning to this chapter's opening gambit, the best thing to drink from is whatever gives you most enjoyment. I have cheerfully drunk one of the world's best ciders from the cut-off bottom half of a plastic bottle while sitting in the ruins of Reading Abbey after an outdoor performance of Romeo and Juliet, so I am certainly not in a position to judge, even if I were minded to. (Not that I'm specifically endorsing plastic bottle cut-offs, but sometimes needs must.)

Nonetheless, the glass you choose can absolutely affect your experience of a perry. So, briefly, here are a few I enjoy.

A glass for every perry and occasion

The pint glass
(Still draught British perry)
This is a bit of an British phenomenon, though you'll also find similar in the USA and Australia.

I should admit that I'm not a *huge* fan of drinking perry in pints. There are three main reasons. Firstly, because perry naturally ferments, when dry, to 6–8.5% ABV, and that's edging towards the spicy side for me in pint form (though your mileage may vary). Secondly, because perries at any strength feel to me as though they have more in common with white wine than beer or commercial cider – which is why I tend to drink more perry from a wine glass. Thirdly, the nature of a pint glass's shape makes appreciation of aromas difficult compared to wine glasses, which are specifically engineered for the purpose.

Half pint and pint glasses are what you are likely to be served perry in when it comes to British draught perry at either the farm itself or at a pub, and what these glasses do very well is communicate *feeling*. There is something comforting to their heft and uncomplicated shape. A sense of 'you don't have to think too much here' that draws focus less to the drink than the setting in which it is served. The British pub, at its best, is about community and conviviality and putting people at their ease, and the pint glass is one of the most important props in this wonderful theatre.

The wine glass

(More or less any perry)

Along with the craft beer-style glasses (see below), a wine glass is my personal preference for home drinking. 'Wine glass' is a generalisation, but for argument's sake let's define it as something with a stem, sides that taper towards the rim and a rounded bowl capable of holding, at its widest point, something like 125–175ml.

The wine glass can be as ceremonial and of-a-place as the pint glass – think of all the restaurants that put them on tables by default – but it is also particularly well-designed for making the most of aroma and flavour. Its shape acts as a funnel, concentrating aromas and allowing you to get a better sense of what the perry is trying to say. Since the glass is only ever partially filled, wine glasses can also be swirled to allow oxygen into the drink, further 'opening' aroma and flavour.

Two-thirds-sized craft beer glasses

(Any perry other than fortifieds, dessert or traditional method)

These are the happy middle ground between pint glasses and wine glasses. Born from the explosion in higher-strength craft beers, and now happily adopted by cider and perry taprooms, these offer some of the heft and feeling of a pint glass, and, unlike a wine glass, can be filled to the brim. At the same time, their tapered shape is every bit as good as the wine glass for swirling, ceremony and concentration of aromatics. Perhaps my favourite glass for any sort of perry is the stemmed Teku – the best of all worlds. And pertinently for the more butter-fingered amongst us, they're also more robust than wine glasses when it comes to washing up.

Some of my personal favourites

Flutes

(Traditional method and other naturally sparkling styles)

The ultimate in *feeling*. Pour something bubbly in a fluted glass and everyone knows it's a celebration. Flutes are all about good cheer, treating yourself and sense of occasion.

However, when it comes to actual appreciation they aren't all that great. Their slender shape doesn't offer much surface area for making the most of aromatics, and if you stick your nose in too deeply you're likely to get a nostril full of bubbles.

Flutes are designed to maximise the visuals of a sparkling drink, which they do magnificently, but their key purpose is in setting that atmosphere. If you want to spend time contemplating the liquid, use another glass. But if you want to feel special, nothing beats the flute.

Copitas

(Ice perries, fortified styles and pear spirits)

Copitas began life as glasses for sherry but have been repurposed right across the world of drinks. They are essentially miniature wine glasses with slightly straighter sides but the same idea of a stemmed glass with a tapered bowl. Given their size they are ideal for drinks served in smaller measures, so I use them for dessert perries, fortifieds and spirits.

Fortified perries call for smaller measures

An Over-The-Top Guide to Tasting

I know, I know. Endless analysis can get a bit boring. Most people, most of the time, just want a drink. I am no different. At the end of a long week all I want to do is sit back, glass in hand, and not think about much.

But I can't help it. When something interesting is in my glass I *want* to hear what it has to say for itself. Or, more pertinently, taste it. You don't have to behave as though you're judging competitions whenever you're drinking. But there is so much flavour, aroma, and sheer pleasure to be found through just a few simple steps.

'Tasting' is just about engaging senses, and a little bit of thought. The more you taste, the more you think, the more you remember what you liked and why you liked it – or indeed didn't – the more enjoyment you may find with every glass, and the more confident you may become in describing characteristics.

Best of all is when you do so with a group of friends or fellow perry lovers (usually the same thing). All of us have lived different lives, exposed to different foods and flavours; no one can dictate your palate for you. If you think you're getting kiwi or cranberry or molasses or petrichor – or all of them at once – then you probably are.

Look

Not a *huge* part of appreciation, though I always enjoy the sight of perry splashing into a glass. But we can glean a few pointers here. Perry deepens as it ages, while oak and phenolics like tannins will also add colour. A young perry that is dark in colour may have oxidised. Conversely a mature, oak-aged fortified or ice perry should be golden-bronze, possibly even creeping towards tawny or chestnut.

We're also looking for 'tears', those beads of liquid that trickle down the sides of the glass. The thicker they are, the sweeter and/or more alcoholic the perry is likely to be.

Finally, clarity. Perry can naturally throw haze, so spotlessly clear perry may be a sign of filtration or disgorgement. Some perries whose procyanidins have been particularly tricksy may be totally opaque and almost milky of hue. I know this might look off-putting, but don't worry, aromas and flavours shouldn't have been affected.

Give the glass a good swirling to get oxygen in, unlocking aromas. This serves the same purpose as decanting, which is also worth considering if you're drinking a younger or more tannic perry.

Smell

Don't be shy. Really get your nose in. Breathe normally and allow aromas to meet you.

We're after intensity first. How powerful are those aromas? Are they leaping out before you're anywhere near the glass, or are you really having to strain for them? The best perries are usually pretty aromatic, though some varieties like Thorn and Moorcroft are naturally more intense.

Then come the characteristics. This is the bit that can feel daunting. The 'what if I'm wrong?' part that we've all feared at some point. Well, you're not wrong. Just allow the perry to remind you of things you've smelled before. Perhaps it takes you on a walk outdoors – flowers, grass, hedgerows, woodland. Maybe it's a fruit basket – citruses, perhaps, or melons, stone fruits, even berries.

Casks, production methods and maturation all impact aromas. Casks might offer toast, vanilla, coconut or notes from whatever those casks held before. As perry ages, its fruits gradually shift from fresh to dried and often from green and yellow tones to deeper notes of tropical fruits; perhaps even savoury spices.

Fortified and ice perries offer luscious tones; a whole world of honeys, marmalades, caramels, moving into chopped nuts, dried fruit and frangipane with oak and time.

A useful hack is to pay attention to anything you smell day-to-day. Whether it's on a walk, in shops, in the kitchen or anywhere else. Smell is our most underused sense, but the one that can trigger the deepest memories. And getting the most out of a perry's aroma is not reserved for a few lucky people. It just takes practice, like anything else.

Taste

Draw a little perry into your mouth. Resist swallowing for a moment. Breathe in gently (trying not to cough, as I did the first time). This achieves the same effect as a swirl – it lets oxygen in and unlocks flavours.

Noses are far more receptive to individual characteristics than mouths. Think how little you can taste when you have a cold. Breathing through your nose can carry all those aromatic qualities through your nasal receptors and fill your mouth with flavour.

Think about what you smelled. Is anything different? Some perries taste like carbon copies of their aromatics, but others change, sometimes remarkably, from nose to mouth. Are you finding anything new, and if so, what?

Where tasting nudges ahead of nosing is in the other factors that contribute to how much we enjoy a perry. How sweet is it? Luscious like syrup, or totally dry? How full-bodied? Mouth-filling, like honey, or lighter, like water?

Then there are what we call the 'structural' elements: tannins and acidity. Tannins are compounds in plants, and also found in red wine and tea – think of a cup you've brewed for a long time. They contribute a 'grippy' dryness you feel on your gums; occasionally bitter in youth but softening with age and adding hugely to body and mouthfeel. Tannins are also preservatives, so can contribute to a perry's ability to mature.

Acidity sounds scary, but it is vital. Without acidity perries can, at best, feel a bit heavy and flat, and at worst be at risk of faults and infection. Perries can range from lip-smackingly sharp and citrusy, to softer and gentler. Like tannin, acidity contributes ageing potential and softens with time. You can feel its presence through how much your mouth is watering.

Finish

The flavours that linger in your mouth afterwards – how long and how strongly do they stay with you? You can still taste the best perries over a minute later. Occasionally, a perry's flavour will actually change in your mouth during the finish. These, usually, are the greatest perries of all.

To spit or not to spit?

Look, this is something we're taking pleasure in. If you're just enjoying a glass with a few friends, there obviously isn't any need for spittoons.

Where I personally choose to use one is if I'm tasting several perries. Occasionally I'm lucky enough to judge competitions, which can mean upwards of 60. If I'm not spitting, I'll be in a bad way.

Using a spittoon also allows me to taste more if I go to a big event or am visiting a producer. Although perry has half the alcohol of wine, I'll still be able to taste far fewer if I'm swallowing everything.

It's my opinion that all big cider and perry tastings should feature spittoons on every table – as is de rigeur in wine. This isn't just about my greediness. Drinks festivals of any sort are usually wonderful events, but with alcohol flowing it's no wonder they can sometimes become anxiety inducing and even unsafe for some people.

Encouraging spittoons in such settings is part of a duty of care. Providing and using them can be an act of solidarity, courtesy and inclusivity.

In short, in the right place and time, don't think of spittoons as 'gross' – think of them as taste enablers, safety equipment and fosterers of a positive community.

Perry with Food

This section could be a whole book or as short as 'just drink the perry you like with the food you like'.

Perhaps the most balanced answer is to say that, firstly, perry's ability to pair with food absolutely deserves to be shouted about. With its natural fruitiness, versatility of flavour, texture and sweetness, and naturally low alcohol, it can work better with some foods than many other more famous drinks. But there is often a degree of gatekeeping and mysticism around food and drinks pairing which I wouldn't want to see perry damaged by. In any case, very few combinations are absolutely disastrous.

I don't want to dwell on matching specific perries to specific foods, but there are a few basic principles which, I hope, will help you find happy matches, should you wish to look for them.

Firstly: think about where your perry has come from, and the food eaten there: i.e., 'What grows together, goes together.' It's a lazy generalisation to say 'perry goes with cheese' (what cheese? what perry?) but it's no coincidence that Normandy, Wales and Gloucestershire make a range of cheeses that complement local perries delightfully. Perhaps most famous is Charles Martell's Stinking Bishop, washed in perry of the same name (also known as Moorcroft).

In the Mostviertel, food and perry have been constructed around each other. The acidity of Grüne Pichelbirne or Dorschbirne perfectly skewers the pork-rich charcuterie boards, rich goulash and starchy potatoes and schnitzel you'll savour in local taverns, while spritzed Speckbirne brings a light freshness to what might otherwise be a heavy meal. Mostviertel perry and food make sense of each other, and there are few gastronomic combinations I find so holistically satisfying.

When pairing perry more broadly, I like to keep these brief pointers in mind:

1. Acid loves fat. That Mostviertel secret. Acidity cuts through oiliness and refreshes you for another bite or sip. Loads of room for experimentation, but my ultimate tip, honestly, is dry Thorn with a massive sausage roll or traditional method perry with the greasiest fish and chips you can find.

2. Meet richness with richness. Light, delicate perries may be overpowered by a hearty stew or curry. Boldness is key here. Think of something like

Rich food calls for big flavours and good acidity

Butt or Flakey Bark, or – better yet – go fortified. The most memorable food and perry pairing I ever had was venison with sweet mostello. This rule also applies in reverse. If your dish is light and fresh, reach for a perry that is also light and fresh. Green Horse, Yellow Huffcap or a young traditional methods with seafood, salads or a picnic is joy personified.

3. Tannin loves protein. Really tannic perry, especially in youth, may feel a little astringent. Put it next to a steak or a wedge of cheddar though, and those tannins bind with the protein, removing astringency, and heightening fruit. The first time I tried this it felt like magic. It still does.

4. Sweet food wants sweet perry. There's a reason 'dessert wines' got their name. Puddings call for a drink to match – nothing dry or tannic here, please – ideally with a thread of acidity to cut through sugars and keep things fresh. Any sweet perry will do, but ice perry is the gold standard. If the pudding is particularly rich, reach for mistelle or mostello. (If your pudding is chocolate, just don't bother with perry. Trust me, I've tried.)

5. Perry loves spice. My ace-in-the-hole tip. Spice heightens the sensation of alcohol, so wines can seem astringent and lose fruitiness. Step forward perry, with half the ABV and just as much fruit. Avoid too much tannin – go all-out on fruitiness and aromatics. Things like Winnal's Longdon, Hendre Huffcap, Speckbirne or AOP Domfront are your friends.

Food and perry matching culture runs deep in the Mostviertel

The World *of* **Perry**

TO step into a wine shop is to voyage by bottle.
I have never been to Tuscany or New Zealand or
Burgundy or South Africa; the foggy hills of Champagne
and the mountains of Argentina are only pictures to me,
but I know what they taste like in my glass. Much of my
love of wine came from exploring the cultures and
countries that grew and made it. I was no geographer
at school, but through wine I discovered the world.

Beer and spirits lovers, similarly, are aware that their
drink is global, that it doesn't belong to one country.
Great whisky is increasingly made outside the traditional
quintet of Scotland, Ireland, USA, Canada and Japan.
British beer drinkers realise they are indebted to the
brewers of America and continental Europe. Our world
of flavour is mind-blowingly diverse.

Yet few perry lovers know much about perry made in
countries besides their own. There are mitigating factors.
Imports and exports are minuscule. Historically, there
haven't been enough people drinking the perry made in
the UK, never mind bringing in bottles from elsewhere.

But as cider has begun to open up, as drinkers have
discovered the zingy sidra of Spain, the keeves of Normandy
and the boundary-pushers of the USA, perry has followed.
It is now made around the world, each country bringing
its own cultures, mindsets, terroirs, traditions, varieties
and innovation to this secretive, insular drink.

UNITED KINGDOM

*'Good perry – if you're lucky enough to find it –
is like drinking angel's tears.'*

(PETE BROWN and BILL BRADSHAW, *World's Best Ciders*, 2013)

I have six glasses in front of me. The first is a deep inhalation of wild, green country on a blue-bright day. It is a swirling eddy of citrus fruit, the leafy breath of hedgerow, the addictive sting of squeezed lime, and the rasp of pear skin. The second is booming and broad-shouldered; ripe tropical fruits, melons and righteous tannin. The third is pure elegance; a stream of golden, creamy bubbles, crisp pear and brioche, and petrichor rising from autumn slate. Fourth is a still, hedonistic gloop of the purest honeys and sticky marmalade, shot through with bright orange peel.

Eagerly, I raise the fifth, and find a monster. Vinegary acetic acid and the solvent, gluey clag of ethyl acetate. I take a tentative sip, to be met by artificial sweetness and the appalling musk of mouse. The sixth is Lambrini.

Where the roads are lined with perry pear trees

Here, in six nutshells, is a rough approximation of the glorious, fascinating, maddening and convoluted hydra that is British perry. At its best, it is easily the equal of anything made anywhere in the world. It offers comfortably the broadest swathe of styles and flavours available from any perry-making nation. Yet, at the same time it is capable of depths that sully the very name of perry in their undrinkable faultiness, as well as mass-produced drinks barely interested in advertising themselves as perry at all.

If that sounds like a qualified endorsement, let me swiftly add that the last few years have seen such an upsurge in the quality, availability and breadth of British perry – in terms of producers, innovation, expertise, presentation, communication and expressions – that there is no country in which I would currently prefer to be a perry drinker.

The modern picture

It is difficult to pin an exact date on when perry's modern revival began. After all, this is a drink which had, as we have seen, dizzying highs as long ago as the 17th century. You could argue that the level of study and interest seen by the Woolhope Club at the end of the 19th century was a high-water mark, and you could certainly make a case for *Perry Pears*, Luckwill and Pollard's work of 1963, being the country's most important piece of literature. It might also be pointed out that Babycham and later Lambrini have been drunk continuously and in significant volume since the early 1950s, though I'd argue that perry more broadly saw no upturn as a result.

Building the 'cheese' for pressing

To my mind, the genesis of today's British perrymaking scene begins in the 1980s with Jean Nowell. Since the 1950s, the industrialisation of perry had seen huge volumes of concentrate shipped in from Switzerland, while the mechanisation of agriculture and the movement towards an increasingly urban society had sounded a death knell for Britain's traditional orchards. *Perry Pears* records a drop from 118,000 to 75,000 trees between 1951 and 1957, and the devastating trend continued, with Somerset orchards decimated in the 1980s as Babycham's light dimmed.

On her farm in Herefordshire's Much Marcle, Jean sought to breathe life into an old tradition. Though she also made cider, she had a particular special for perry, and among her most significant contributions to the modern perry era was the inspiration and mentorship she offered a group of new makers who became some of the best in the world: people like Tom Oliver and Kevin Minchew, as well as Mike Johnson of Ross-on-Wye and James Marsden of Gregg's Pit.

This critical fostering of a cider and perrymaking community was underpinned by the organisation – by Jackie Denham, heavily supported by Jean – of the Big Apple celebration in Much Marcle in 1989, and the Big Apple Trials in 1992, a festival and a peer-reviewed cider and perry competition that continues to this day.

in pears, pre-sorting

At around the same time, CAMRA formed 'the APPLE committee' in 1988, formalising a commitment to championing cider and perry nationally with the same resolve and vigour with which they had formed to campaign for the protection and promotion of real ale.

To preserve the diversity of perry pear varieties, and save the most endangered specimens, Charles Martell began a collection in 1991, rediscovering and planting 59 by 1998. In 1999 Jim Chapman began a second collection at his cottage in Hartpury, Gloucestershire, planting a third collection in 2003 and establishing the Hartpury Orchard Centre, now home to the National Perry Pear Collection. Jim and Charles continue to seek out perry pears, and the collection at the Centre now numbers well over 100 varieties.

Despite this, perry always clung onto the coattails of cider, for the most part found exclusively in tucked-away corners of the Three Counties and secondary to its apple-based cousin even there. Then, in the mid-2000s, when all cidermakers, from the biggest to the smallest, reaped the benefits of the so-called 'Magner's effect', traditionally made perry saw its sales decimated by the rise first of industrial 'pear cider' and then of the alternative fruit ciders that followed in its wake.

John Edwards at the mill

Then came the rise of 'craft'. Whatever your take on the word, there's no denying the massive effect that 'craft' has had on the drinks market of the last 20 years or so. As craft beer crossed the Atlantic from America, so craft spirits – particularly gin and single malt whisky – rose to meet it.

As ever, cider was late to the party. But influenced by makers mentored by Jean Nowell, as well as producers in the south-west and south-east, inspired by the phenomenal craft cider movement taking place in the USA, and buoyed by writers such as Pete Brown and Bill Bradshaw with *World's Best Ciders*, Gabe Cook with *Ciderology*, Susanna Forbes with *The Cider Insider*, and the ever-present online commentator James Finch ('the Cider Critic'), a revolution began. Behind a rallying cry of 'rethink cider' devised by Forbes and Jane Peyton, Manchester Cider Club was formed in 2018 by Dick Withecombe, Cath Potter and Nicky Kong, becoming a model for subsequent cider clubs nationwide.

Most importantly, the number of small, aspirational makers skyrocketed, enabled particularly by the emergence of online cider merchants, whose role in the changing perception of UK cider and perry is impossible to over-state. For the first time, drinkers in every corner of the UK could buy mixed cases of cider and perry from the country's best makers. Significantly, these merchants – first The Fine Cider Company, then Scrattings and especially The Cat in the Glass – weren't solely focused on bag-in-box or smaller bottles. Instead, they stocked drinks often presented in wine-like 750ml bottles; ciders and perries that considered themselves to have been made with the same care for process and ingredient as good wine, and packaged and priced accordingly.

Between 2018 and the present day, 750ml bottles of cider and perry went from something seldom seen in this country to an almost ubiquitous choice for the best makers – just as they are in all other traditional cider and perrymaking countries. A fresh alignment with wine was a redirecting of the march away from the orchard that began when breweries started buying cideries in the 1960s and turning cider into something more industrial. The result has been a resurgence of interest across the UK, and attention from retailers who might previously never have considered it. It's a rare British wine shop these days whose shelves don't boast at least a few of the country's finest apple-based products.

*No perry pear goes unchecked
at Little Pomona*

This time, perry was a beneficiary of cider's fortune. Though usually featured as a side note, increased national awareness of cider begat a fresh fascination in the bounty of the pear tree – and especially in the differences of flavour, texture and experience that perry offered. As the cider and perry revolution has continued, the contrast between the two drinks has fallen into ever-sharper relief.

Today, it is increasingly common to see perry afforded its own tastings and events and to be considered as the distinct drink that it has always been. While the inherent support of cider has been a boon, and while it is almost invariably made by the same people, perry is beginning to enjoy the spotlight as makers celebrate its individuality – nowhere more prominently than at the annual Festival of Perry at the Three Counties Malvern Show, where Chris Atkins cultivates a bar of well over 50, with not a cider in sight!

From Merseyside to Kent to Gloucestershire to Cornwall, from Monmouthshire to Manchester and even as far north as Fife, a perry resurgence – the most significant for 350 years – is taking place.

As numbers of producers have grown, so the perrymaking community has spread, sharing knowledge and experience along the way. Even in the last five years the average quality of perry to be found in Britain has risen out of sight of what it once was, and the range of varieties, styles and flavours is without international peer.

What's more, the side-by-side cultures of draught pints combined with the rise of the 750ml bottle – increasingly seen at the highest-end restaurants – offers perry an even more impressive spectrum of identity. Drinkers can enjoy a gloriously refreshing glass from keg or bag-in-box at a pub, or pore over something complex, aged and perhaps served in a smaller measure at a restaurant or in the comfort of their own home. There are perries bottled as single varieties,

Scratting at Hollow Ash

or as skilfully composed blends. We have perries made in every style –
even ice perries and mistelles.

Regional flavours are becoming more distinct, with producers in the
east of England no longer nervous of presenting their lighter, tannin-free
creations made from dessert pears, but showcasing them proudly as
Eastern Counties perry. We are discovering perry's incredible capacity to
pair with a huge range of foods – not just the local meats and cheeses, but
also spicier dishes such as the marvellously varied cuisines of Mexico and
the Far East.

Make no mistake, this is the best time in living memory to be a perry
drinker in Britain. We may still have the world's biggest producer, and we
may still have a (dwindling) handful of the world's worst, but we have a
range that no one else can match and a top table of quality making an
increasing case for the world's finest too. It's been a hard road getting here,
but my goodness it's been worth it. And in this drinker's opinion, the good
times are only going to get better.

Ross-on-Wye's Becky entertained by the author's efforts

The Three Counties

The hill doesn't look anything special. Another rolling mound in the Gloucestershire landscape. If it wasn't for the limpet of pine trees studding the peak you'd barely register it. Those pines were planted in 1887 for Queen Victoria's Jubilee, and they've made this humble knoll recognisable for miles around. But really, they ought to be pears. Because this is Yartleton Hill – or, as it is now more commonly known, May Hill.

The (somewhat biased) saying goes that if you're in sight of May Hill, you're in perry country, where the best is made and drunk. That means the Three Counties: Herefordshire, Worcestershire and Gloucestershire.

Pears go back a long way here. Worcestershire was once so covered with them that Queen Elizabeth I had three added to Worcester's coat of arms. They're still there – and on the local rugby club's, too. Herefordshire was the crucible for perry's enlightenment years in the 17th century, and Charles Martell's *Pears of Gloucestershire* shows just how many of the greatest modern varieties have their origins in that county.

May Hill, the heart of British perry

Unlike cider, which is as deeply ingrained in the drinks culture of the south-west, English perry has always been mostly peculiar to these Three Counties. (I say 'English' because Monmouthshire, over the border in Wales, would arguably be justified in a discreet cough if I said 'British'). Even though perry can be, and is, now made all over the UK, the Three Counties remains its true heart.

Why should that be? The myth is that it's the work of the gods. The story goes that when the world was made, they sat on the crest of May Hill, where a young god brought the god king a fruit, claiming it made a drink of stars and nectar. Biting into it, the god king retched at its bitterness and spat the mouthful out, spraying perry pear pips around the hill.

Alas, as ever, the truth is more prosaic. Firstly, this is simply a good place to grow pears. Bannau Brycheiniog, the Black Mountains and the Malvern Hills offer protection from excess rain, and a warmer, sunnier microclimate than in many parts of our often-chilly island. What's more, the soil types of the region lend themselves to pears, and, perhaps most critically, include types which *do not* lend themselves to apples.

This may be the nub of it, and the real magic of May Hill. Around it, and to its south, along the Gloucestershire-Herefordshire border, is a band of Old Red Sandstone and intensely thick, impervious subsoil. Apple trees don't like it, but pear trees do. Spreading out into Gloucestershire's Severn Vale is yet more expanse of heavy clay. Again, apples don't do well here, but a good number of pear varieties are perfectly happy.

And so we have a combination of abundant perry pear varieties left standing when those of the Eastern Counties were grubbed up for dessert fruit, a cauldron of intellectual pomological interest, intense planting and grafting driven by the need to find a native wine, and a terroir that didn't really suit the otherwise ubiquitously planted apple. Welcome to perry pear country.

Herefordshire is full of great small producers

Herefordshire

Despite the fact that Gloucestershire and Worcestershire's pear and perry history is every bit as ancient, though both are home to good modern producers, and though Gloucestershire houses the National Perry Pear Centre, as far as the drink itself is concerned, its modern stronghold is, without any shadow of a doubt, Herefordshire.

Herefordshire is one of the United Kingdom's most overlooked and underrated crown jewels. Untroubled by the motorways that run past it to the south and the west, it is one of those rare counties you are unlikely to simply pass through. You have to know that Herefordshire is there and visit it directly. Unlike the flatter lands to the south-east, it is undulating country; a rough-hewn borderland of worn hills and ridges, looming hedgerow, thick clay, secret woodland and the ancient, earthy tones of oak and scrub and pasture, cleft in two by the River Wye that feeds it.

Broome Farm pears

As a seat of gastronomy, it is formidable. It is home to one of the world's iconic cow breeds and an embarrassment of produce besides. But it is in cider and perry that it truly stands apart. Aside from boasting the largest cidermaker in the world (Bulmer's, now owned by Heineken) and the largest producer of fresh-pressed juice perry in the country (Weston's), it also has an astounding number of the best, most forward-looking producers. Though other counties, especially Somerset, might challenge it for the somewhat subjective title of 'best' cider region, when it comes to perry there is no debate. Herefordshire is the UK's standard-bearer.

It's worth acknowledging that many of these producers – including some of the very best – are tiny. By current UK law, cider and perry producers are exempt from paying duty if they make less than 7,000l, and so that is what many of them produce.

But Herefordshire also boasts producers who are not only larger in output but whose approach to perry (and cider) as both a category and community has inspired and galvanised the rest of the country, has raised the national standard immeasurably in a relatively short time, and has fostered the sharing of knowledge and experience between producers. People like Mike and Albert Johnson at Ross-on-Wye, James and Susanna Forbes at Little Pomona, and Tom Oliver at the eponymous Oliver's Cider have made high-quality perry more readily available than it has ever been before. They have been the rising tide on which smaller producers have been lifted to national recognition.

Removing rejected pears

It is in Herefordshire that you will find many of the key figures on the Three Counties Cider & Perry Association's committee, establishing conferences like CraftCon for the meeting of cider and perry minds. It is Herefordshire that boasts the Big Apple Events, the Putley Trials and other key peer-reviewed competitions such as the annual Yew Tree Trials. And it is Hereford that is home to the magnificent Museum of Cider, where Pomonas of the 17th, 18th and 19th centuries are housed, along with beautiful sets of 18th-century crystal glasses; a stunning demonstration of the regard in which perry was once held.

Defining a characteristic 'Herefordshire' style is as futile a task as defining a UK style more generally. You'll find every style made here besides fortified; Once Upon a Tree have even bottled an Ice Perry, called 'The Wonder'. Little Pomona alone offer still, pét nat, traditional method, perrykin and co-fermented perries, while Tom Oliver runs the full spectrum of sweetness, from the most luscious to the most raspingly dry. I'd be surprised if any perrymaker on earth bottled the same range of single varieties as Ross-on-Wye, whose output is emphatic in its rebuttal of the generalisation that perry is defined by delicacy and florality.

Cwm Maddoc's Clare at the sorting table

Ultimately, it is that spirit of curiosity and adventure, that willingness to engage with the full spectrum of potential style and flavour, alongside a reverence for the bounty of ancient trees and treasured varieties, that is Herefordshire's true ace in the hole, and has been ever since the likes of Beale and Hartlib were writing about the first drinks fermented in bottles. It is a marvellous and ever-satisfying paradox that within this gentlest, softest and most soul-nourishing of counties there blazes such relentlessly bright and dynamic fire. There may be regions overseas that challenge for perry quality, but nowhere on earth does tradition and innovation so seamlessly and prolifically intertwine.

Wales

When people talk about British perry, it's generally in terms of the Three Counties. But there's a fourth, whose history and heritage deserves to be considered in the same light: Monmouthshire, across the border in Wales.

It's hardly surprising that pears grow well here. Geology and climate do not respect borders, and the red sandstone and clay soils and patterns of weather are much the same here as they are in neighbouring Herefordshire. And, of course, historically, England hasn't shown much respect for borders either, the dividing line between England and Wales having shifted several times over the centuries. Inevitably, pear trees grew across the political divide, with most of the best varieties finding a happy home in both countries.

The age of many of the existent trees – easily rivalling their centuries-old English counterparts – illustrates the point. *Perry Pears* mentions that perry has been made here for at least 400 years, taking it back to the same time that Beale, Hartlib and friends were discussing it in depth in England.

'What sets Monmouthshire (and parts of southern Powys) apart from the Three Counties is that until the latter part of the 20th century, perrymaking was a rural, farm-based practice,' Mike Penney, perrymaker at Troggi tells me. 'It was largely uncommercialised, without widespread distribution.'

Perry pears have no borders

Welsh perry remains, for the most part, an inside secret – more so than English – even in Wales itself. Many of its best makers – Mike himself, Phill Palmer at Palmer's Upland Cyder, Three Saints and Llanbethian Orchards – can be, even at the time of writing, elusive creatures to the online buyer.

They are worth the search, however. Some of the best and most interesting perries in the world are being made in this country's soulful valleys – a fact of which perry drinkers are becoming increasingly aware. The Welsh Perry & Cider Society (WPCS), founded at the instigation of Dave Matthews in 2001, has done sterling work in uniting the country's small makers, sharing their creations at festivals and flying the flag for Welsh pears and perry.

Although varieties overlap with those of England (Blakeney Red is the most common perry pear here too) Wales is, nonetheless, rich in its own indigenous pears. Dave, who left Wales and began making perry at Bartestree in Herefordshire, cites Welsh Gin and the lime-scented Potato Pear as two favourites, while other makers find wild Welsh pears to be particularly adept working together in a blend. There are even pears that may have begun life as English varieties but now grow best in Welsh orchards. Betty Prosser is one such juicy, opulent treat, and is among my favourite varieties. Although cited as a Gloucestershire pear originally, two of the four makers I'm aware of using it – Palmer's and Monnow Valley – are Welsh, while a third, Herefordshire's Cwm Maddoc, source their fruit from Monmouthshire.

Though perry in general is worthy of far more attention than it gets, my feeling is that Welsh perry in particular is an under-celebrated gem, one that shares the same breadth of style and flavour as its more famous neighbour. But if British perry is indeed ascending, it surely can't be long before Wales' stellar output gains its deserved place in the firmament.

Norman the perry dog

SELECTED UK PRODUCERS

I'll admit it; I've included more producers here than I have from any other country. This is partly because the UK perry scene is the one in which I am most deeply steeped, and the one that I have had greatest access to, but I also felt that the remarkable diversity of UK perry's style and flavour could only be reflected by including the broadest spectrum of makers.

That said, this is by no means a conclusive list, though all those included here have given me magical perry moments, for which they have my hearty endorsement and heartfelt thanks.

Herefordshire

Artistraw

Lydia Crimp and Tom Tibbits are two of those people we'd all like to pretend we're going to be a bit more like one day. They transformed a slope on the Herefordshire-Wales border near Hay-on-Wye into a little utopia of fruit trees and vegetable garden, campaigned for the health of the River Wye (and seemingly infinite environmental concerns besides), and make beautiful natural ciders and perries to boot. The hugely talented Lydia even makes her own natural paint with which she designs their stunning labels. Perry is a smaller concern for them than cider, but they have long been a reliable source of full, vinous, cold-racked pét nats that call for sitting on the grass with a picnic, ignoring real life as resolutely as you can.

Artistraw's Tom and Lydia

Bartestree

Sadly, over the course of writing this book, Dave and Fiona Matthews decided to call time on commercial perrymaking, but their impact on the British perry scene, and the phenomenal quality they produced, is too overwhelming not to include. Not only was Dave largely responsible for the formation of the Welsh Perry & Cider Association, but their later work in Herefordshire earned them numerous awards. Always marked by a ripe fullness of texture and pronounced generosity of pure, in-your-face fruitiness (irrespective of variety), Bartestree's perries will be missed by all who tasted them, and will no doubt remain a personal mental yardstick for years to come.

Bartestree's Fiona Matthews

Butford Organics

My memories are a little hazy (that's perry for you) but I'm fairly certain it was with a naturally sparkling Butford Organics that I had my Damascene perry moment. Organic agriculture is no easy feat, and Martin Harris has certainly had trials to contend with, making no perry at all for a couple of

Martin and Janet at Butford Organics

years thanks to nefarious ermine moths, but his results are frequently voluminous. Behind my all-time favourite Hendre Huffcap and a swathe of single varieties besides, Martin's handiwork unquestionably deserves to be considered amongst Herefordshire's finest. Not to mention its partial responsibility for this book.

Gregg's Pit

With 14 Champion Perrymaker trophies at the Three Counties' peer-judged Big Apple awards, James Marsden is perhaps the most decorated perrymaker in recent UK history. His small orchard boasts some truly historic trees, including the 'mother tree' of the Gregg's Pit variety, over 250 years old. A meticulous maker, whose still draught perries and especially pét nat and traditional method bottlings are invariably among the most pristine, elegant and pure of fruit made anywhere in the world. All are buy-on-sight fare, but his pét nat blend of Brandy, Blakeney Red and Winnal's Longdon, and his traditional method Thorns are doubly so.

Gregg's Pit's James and Helen

Hollow Ash – Cwm Maddoc

This is one of my greatest insider tips. Jeremy Harris and Clare Adamson are far too humble to admit the quality of their perry – they've told me off more than once for shouting about it –so I can only apologise to them for repeating for the umpteenth time that they are two of the best producers making this drink anywhere in the world. Their pét nat perry is always delicate, pristine and utterly sensitive to its fruit. Gin, Oldfield and Thorn are particular specialties, but my favourite of all is their rounded, amply fruited Betty Prosser. Keep an eye out, too, for any vintage of Cefnydd Hyfryd, a new Welsh variety they unearthed in someone's garden.

Jeremy and Clare at Hollow Ash – Cwm Maddoc

The Houghton Project

Since 2002 the team at the Houghton Project have done inspirational work teaching rural skills, including the making of cider and perry, to people with additional needs. That alone would merit inclusion, but what's particularly important to note is that it happens to be perry of superb quality. The project's participants have visited the likes of Oliver's, Ross-on-Wye, and Little Pomona, and the perries they have subsequently made – generally medium-sweet blends of varieties including Gin, Blakeney Red and Thorn – have not only competed with these world-renowned makers, but matched or beaten them in competitions.

The Houghton Project team

Little Pomona

It's safe to say James and Susanna Forbes have revolutionised cider and perry since they left the world of wine to make natural drinks in northern Herefordshire. Now joined by former winemaker Laurence Cocking, they are amongst the most imaginative of all makers, drawing on their vast experience with other drinks, and unshackled by tradition. Groundbreaking creations include not only beautiful pét nat, traditional method and still perries, showcasing an array of English and French varieties, but thirst-

Little Pomona team

quenching perrykins and co-fermentations with grapes and damsons, augmented by a category-leading barrel programme.

Quick to champion other makers and drinks categories as well as perry's place on the table, Little Pomona epitomises the highest standards of perrymaking and the most admirable of broad-tent mindset.

Newton Court

All Newton Court's perries come recommended, but their Black Mountain – a pét nat keeve, or 'Normandy method', as the label has it – is, for me, one of the classic evocations of Three Counties perry; the sort of bottle I'd pour someone to explain what this drink, and part of the world, is all about. Long cherished by those in the know, they are now going from strength to strength, both in terms of the ambition of their creations and their sparkly new visitor centre and restaurant. A perrymaker to keep firmly on your radar.

Oliver's

What more can be said about Tom Oliver? Perhaps the most famous and revered of all perrymakers, his creations are simply some of the most complex, balanced and downright delicious drinks of any sort, and have won international fandom accordingly. Most astonishing is that he makes them in tandem with his career as tour manager and sound mixer for The Proclaimers!

Although Tom does bottle occasional single varieties – look out for his Coppy – his heart lies in blends and the harmonies he can mix with them. Whether still or sparkling, sweet or dry, barrel-aged or unoaked, they are never less than exceptional. And his keeved perry – from any vintage – is a bottle to produce when you want to witness jaws dropping.

Wisely, Tom has always extended his curiosity to other drinks categories, collaborating with some of the UK's best brewers such as Mills Brewing and Cloudwater. Their joint creations make hens' teeth look commonplace, but if you find one, don't leave it on the shelf.

Tom Oliver

Redvers

Over 100 years ago Redvers Aspey picked pears and pressed perry in Herefordshire's Yarkhill. A century later his great grandson, David Nash, has picked up the torch to delicious effect. It's quite something to be harvesting from exactly the same trees as his ancestor, but that's perry pears for you. With his single variety pét nats (including a stunning Blakeney Red that manages to be both luscious and crisp) David has even begun winning first prize at the fiercely contested Big Apple awards. Redvers, I suspect, would be proud.

Redvers

Ross-on-Wye Cider & Perry

Easily a contender for my favourite perrymaker in the world, and not just because I got engaged in one of their orchards. The Johnsons at Ross-on-Wye – Albert and his father, Mike – along with John Edwards, are not only some of the best makers in the world, but some of the most universally beloved. They're single variety specialists, dedicated to championing the distinct flavours of individual pears. Their perries are almost always dry and predominantly bottle-conditioned. They also fly the flag for keg conditioning – live perry on draught – and their keg-conditioned Winnal's Longdon is an all-time personal favourite.

When I think of Ross-on-Wye perries, the word that comes to mind is 'vivid'. They have made some of the most intense, textural, full-throttle, full-flavoured perries I've been lucky enough to taste. Whether it be Thorn, Butt, Gin or their treasured Flakey Bark, Ross-on-Wye have conjured the most vibrant and arresting version this taster can remember.

Ross-on-Wye Cider & Perry Company

Seb's

Not least of the reasons the Ross-on-Wye festival holds a special place in my heart is that it is one of the few opportunities of my year to taste perries from a handful of superb makers whose wares aren't always easy to buy online. One such maker is the eponymous Seb, whose dry, bottle-conditioned perries from organic, unsprayed orchards are always an early draw. His 2020 vintage Butt was so good we went back for it three times over the course of the weekend and snuck a couple more into the boot when we drove home.

Gloucestershire

Bushel and Peck

Sometimes you want a juicy, easy-sipping, lazy weekend, not-too-much-thought kind of perry. Sometimes you want something complex, compelling, intense, arresting and spectacular. Admirably, Bushel & Peck endeavour to cover both bases. Their basic range, cleverly titled for each bottle's respective style, features a 'Smooth and Subtle' perry that certainly lives up to the name, while their limited editions allow them to explore the highways and byways of single varieties, barrel ageing and various sparkling styles. In short: a perry for everyone.

Capreolus

Barney Wilczak deserves an entire book of his own. Distilling eaux-de-vie from whole fruit located within 50 miles of his home, he is perhaps the most precise, meticulous drinks maker I have encountered, and unquestionably one of the most interesting distillers in the UK. His spirits, sometimes yielding only 1l from 30–45kg of fruit, made with obsessive selection, wild fermentations, astonishingly slow distillation and painfully narrow spirit cuts are more like essences; evocations of fruit that have won admirers even at Michelin-starred restaurants.

Capreolus

185

His perry pear eau-de-vie, distilled as individual varieties before blending, somehow manages to conjure not only the whole pear – flesh, juice, skin and all – but a sense of the orchard itself; what the French call 'sous bois'. Given the production meticulousness, these spirits aren't cheap, but my goodness, you must try one if you get the chance.

Castle Wood Press

Never mind 'in sight of', Rob Castle picks and presses his perry pears on the very slopes of May Hill itself. And if you want to taste his creations, it's to May Hill – or the Ross-on-Wye festival – you'll have to go. They are worth the trip in and of themselves. Dry, natural, bottle-fermented, often boasting iconic handmade labels, these are intense, textural things that encapsulate with a rare clarity the whole of the variety from which they're made. Rob's iterations of the classics – the likes of Gin, Butt and Thorn – are never short of top notch, but it's his rarer varieties like Rock, Judge Amphlett and Flakey Bark (the only one I know of currently made by anyone besides Ross-on-Wye) that I usually make a beeline for first.

Charles Martell

One of the most important characters in British perry's modern history, Charles Martell was instrumental in establishing and championing the National Perry Pear Centre as well as discovering new varieties and rediscovering varieties thought lost, including Dymock Red and Flakey Bark. A world-famous cheese maker, his 'Stinking Bishop' is so called for being washed in Stinking Bishop (Moorcroft) perry. Also an excellent distiller, his pear spirit, and, particularly, 'Poireau' mistelle, are among the best perry products you are likely to taste.

Charles Martell

Mills

Not a cidermaker, but one of the most talented brewers in Britain. Specialising in spontaneously fermented brews and constantly looking to reflect their place and incorporate the flavours around them, Jonny and Genevieve Mills found a natural sparring partner in the ever-inquisitive Tom Oliver. Their combination of perry pear juice with Saaz-hopped Pilsner wort was one of the cleverest, most delicious drinks I've ever come across. Who would have thought perry and beer could find such a happy marriage? Yet more proof of how much there is to be gained by looking across the drinks divide.

Jonny Mills

99 Pines

Another denizen of May Hill, based in Taynton – home to the famous Taynton Squash – Phil Kester is one of the newest makers on this list, having only launched in 2022. Named for the distinctive trees that make

May Hill Gloucestershire's most recognisable landmark, 99 Pines has the rare distinction of being entirely focused on perry. A community organisation that donates all profits to charity, sourcing local fruit and using a traditional old rack-and-cloth press, their inaugural bottlings (especially a Taynton-Blakeney blend) suggest a splendid addition to the British perry pantheon.

99 Pines' Phil with some perry-loving bystander...

Orchard Revival

There are a few people whose cider and perry recommendations
I trust implicitly, and Alison Taffs, who owns and runs the CAMRA
multi-award-winning Hop Inn in Hornchurch (a cider- and perry-
lover's must-visit) is one of them. So, when she lavished praise on
Orchard Revival I immediately sat up and took notice. If you can't
get to Hornchurch you'll need to make your way to Gloucester,
but it's a pilgrimage with significant reward. Tim Andrews'
draught creations and bottled 'Pioneer Perry' – from traditional
orchards he is helping protect and restore – are special indeed.

Ragged Stone

Chris Atkins of Ragged Stone is a true perry obsessive. He not only
creates a bewildering array of single variety and blended perries
in bottle and draught (look out especially for their rare, bold,
Rock), but he even moved his production to the National Perry
Pear Centre in Hartpury itself. A champion for all perry, Chris has
mentored talents including Lucie Mayerová of Naked Orchards,
and, perhaps most importantly, engineers the Festival of Perry at
the Malvern Autumn Show, the UK's biggest harvest celebration,
where makers talk perry to thousands of visitors, world-record
displays of varieties are put on show, and over 50 different perries
both British and international are available to taste. Epic.

Severn

I have a soft spot for Severn Cider's perry. Sweetish, super-juicy
and supremely approachable whether still or sparkling. They pick
their fruit in Blakeney, the place that gives its name to Britain's
most widely planted perry pear, Blakeney Red, unsurprisingly
the predominant variety in their flagship blend. I remember
visiting, following the meandering Severn River, and admiring the
slopes of fruit trees that rise upward from the bank. Everything
charming, easy-going, gentle – a metaphor for their perry itself.

Wales

JKL

You'd expect someone with Ben Llewellyn's wine background to do exciting things with perry. The 'L' of JKL – the 'J' and 'K' are his colleagues Henry Johnson and Alex Khan – Ben has made some gorgeous, clearly wine-inspired still and lightly spritzed perries from Henry's home farm fruit, after training with James Marsden at Gregg's Pit, whose output Ben cites as 'easily the best perry there is'. Rather appropriately, for a wine professional, he has predominantly used Wales' Burgundy pear, supplemented by Thorn and the sole known example of Llanarth Green, a floral, juicy pear that reminded me of Loire Chenin Blanc. Some experiments – ice perry, even ripasso perry fermented on pulp – are yet to see the light of day. I'm waiting…

Pressing at JKL

Llanblethian Orchards

I'm not sure I can praise Alex Simmens' perry more highly than to say I once made an impromptu 250-mile round trip just to buy some at a farmer's market. Thankfully, his blends and single varieties are now a little easier to find online. Alex is another maker who likes to play around; draught, bottle-conditioned, pét nat and even ice perries all feature in his ever-changing repertoire. Aside from their quality, Alex offers a fantastic level of trans-parency, featuring all his varieties, ingredients and processes on his labels. An example I hope perrymakers will increasingly choose to follow.

Alex Simmens, Llanblethian Orchards

Monnow Valley

After a few years harvesting for another producer, in 2007 Kevin Garrod began his own cider and perrymaking venture, going commercial in 2015. Hunting perry pears in the small orchards of Monmouthshire's Monnow Valley, he started by making blends before curiosity around the potential flavours of single varieties got the better of him. Using a range of pears, from Welsh pears to such varieties as Thorn and Taynton Squash, he's also one of the very few makers working with Betty Prosser.

Kevin Garrod, Monnow Valley

Palmer's Upland

Ever-friendly Phill Palmer is a fixture of cider and perry events and awards around the country – probably because he seems to keep winning so many. An early member of the WPCS, Phill waxes lyrical about the fledgling days of makers sitting around in each other's barns and kitchens, tasting and comparing notes. Much of what he makes is draught blended perry – he suggests most Welsh pears are best as blends – but his bottle-conditioned single variety fizz is always worth looking out for. I remember a 2018 Betty Prosser with special fondness.

Skyborry

Welsh? English? Based in the border town of Knighton and using fruit from both Welsh and Three Counties orchards, this Powys producer is an excellent advert for Anglo-Welsh co-operation. They're also an excellent advert for perry, cited by Wilding's Sam Leach as the makers who made him want to do perry himself. Usually pét nat and deploying both English and Welsh varieties – I particularly enjoyed their 'Ultralight Beam', made from Berllanderi Red and Green – their signature, irrespective of which pears they use, is a wonderful balance of ripe, fleshy juiciness with elegant freshness. Gorgeous stuff.

Adam and Dani of Skyborry

Three Saints

The presence of an ancient perry pear orchard on her Gwent farm naturally led Jessica Deathe down the rabbit hole of this marvellous drink's history and production. Since 2004 she's become one of Welsh perry's leading lights, her sweet blended 'Laughing Juice' (a super name for perry) is a festival feature. Though the range is ever-changing, all of Jessica's perries, it seems to me, tend towards a supremely juicy, approachable style, often lower in alcohol. Resolutely offline, Three Saints is another perry you have to go hunting for – but perry pilgrimages are always the best sort.

Troggi

When I ask Welsh makers about perry, Mike Penney at Troggi is the first name that comes up. A founding father of the WPCS, 'he was making bottle-fermented perry years before anyone else,' Dave Matthews tells me. Introduced to perry pears by the vendor who sold him his Victorian press in 1988, Mike has watched modern Welsh perry's story unfold from a central position. Like most Welsh makers, he predominantly uses English varieties, citing Blakeney Red, Gin, Brandy, Butt and Oldfield as favourites, but he has a special fondness for the very tannic Welsh variety Little Cross Huffcap. His draught is exemplary, a fixture at CAMRA festivals where it is always quick to disappear, but his bottle-fermented sparkling will have you believing in magic.

Somerset

Burrow Hill – Somerset Cider Brandy Co

The Temperley family don't do things by halves. Not content with being the UK's leading distillers of apple brandy and one of the country's most prominent aspirational cidermakers, they have also gone against the Somerset grain by planting their own perry pear orchards of over 20 varieties including Thorn, Brandy and Hendre Huffcap. As well as a delicious, sparkling 'session' perry, they make a traditional method of startling elegance, and – they're distillers after all – an unaged, delightfully floral perry pear eau-de-vie. I await barrel-aged perry brandy with no little impatience.

Downside

My all-time favourite perry? Almost impossible to answer, but Paul Ross's still, dry Downside Special Reserves 2016 and 2017 might just take it. Astonishingly aromatic, gorgeously textured, they boasted flavours unlike any perries I have tasted before or since. Paul is one of the very few producers who makes his perry from a blend of English, French and German varieties, having travelled to other regions and been won over by the likes of Jörg Geiger's Champagner Bratbirner and the Plant de Blancs of the Domfrontais. I missed Downside immensely when Paul closed his operations to begin making cider and perry for another producer, and was delighted when he started his own production again in 2022.

Paul Ross, Downside

Hecks

Perhaps the proudest standard-bearers for perry in cider-dominated Somerset, Hecks' iconic farm shop is firm must-visit territory. There you can choose from a range of draught single variety and blended perries (like Ragged Stone, their Rock is a bold beauty). The Hecks family's 31 single variety pouches gave my wife and I many happy hours of blending fun during 2020 lockdown, though we soon discovered it was best left to the experts. Besides their draught, their rare, special-edition keeved perries, especially an Oldfield highly recommended by Gabe Cook – 'the Ciderologist' and one of my perry mentors – are essential drinking.

Nempnett

One of the very first makers I encountered on my perry journey. Though they took a short break during the pandemic years between 2020–2022, Keith Balch and Debbie Chivers had previously been winning CAMRA Gold National and Regional Championship awards for their draught and bottled perries. As of the 2023 vintage they're back with a vengeance, and inspired by the rethink cider movement are looking to produce a larger number of 750ml sharing bottles, feeling it should be drunk like wine rather than by the pint. With access to their own young trees, as well as old Long Ashton Research Station orchards in Somerset, they work with over 24 varieties, making blends and single varieties (including rare Claret pear) and even a few natural keeves. Everything is wild fermented and traces of sulphites are sensibly added where necessary. It's so good to see them back.

Wilding

Champions of the natural movement and dedicated to making minimal-intervention ciders and perries from traditional Somerset orchards, everything Sam and Beccy Leach make is underscored by a desire to express the entirety of their fruit. Though Somerset isn't perry-rich, Beccy's first cousin once removed is none other than Tom Oliver, so it's no surprise they've turned their hands to perry, and their explorations of old Somerset orchards are unearthing a surprising and ever-growing number of varieties. Their perries are generally cold-racked (occasionally keeved) for natural sweetness and already feature a number of full-throated, breathtakingly juicy releases. Perrymakers to keep an eye on.

Devon and Cornwall

Bollhayes

Bollhayes were early pioneers of restoring traditional method cider to the UK, bottling their first in 1994. Alex Hill's orchard in Devon's Blackdown Hills boasts two pear trees – a Thorn and a rare Pine – perfect for making pristine, fresh, clean-lined, dry traditional method perry that offers a beautiful alternative to champagne. With a scientist's approach to hygiene and an artist's approach to blending, Alex's perry handiwork is all too rare, but worth every minute of the search.

Find and Foster

Admittedly, at the time of writing, Polly and Mat Hilton have only released two perries. But given that the first, in particular, would sit comfortably in any list of the best I've ever tried, it would be a sin not to include them. Having set out to restore Devon's devastated orchards, Find & Foster have become one of the most highly regarded producers in the country, making ciders of breathtaking elegance. Their perries – pét nat blends of Butt and Blakeney Red from just four trees – show the best of those varieties; scintillating fruit, minerality, purity and clarity. I remember thinking of their debut edition as a unicorn perry, and if there is any justice in the world, it will prove the first of many.

Find and Foster

Gould

Cornwall only has a few scattered perry pear trees, but when Jonathan Gould heard Charles Martell talking on the radio in 2007, he was inspired to plant his own. It wasn't until 2019 that he had enough fruit to start making perry, but he raced out of the blocks with what was, when I tasted it, some of the best I'd tried that year. Not confined to English varieties, Jonathan has also planted French pears, and indeed it was AOP Domfront that inspired his production approach: pét nat with only fallen fruit (no shaking of, or picking from, trees). Having played with mistelles and ice ciders, Jonathan's looking to explore the same with perry. I can't wait.

Rull Orchard

The irrepressible Mike Shorland is one of the most enthusiastic characters in British cider and perry. This former construction worker had a Damascene moment one day and poured his life savings into starting a biodiverse organic orchard and cidery in Devon with his partner, Claire. Though his cider is good, to my mind his bright, elegant, citrusy traditional method perry is the pick of his output to date. Never afraid to try something unusual, he is also the only perrymaker I've come across who's experimented with ageing perry in tequila barrels. It worked, too; Perryote is a riot of fruity, oaky fun.

Rull Orchard

Vagrant

'If you make cider, perry feels like a logical extension,' James Fergusson of new Cornish cidery Vagrant tells me. Initially put off by perry's notoriously troublesome reputation, he was persuaded by the quality he tasted to finally give it a go. With few perry pears available, he bought Duchesse d'Angoulême pears from Kent and with them made one of the best culinary-pear perries this author has ever encountered. Dry, still and near-vinous in texture, with freshness, minerality, light stone fruit and even a twist of beeswax and herbs, it reminded me of great Italian white wines – even Spain's Albariño. A monumental first effort. More please!

Vagrant's Tessa

East England

Blue Barrel

Beginning their journey in a community orchard in Nottingham, and now making cider and perry not only with Nottinghamshire fruit but with apples and pears from their current home in Cambridgeshire, Emma and Leo Jordan were inspired (like so many British makers) by the Johnsons at Ross-on-Wye to make perry. One of the friendliest couples on the UK scene, their pears come from a range of sources, including an ancient perry orchard in Nottinghamshire, wild trees on industrial estates in Nottingham itself, and, one day, trees they've planted in their new home. Varied terroir, you might say.

Emma and Leo Jordan of Blue Barrel Cider

Nightingale

Sam Nightingale is perhaps the most exciting maker in a region rapidly discovering its voice. His elegant sharing-bottle creations championing Kent's dessert varieties sit happily in company with the best made anywhere in Britain, and his endlessly sessionable cans are a fridge door staple. His perrymaking journey, with Concorde, Conference and Commice pears, has been a gradual one – these are unforgiving varieties to work with – but persistence has rewarded him with a beautiful, aromatic, floral and sherbety gem. A celebration of Kentish fruit.

Turner's

Turner's prefer 'Pear Cider' as a term, but whatever you call it, this elderflower-scented, easy-drinking Kentish perry is a crisp glassful of joy that tastes somehow like the light shimmering off ripples in a stream. A perry to slip into a picnic hamper, though it's dangerously moreish sipped on its own, it calls for nibbles, charcuterie and salads. Acidity balanced with just a touch of sweetness; I can't think of anyone who wouldn't take a second glassful.

Whin Hill

North Norfolk isn't the first place you'd think of looking for an orchard of perry pears, yet Whin Hill boast a stunning one. With around 144 trees, mostly Thorn and Brandy, augmented with Winnal's Longdon, Helen's Early, Moorcroft, Yellow Huffcap and more, it services a stunning, perfumed, richly fruited and well-structured blend like no other in the Eastern Counties, and which, while sharing DNA with the perries of the west, takes on its own distinct inflection of flavour. The expertise of makers Mark and Lisa Jarvis? The Stanhoe terroir? Probably a bit of both.

West and North England

Brennan's

Who knew that there'd be an orchard of Yellow Huffcap trees growing a short drive from where I grew up? As a native Merseysider, I couldn't leave Brennan's out, but given the Brennan brothers are some of the nicest people in perry, and their perry is such a refreshing, lip-smacking, citrusy joy, there's no question they're in here on merit. Based on an army camp just north of Liverpool, they're surely the only perrymaker in the world who need to pass a checkpoint before pressing can commence.

Dunham Press

Thanks to the efforts of Dick Withecombe, Cath Potter, Nicky Kong and others, Manchester has, unexpectedly, become a major cider and perry hub, packed with brilliant pubs, knowledgeable drinkers and a nation-leading cider club. It's no surprise that this group of passionate enthusiasts includes some seriously talented makers, and Dunham Press is particularly special. Using old, traditional orchards in Dunham Massey, they make very good cider – but their Peterloo Perry is the real head-turner. A still blend, it's bagged Champion Perry against Three Counties rivals at both the Manchester Beer and Cider Festival and the National Fruit show. A northern standard-bearer.

Hogan's

Warwickshire's Hogan's are very much the face of what large-scale cider and perry in the UK could, and ideally should, be. Eschewing concentrates, using fresh-pressed fruit, bottling a diverse range of creations with high juice content, showcasing varieties and methods, creating space for high-end, playful and aspirational editions … and being lovely people to boot. Their standard perry is a former trophy winner at the International Cider Challenge and the epitome of the light, delicate, yet bursting with in-your-face fruit style that is so irresistible. Occasionally they bottle special edition 750ml offerings, which are always worth picking up.

Mosser

Planting fruit trees anywhere is an act of faith. Planting them on a mountain in Cumbria you could be accused of bloody-mindedness. But that's precisely what maker Mark Evens did, recording the tribulations vividly, fascinatingly and very entertainingly in an article titled 'How not to grow fruit trees' on Mosser Cider's website. His own plantings, thus far, have predominantly been apples, but his perries are still Cumbrian fruit – Thorn and Blakeney Red from North Cumbria's Acorn Bank. I never need an extra excuse to visit the Lake District, but perry seems an especially good one.

Mosser

Scotland

Fleming's Fife Cider

Scotland's perry connection, though faint, goes back further than you'd think. The monks of Newburgh, Balmerino and St Andrews in Fife planted orchards of pears that were certainly used to make it. Today, Scotland, led by the likes of Anstruther's Æble cider shop, distributors like Hard Pressed Cider and a swathe of determined, brilliant producers, is having a major cider renaissance. Perry is still hard to find, but Robbie Fleming of Fleming's Fife Cider has made some beautiful examples, drawing on local Fife culinary pears as well as Gloucestershire-harvested Butt to make dry, naturally sparkling perries fermented with ambient yeasts. Judging from his first releases, Robbie's done those monks proud.

Fleming's Fife Cider

Naughton

This entry is a bit of a tease, but consider it a tip-off to set your watches. Naughton is one of the most exciting new producers to enter the world of cider and perry recently, managed by Peter Crawford, one of the UK's leading Champagne experts. Inspired by the famous French fizz, he has made stunning traditional method ciders, and has recently turned his attention to perry. He tells me he finds it even more exciting to make: 'I feel it charts the phenolics and mouthfeel of wine more than cider.' He's currently ageing both stainless-steel and oak-fermented blends of English perry pears on their lees in bottle, but is most excited about a single variety of a French pear that has just begun its secondary fermentation. Its name, appropriately, is Champagne.

Naughton's
Peter Crawford

Diggers

Perthshire's family-run Diggers have been a central part of Scotland's cider revolution and were behind the first ever Scottish perry I tasted – the subtle, sherbety and deliciously elegant Aster, wild fermented from hand-picked pears and bottle-conditioned. Wonderfully, in addition to their commitment to only using Scottish-grown fruit (their pears come from the historic Carse pear orchards), Diggers have planted an incredible 2,800 trees themselves,

at Little Kinnaird in Forgandenny and Guardswell Farm. It'll be a little while before those trees start properly cropping, but once they do, I suspect Aster will prove the first in a long list of recommended Diggers perries.

Digby, Diggers

Linn

'Perry is our secret weapon,' Jack Arundell and Eilidh Izat of Fife's Linn Cider tell me. 'We are really lucky to have a wide variety of pears available to us although not all or possibly none are classically considered perry pears.' Gathering their fruit from walled gardens and even ancient trees in the grounds of cathedrals, Linn follows the time-honoured Central European approach of blending pears with eating apples in their ciders to add aromatics and body to the sharp apple notes. They've further experimented by marrying pears with bittersweet cider fruit. They've also harvested in Herefordshire to make (outstanding) pure pét nat perry from French and English variety perry pears and hope to one day plant a pear orchard. One of Scotland's newest makers, they could yet prove one of the most exciting.

FRANCE

'Such excellent perry, that not only does it resemble in colour
the white wine of Anjou, but also in taste, and in all its other
qualities: so that often the best gourmets of France are deceived.'

(De vino et pomaceo libri duo, 1588)

A gorgeous, green-glass 750ml, whose elegant curves and long, slender
neck recall a wine – no, *Champagne* – bottle, complete with cork and cage.
A gentle twist, that heart-filling pop and a rush of frosty-white mousse.
It glows in the glass like living gold, and on its perfume are the scents of
tangerines picked from the tree, sun-warmed grapefruits, and a June
rose garden. Bubbles tingle, gentle sweetness tempered by a refreshing,
ripe-citrus lilt of acidity, and wave after wave of peach and mandarin
and greenhouse blooms. It is nectar. You take another sip and give silent
thanks for French poiré.

The classic poiré look

Ask me about English perry and I don't have a specific image in my head. The scene is too convoluted. But mention French and a clear picture emerges. Broadly speaking, almost all French perry has at least a helping of sweetness – more often than not a generous one. It is (almost) invariably sparkling, generally pét nat, and ubiquitously served in 750ml bottles. What's more, a huge percentage of France's perry output is dominated by just a single pear: the Plant de Blanc.

This sounds rather homogenous, and certainly I've spoken to a few English makers who have levelled somewhat ungenerous accusations of 'it all tasting the same' at French perry. Stealing from Æsop's fables, it's as if English perry is the fox, who knows a range of tricks of differing effectiveness, while French is the hedgehog, who does just one, but has perfected it.

That generalisation, though, conceals a more complicated picture. For the last 20 years or so, producers have gained confidence. Confidence that perry is more than just sweetish fizz for pairing with crêpes. Confidence in the flavours and styles nurtured over generations. And confidence to begin overturning those historic norms in search of the new.

What's more, it is underscored by a far more rigid concern for quality and ingredient than is afforded by the ever-insouciant British government. In France there is a minimum juice requirement of 50%, with even the biggest producers generally using more. Although concentrates, dilution and pasteurisation exist, they're far less endemic than within the British scene, and more frequently found in French cider than perry in any case.

Today, French makers are bottling disgorged méthode traditionnelles alongside their pét nats. At the sweetest end of the spectrum there are experiments with ice perry – poiré de glace – while among many producers there is a general trend towards gradually drier bottlings. Some makers are coaxing Plant de Blanc to its most symphonic expression, while others

Bottling

are experimenting with other pears, even as single varieties – from rose-scented Fossey to lip-smacking Vinot and deep, sonorous De Fer.

Though the tiny south Normandy appellation of AOP Domfront is French perry's heartland, you will find it fermenting in the rest of Normandy, in Brittany, the Loire Valley, and, increasingly, other places besides. Pears don't take as well to high-density basse-tige (low branch) orchards – another reason fewer pears grow outside Domfront, and that industrial producers are less interested – so it is a sign of the changing perception of perry that a growing number of makers are planting trees and taking perry seriously.

In France, of all countries, it's no surprise to find perrymakers not only thinking like winemakers but collaborating with them and co-fermenting pears with grapes. Indeed, many winemakers have added perry to their own repertoires, especially in the Loire. Natural winery Les Capriades makes beautiful pét nat from local pears, while Côme Isambert, in Saumur, was behind one of the best French perries I ever tasted.

And France boasts a trump card: the distillation of Calvados, as well as a swathe of mistelles – pear juice fortified with Calvados and aged in oak casks – as richly satisfying as sherry, Port or Madeira.

Far from a one-trick pony, this most traditional of drinks-making countries could be the most exciting, dynamic perry destination of all.

Planting in a traditional meadow

The Domfrontais

Though in cider terms it vies with its neighbour, Brittany, when it comes to the fermented pear, Normandy reigns supreme. But even in Normandy, perry plays second fiddle. In 1588, in Julien le Paulmier's treatise on wine and cider, *De vino et pomaceo libri duo*, it was acknowledged that areas of significant cider production, such as coastal Cotentin, made little perry, and that what they made was considered poor stuff. Though producers throughout the region might offer one or two, it is very much subsidiary to their apple-focused output. Except in one tiny pocket on the region's border: the Domfrontais.

You couldn't really call this country 'rolling'. At most you could say it ripples like a pastoral sea; agricultural tillage in every direction, fringed with tree line, studded with cows, and rising, as if on a swell, to the hill on which the town of Domfront en Poiraie perches, its ancient castle and octagonal-steepled church dominating the skyline.

Even by the standards of perrylands around the world, this is quiet country. Though every inch of the countryside seems worked, there is a haunting silence as you walk through the lanes. Pear trees are everywhere, and staggering; muscular behemoths that tower over the handful of far-smaller apple trees. Most are at least centurions – the biggest were here a hundred years before Napoleon. All are grown the tall, traditional way – haute-tige (high branch) – wide spaces between each. Unlike the Mostviertel, where trees mostly grow in individual rows along the line of fields, orchards are a common sight here, the size of the beasts within giving them the look of paddocks for Ents. By law, pear trees must make up at least 25% of any Domfrontais orchard. In practice, as becomes increasingly apparent the more you wander, they generally account for far more.

Many varieties cluster like grapes on a vine

Why were they planted here in such numbers? Historical sources are vague. There's one unverifiable suggestion that it was because under the ancien régime, before the French Revolution, pears weren't subject to tithe. Certainly, pear trees were then so common that farmers reduced their grain crops in favour of them, and one politician talked of 'pear tree forests'.

The likeliest answer seems to be that, like the land around England's May Hill, this was soil better suited to pears than apples. Mainly deep, wind-blown loess over schist, or thick clay over granite, it holds a lot of water for a long time, and that soil gets cold. Apple trees don't do as well here as in the softer, better-draining areas to the north, but pear trees are delighted. What's more, arable plants such as corn and buckwheat are also fans – and the height of haute-tiges pear trees, alongside the space between them, meant crops could grow together in harmony.

Towering traditional French pear tree

Their height is a boon for dairy farming too, since cows happily graze beneath the pears without stripping the fruit. Almost every farm in this part of the country is mixed agriculture; it's a rare Domfrontais grower who doesn't have a small herd as well. Unsurprisingly, local cheeses – Camembert, Bûchette Basilou and Bleu de Saint Jean – go perfectly with poiré; the drink's acidity slicing through the creaminess of the cheese, its fruit and fizz adding lightness and perfume.

Though perry has been mentioned here for a thousand years, a demonstration of its lamentable insularity comes at the end of the 19th century, when the writers of the Herefordshire Pomona described France as not taking much interest. Somewhat misleading, given that, in 1908, the French horticulturalist Charles Baltet describes an average national production of 2 million hl a year. In the same treatise he mentions several varieties as especially high quality, even singling out those particularly good for sparkling perry. Clearly less parochial than his English counterparts, he praises the perries of England, Germany and Switzerland as 'full-bodied, sparkling juice which will compete with our Champagne'; remarkably magnanimous, not least because Baltet also attests to perry being made in Champagne itself (though I don't believe Napoleon called that one 'Champagne's other Champagne').

As late as 1928 the Encyclopédie Agricole Cidrerie attests to 1 million hl of perry produced across the départments of Orne, Manche and Mayenne, writing, 'pears find their best use in the production of a heady drink called perry ... reminiscent of certain white wines from Anjou'. In fact, enough perry was being pressed that unscrupulous winemakers from Anjou and Saumur in the Loire were using it to bulk out their wines. When I first got into perry I was struck by the similarities between some perries and Loire Chenin Blanc. Perhaps I had it the wrong way round. Perrymakers even recall testimonies from the stationmaster of Fers that, in the

The ubiquitous cork and cage

19th and early 20th centuries, tanks of perry regularly left for Champagne where unscrupulous vignerons used it to illicitly pad out and add fruitiness and possibly other qualities to their sparkling wines.

Certainly, perry, drunk knowingly as such, was largely a regional concern, the drink a distant third place to cider and wine (never mind beer or spirits). When microscopic insects called phylloxera wiped out most of France's vineyards in the late 19th century, it was cider that primarily stepped in to fill the gap. As soon as vineyards had recovered, wine regained its primacy, helped by intensive government promotion. Perry dwindled in the decades thereafter, both in quantity and quality.

The boom of the bootleggers

So, what were the pears primarily used for? The answer is distillation – predominantly of the illegal variety – on a scale to make bootleggers in prohibition America wince.

Normandy is Calvados country: cider and perry distillation has been recorded here since 1553. At the start of the 17th century, distillers formed a guild and when grape brandy was devastated by phylloxera, Calvados transformed its rough-and-ready image into something more sophistica-ted, increasing production astronomically. Although Cognac and Armagnac ultimately regained primacy, by 1900 there were an astonishing 100,000 distillers in Normandy.

In 1875, just as French spirit lovers needed a replacement for Cognac, and pear growers were starting to see major financial potential, the French government passed a hugely unpopular law. From now on, farmers could make as much spirit as they wanted for personal consumption, tax free, but on every litre sold the new tax quadrupled the previous price required for profit. In 1916 the law was tightened to a maximum of 10l for personal consumption, with regular checks from custom officers.

Given there were, at this point, well over a million pear trees in the Domfrontais alone, given the number of French bistros almost doubled during this period to 500,000, and given the region's labyrinth of sunken lanes and poorly kept roads far from big cities, what happened next was inevitable.

The département of Orne, a fifth of Normandy, was the leading producer of spirit in the south of the region, and the Domfrontais made over half of its output: an astonishing 176,333hl. (For context, in 2021 there were 651hl of Calvados Domfrontais distilled.) Over 90% was illegal.

Fully ripe French perry pears

Visiting this gentle countryside, it is impossible to imagine it having been, within living memory, another wild west. Yet the scale of smuggling was incredible. Spirit was sold to bistros and the miners of northern France. It was doctored with caramel, with cherry and apple sticks to give the impression of maturity, and white spirit was sold in bulk to transform into fashionable pastis.

Farmers and smugglers hid stills and spirit anywhere imaginable: children's bedrooms, flattened barrels stuffed into wall cavities, bales of hay. Fire brigades would constantly be called to deal with barns being consumed by flames, like fired brandy over Christmas pudding.

The reward was worth the risk. Spirit was by far the most lucrative source of income. One bootlegger, Pierre Dubourg, modified his Citroën DS 19 to avoid pursuit. It could billow smoke, drop oil and nails, shine dazzling lights, change registration plates as it drove ... and carry 400l of illicit Calvados. Nicknamed 'the James Bond of smugglers', Pierre was finally arrested in 1987, and discovered to have a whole fleet of modified Citroëns.

To farmers, smugglers were the heroes and customs officers the enemy. After all, it was the farmers who were distilling. Most hated of all were the legally encouraged surprise home visits. In February 1935, 5,000 distillers gathered at a farm in tiny Mantilly – their aim to revolt in the name of freedom to distil. Massive demonstrations followed, including a scarcely believable gathering of 15,000 distillers at Saint-Hilaire-du-Harcouët, where windows were smashed and a guard bus set on fire. To place the number in context, the population of Domfront en Poiraie today is 4,000.

The Domfrontais is covered with trees like this

In the face of these numbers, and with customs officers being menaced, assaulted and even kidnapped, the government deployed the army to restore order. But in June they relented and abolished home visits.

Smuggling remained endemic throughout the latter half of the 20th century. Jérôme Forget recalls men driving around the countryside with vans full of illicit spirit in 1996. But with improved roads and more enforceable regulations, the practice dwindled – and with it the pear trees.

France's perry-in-law: the rise of AOP Domfront

It's ironic that the survival of the Domfrontais' perry pear trees was directly linked to the fortunes of illegal distillation. But as other, more law-abiding spirits regained popularity, and the bottom fell out of the illicit pear brandy market, so the farmers looked at their fields of pear trees and wondered whether they were worth keeping.

Usually their answer was no. What's more, partially to combat the smugglers, and to encourage the planting of corn, the government had incentivised the destruction of pear trees with a subsidy of 23 Francs per uprooting. The Domfrontais was hit particularly hard, since the Common

Probably over 300 years old

Agricultural Policy, installed by the EU to provide aid to agricultural holdings, classes orchards as a minimum of 80 trees per hectare. The trees of the Domfrontais are widely spaced, with many orchards numbering no more than 40 trees per hectare, so are classed by the EU as 'meadows', ineligible for financial assistance.

Pear trees were grubbed up in thousands, sold for high-end furniture and replaced with corn. This was compounded in 1999 when a storm ripped out another 100,000 trees. In the 1960s the collective orchard of the Domfrontais numbered 1,387,000 trees. By the year 2000 only around 100,000 were left.

What stopped the rot? Ironically, given the escapades of the preceding 125 years, it was a refocussing on perry – and France's strictest drinks regulation.

Though pear spirit had been distilled by the thousands of hectolitres, and Calvados had been (briefly) the darling of high-end French brandy drinkers, perry had been reduced to ignominy. A little was made, but only for the refreshment of farm workers. As a drink in its own right, it had no status. Barely anyone outside the farms was aware of it.

In the 1990s there was a kickback. Makers like Jérôme Forget, the Pacory family and others were not only reconsidering perry's potential, but – alarmed by the destruction of pear trees – wanted to gain protection and recognition for their drink and for the plants and place that nurtured it.

A classic Domfrontais perry farm

How to achieve this? The answer is through something called an Appellation d'Origine Protegée (AOP, sometimes AOC). In English this translates as a Protected Designation of Origin.

AOPs are the strongest protections that France offers to food and drink. They're most famously applied in wine, where there are over 360, but they can also be for anything from cheeses to strawberries.

An AOP is a legally protected status given to particular produce from a specific place. To bear an AOP, that produce must conform to tightly regulated rules regarding where it is grown and exactly how it is made. The first in wine was Châteauneuf du Pape in 1936. It governed the appellation's area, the varieties of grapes allowed, and the methods of winemaking. It was even updated to prohibit UFOs from flying over or landing in the area – seriously.

There are few AOPs for cider. Normandy has Pays d'Auge, Cotentin and, recently, Du Perche. Brittany has just one – Cornouaille. And the Domfrontais boasts the only AOP status afforded to a perry.

'It was important in identifying this particular region,' says Jerôme Forget. 'And in recognising or honouring the efforts undertaken in

Perry continues to mature in bottle

preserving traditional orchards. It was also important in preserving the "savoir faire".'

As the then-president of AOP Poiré Domfront and AOP Calvados Domfrontais, Jerôme was at the forefront of securing appellation status and determining its parameters. To earn AOP Domfront status perry must be made from pears grown within the Domfrontais. Those pears must be harvested after they have fallen from the tree to ensure full ripeness – no picking – and must include a minimum of 40% Plant de Blanc, though in practice most AOP Domfront contains well over 60% and is often a single variety. Artificial carbonation is prohibited – fizz is mandatory, but must be naturally induced – as is the use of pasteurisation or concentrate. The required sugar ripeness of the pears is stipulated, as is the maximum yield per tree. And perries must be fermented using only wild yeasts, rather than pitching specific strains.

'Plant de Blanc was the pear everyone had,' Jérôme admits, when I ask him why it was singled out. But he's quick to underline its remarkable quality. 'It's the queen!' adds Camille Guilleminot, co-founder of cider and perry subscription service, Calyce Cider. 'It brings all its roundness,

A bit of grass is always harvested too!

lightness and lively effervescence.'

The impact of the AOP has been hugely positive. Another 60,000 trees have been planted since 2002; perry has been taken more seriously and has started gaining wider recognition, with bottles of AOP Domfront appearing on the lists of Parisian restaurants. Regional tourism has increased, and quality has been tightly governed. By my reckoning, and that of many in the know, there isn't a higher average quality to be found anywhere in the world.

Detractors of AOP systems argue that over-regulation can stifle creativity and breadth. Certainly, within French wine, in tandem with the modern natural wine movement, there has been a pushback from many producers against what they see as the homogeneity of appellation-governed drinks. When I ask Jérôme about this, he acknowledges that the Plant de Blanc stipulation has led to other varieties being neglected in new plantings at that one pear's expense. But he makes it clear that the benefits have far outweighed any negatives.

'Producers can do what they like,' he tells me. 'I'm in favour of keeping the AOP the way it is. I am, however, keen to explore the possibilities of other varieties – they offer a whole spectrum of taste, colour and aroma. It would be boring just to keep on doing the same thing. I think that Poiré Domfront and other types of poiré can go hand in hand, providing values remain the same.'

There's an irony that Jérôme, instrumental in organising the AOP, is one of the keenest producers to explore perry beyond its boundaries. But he's far from the only one. Makers all around the Domfrontais are exploring the possibilities that the region's tapestry of pears affords. Not least Jacques Perritaz, a Swiss maker who found global recognition with his Cidrerie du Vulcain brand and bought a farm in the Domfrontais – La Prémoudière – specifically to gain access to its pears. With the skill of a 20-year practitioner, the irreverence of an outsider and an endless fund of curiosity, his early fermentations – championing delicious varieties besides Plant de Blanc – are bristling with promise and possibility.

What's more, the quality of Domfrontais perry and pears now reaches beyond the appellation. Producers elsewhere in Normandy are planting Domfrontais varieties or harvesting within the appellation itself. Makers who have previously used pears to bulk up spirit, or add

That graft mark towers above a person

acidity to their ciders, are re-evaluating the potential of perry in its own right and looking to AOP Domfront as their lodestar. Meanwhile, Domfrontais producers are continuing to raise standards and experiment with methods and varieties, even as they perfect the style that they do best, and which has earned them international renown.

Domfrontais poiré may still be niche. It may still pale in quantity beside Norman and Breton cider – not to mention French wine – but to my mind it is one of the country's great libatory treasures and one of the brightest stars in all of perry's firmament. It has been long in the reviving, via brandies and bootleggers and devastated orchards, but in AOP Domfront France has the perry champion this remarkable drinks-making nation deserves.

Calvados Domfrontais: perry in spirit

Deep, rich, sonorous nosefuls of orchard floor and dusky barrel cellar; honeys and caramels gliding across a rich, oily texture, all lifted and ener-gised by the unexpected perfume of fresh flowers, pear fruit, and a prickle of fire. That's Calvados Domfrontais to me; one of the rarest and most distinctive of all spirits; the meeting of pear and oak and flame and time.

Although pear spirit is no longer such colossal (or illegal) business in the Domfrontais, it nonetheless remains an indelible aspect of France's perry landscape. For a huge number of makers, Calvados Domfrontais accounts for at least half of production, if not more, and is responsible for far more of their income than perry.

The first mention of the cider brandy that would become known as Calvados comes in the 1500s, when a squire and forester named Gilles de Gouberville made a diary note of a spirit distilled from apples the same way as the grape brandies from further south. Following the division of France into départments after the French revolution, the newly formed Calvados, in the region of Normandy, gave the spirit the name it still holds today.

Despite being heavily taxed, and even prohibited in regions outside of Normandy, Brittany and Maine, predominantly to safeguard the interests of grape brandy, Calvados held on. And though it didn't retain the status of premier French brandy that it briefly held during phylloxera, it remains a spirit celebrated and drunk around the world – a position the cider and perry from which it is made has yet to emulate. Not to mention the time-honoured (and rapidly reviving) French tradition of 'café-calva' – a spot of Calvados in the morning coffee.

Slumbering in ca.

Distillation is also governed by appellations, and for Calvados there are three. The generic Calvados AOP, the smaller, highly rated Calvados Pays d'Auge AOP – both distilled almost entirely from apples – and, as of 1997, Calvados Domfrontais AOP.

Calvados Domfrontais is comparatively tiny; responsible for just 1% of all Calvados production. But it boasts perhaps the most distinctive character of all, thanks to the minimum 30% of Domfrontais perry pears, which, by law, must be included in every bottle. Most Domfrontais producers would like that percentage to be higher – and indeed most use from 60% to 100% pears – but industrial makers across Normandy lobbied powerfully for the lower number.

Those pears imbue Calvados Domfrontais not only with a unique freshness, but with tones of honey and golden syrup and tarte aux poires and dried flowers that no other Calvados style can emulate, all dancing atop classic Calvados notes of oak, dried fruit and spice.

That fragrance and elegance is further enhanced by the use of a column still, rather than the alembic pot-stills used for Calvados Pays d'Auge and, occasionally, Calvados AOP. Collected at a maximum of 72% ABV, to preserve spirit weight, there is nonetheless a higher-toned lightness and freshness to the base spirit of Calvados Domfrontais that perfectly suits the character of perry pears.

Calvados Domfrontais must then spend at least three years maturing in oak casks before it earns appellation status. During this time, it not only takes on flavours from both the wood itself and from whatever was housed in the barrel previously, but the porous casks allow micro-oxidation to slowly soften any harsher tones, while small amounts of spirit evaporate away – the so-called 'Angel's Share' – further developing flavours. Though the youngest Calvados Domfrontais may be three years old, most is far older, some ageing up to 50 years or more, evolving notes of dried fruits, spice and even gamey rancio tones, as well as developing in body and structure as the years drip by.

Like a reused teabag, the more frequently a cask is emptied and refilled, the less oak flavour it imparts. The common practice for Calvados Domfrontais is to use fairly old barrels so that flavours of the spirit are not overwhelmed by oak.

When it comes to bottling, makers will usually blend casks of different ages and vintages, with the youngest constituents of the blend dictating the legally permitted stated age. These can be bottled as 'Vieux' or 'Réserve', indicating a minimum of three years' ageing, VSOP, indicating four, XO or Hors d'Age, indicating a minimum of six, or specifically marked with age or vintage.

Father-son distilling team at Pacory

The spirit is usually diluted to a minimum strength of 40% ABV. *Some Calvados* As in the worlds of single malt whisky and bourbon, some producers are *ages for decades* exploring whether more character and body can be expressed by bottling with less dilution.

Where makers have bottled higher strength examples, the payoff in flavour and texture is extraordinary. But dilution means spirit can stretch further, as well as reducing the required duty. In any case, most drinkers are used to lower strength, meaning 40–43% is likely to remain the norm. To devotees, though, the opportunity to taste pure Calvados Domfrontais straight from cask is reason enough in itself to visit the Domfrontais.

The pommeau with no name

Meet a drink made in meaningful quantity nowhere else in the world. Mistelle is the natural middle point for grower-distillers, blending fresh, unfermented juice with fruit brandy to achieve a deep, rich, sweet yet beautifully balanced fortified drink around 17% ABV.

Pommeau, as apple juice-based mistelle is known in these parts, is a true regional speciality, protected by appellation law. But unlike cider, perry and Calvados, which have separate appellations governing different areas of Normandy, for pommeau a single AOP covers the whole region. To qualify, a drink must be made from roughly one part Calvados to two parts apple juice, meaning that even in the Domfrontais pommeau will be dominated by the flavours of apple.

Unsurprisingly, though, in this pear-obsessed region, it's common to find producers blending pear juice with Calvados Domfrontais, and since this drink isn't governed by appellation law, it doesn't have a specific name. You'll find it under various titles from producer to producer. There is also no legal limit on ageing, so some will deliberately make a younger, fresher style which suits the high-toned, perfumed notes of pear juice perfectly. Others, like Pacory, will age it nonetheless, developing unctuous, honeyed, near-mead-like and dried tropical fruit characteristics.

The use of perry pear juice gives this drink a refreshing zip of acidity and a more sinewy, gently tannic body than pommeau, which, to my taste, better balances sweetness and strength. Though it may not carry its own appellation, the Domfrontais 'pommeau but with pears' deserves every bit as much acclaim as its apple-based cousin.

Gorgeous fresh-oak casks

France is home to some of the world's greatest perries

SELECTED FRENCH PRODUCERS

The Domfrontais

La Cave Normande

My idea of a classic Domfrontais maker. From their ancient orchard, and trees replanted after a devastating 1999 storm, this family makes beautiful single variety AOP Domfront from Plant de Blanc as well as easier-drinking Poiré Fermiers and outstanding 'Cuvée Tradition' blends that show off other pears. The Calvados Domfrontais is very good indeed, aged at least 10 years and comprising a minimum 80% pear spirit to make the most of the appellation's perfumed individuality. And that feeds into their Fleur de Poire mistelle, one of the most honeyed and floral you'll find. Superb all round!

Domaine Didier Lemorton

Though they do make very good perry, what makes this producer unmissable from any self-respecting work on the Domfrontais is the exceptional quality of their Calvados. This fifth-generation producer makes some fruit-driven, lively, youthful Calvados Domfrontais made from 70% pears, whose blissfully floral perfume demands generous glasses on the first day of spring. But the real draw is their back catalogue of ancient, venerable bottlings, many vintage dated – some averaging 60 years or over. Benefitting from older barrels that don't over-oak the spirit, allowing the pears to age, ameliorate and still do the talking, these are rich, stately spirits that are a privilege to taste.

Jacques Perritaz – La Prémoudière Le Vulcain

If I had to nitpick I'd say the Domfrontais could benefit from some outside influences disrupting the status quo, and Swiss maker Jacques Perritaz is just that. Already world-renowned for his work at Le Cidrerie du Vulcain, the bounty of perry pears drew him to the Domfrontais. Like 'a kid in a candy shop' in his first vintage, 2022, he fermented as many pears as he could, from tangfastic Petit Blos to Fossey and melony, juicy Du Cloche. Not tied to tradition, Jacques plans to plant quinces and already co-ferments with redcurrants. A brilliant addition to the region's stellar cast.

Jérôme Forget – Le Ferme de l'Yonnière

Having learned – indeed been central in setting – the rules of AOP Domfront poiré, Jérôme Forget now determinedly breaks them. Not that his AOP isn't delicious – it's superlative. His 2016 is perhaps my all-time favourite. But his range is the most convincing of arguments for also making perries that live outside appellation law. Whether through lemon-and-lime-scented Vinot, rose-petal-haunted Fossey, or ultra-rare and notoriously difficult to harvest De Fer, you'll find flavours in Jérôme's range that you won't anywhere else. What's more, he's simply a legend of world perry. Le Ferme de l'Yonnière was top of my wishlist to visit when I first explored the Domfrontais. It'll top the list again when I next return.

Jérôme Forget of Le Ferme de l'Yonnière

*Frederick and
Simon of Pacory*

Pacory

Whenever I ask one of my French perry pals for a recommendation, Pacory
seems to top the list; with good reason. Third and fourth generation makers
Frederick and Simon cultivate one of the most satisfyingly complete and
high-quality ranges in the world. They're an advert for Plant de Blanc,
exploiting its versatility as a single variety in not only a fresh, thrilling,
early-harvest bottling but a juicy, ripe, late-harvest cuvée and disgorged
traditional method. Simon trained in Canada and brought back the idea of
an ice perry – Pacory's is as luscious and vivid as they get. Their Calvados
Domfrontais is superb, whether long-aged or young and fresh, and their
tropical fruited and frangipane-toned Grim' de Poire is my favourite pear
mistelle. Can you tell I rate them?

Rest of Normandy

Antoine Marois

Humble-to-a-fault Antoine is perhaps France's answer to Devon's Find &
Foster on several levels: in the meticulousness of his production; in his
care for making gorgeous, natural drinks from old, endangered trees; and
in not making much perry. But, like Polly and Mat, when he does make
some, it is out of this world. Appropriately named Ad Astra, it's a single
variety Plant de Blanc from Domfrontais fruit (though based further
north, Antoine believes there's no matching the Domfrontais when it
comes to pears). Outrageously aromatic and a little drier than the
Domfrontais norm, this is one of France's elite perries.

Maison Sassy

French cider and perry is gradually beginning to shed its sometimes-old-fashioned image, thanks in no small part to producers like Maison Sassy. Their eye-catching branding resolutely appeals to younger audiences while celebrating Norman cider, Calvados and perry. A good eye for marketing isn't at the expense of quality though; their multi award-winning poiré, made from 12 varieties of pear, mainly Blanc, Antricotin, Vinot and Belle-Verge, is a mouth-filling juice-bomb, low on alcohol but high on flavour, and bursting with pear fruit. A superb gateway to the world of Norman perry.

Templar's Choice

Having spread his decades-long experience across two of the drink's modern heartlands – Gloucestershire in England, then Normandy in France – you'd expect Adam Bland to know his way around a fermented pear, and he certainly does. Formerly known as Bland's, before deciding 'Bland' wasn't the best association for good cider and perry, Adam's orchards sit right on the border of Camembert, and his super-aromatic, unusually vibrant (by Normandy standards), zingy, green-fruited perry is the perfect foil for that world-famous creamy cheese. This being Calvados country, he's also a distiller, and his 100% perry pear brandy is a deep and soulful delight.

Les Vergers de la Morinière

A standout when I visited the marvellous CidrExpo – a cider and perry exhibition held in Caen that was probably the best of its kind I've ever attended. Headed by fifth-generation perrymaker Astrid Hubert, Les Vergers de la Morinière make a supremely elegant traditional method poiré, as well as two more that take the marvellously innovative step of using mandarin or cherry syrup for the dosage post-disgorgement. The results are beautifully refined perries offset by the light, complimentary influences of other fruits. Look out also for their luscious pear mistelle.

Maine

Eric Bordelet

If my life depended on picking a perry that a randomly chosen drinker would love, it would be Eric Bordelet's Poiré Granit. Eric is a former sommelier who must be one of the most meticulous makers of any drink when it comes to understanding his terroir and nurturing fruit and production. A champion of the importance of place – Granit is named for the soils the pear trees grow on in his Maine orchards – he uses a blend of varieties from trees that are around 300 years old. His 'standard' poiré (there's nothing standard about it) is world class, but Granit is world leading: a masterpiece of precision, balance and intensity that ages astonishingly.

The Loire

Les Capriades

When I first got into perry I was frequently struck by how some of them reminded me distinctly of many white wines of the Loire. It felt appropriate, therefore, to discover that there were indeed first-rate perries made by Loire producers, often with varieties specific to the area. Pascal Potaire and Moses Gadouche at Les Capriades are a wonderful example, bottling pét nat perry made from local varieties Carési, Crassot Rouge and, particularly, Poire de Loup. Drier than their Norman counterparts, with a splendid freshness and acidity beside rounded mouthfeel, this is a special perry, proudly of its place.

Côme Isambert

The first time I travelled to Normandy, Camille Guilleminot, my mentor in French cider and perry, gave me a bottle that wasn't from the region, but from a maker called Côme Isambert in the Loire. That perry remains an all-time reference point. Having trained at a world-renowned biodynamic winery, Côme, with partner Gretchen, makes low-intervention natural drinks from pears, grapes and other fruits in a cave (literally) in Saumur. Naturally curious, he makes perry from Normandy fruit, but also plays with pear-grape co-fermentations and collaborates with other innovative makers.

Julien Thurel

Julien is another in France's impressive cast of orchardists and makers who marry a natural, organic, minimal-intervention approach focused on fruit and terroir with scrupulous care and attention to best practice in fermentation. The result: pristine pét nat perries of stunning energy and ethereal aromatics. Generally high-toned, fresh, and, like other Loire producers, drier than the Normandy average, Julien bottles single varieties from lesser-spotted pears like the juicy, crunchy Poire d'Angouisse, as well as complex cuvées. All are naturally-sparkling, aged on lees, and crystalline in their precision and purity of flavour.

AUSTRIA

*'She poured for me with the jug, that my throat would again
be bright and cheerful. I drank her perry very heartily:
she was happy about that.'*
(Neidhart von Reuenthal, 1240)

About an hour's train ride west of Vienna, amidst the pastoral green foothills of the Alps, is perhaps the best-kept secret in the world of cider and
perry. Bewilderingly little-known outside its own country, yet so steeped in
perry culture that it owes its very name to the drink, this is the only region
on earth in which perry has primacy over cider. Welcome to the Mostviertel.

The Mostviertel is so unassuming a place that on my first visit,
spending a night at a bar in the central town of Amstetten, I was asked
on three separate occasions what I was doing there. When I mentioned
I'd come for perry – *most*, or *birnenmost*, as it's known in these parts – they
all seemed bewildered.

The rolling hills of the Mostviertel make for some of perry's most scenic countryside

Perhaps that's understandable. After all, I wasn't drinking perry at the time – there was none to be had at the bar. The main drinks were weißbier and lager, supported by a handful of spirits. I'd asked for perry at a few different bars, but by this point I'd given up. Beer it was.

Yet pears are everywhere here; virtually religious icons wherever you look. Pears sewn into lace curtains, carved pear door handles, bars of pear-scented soap in the shape of pears. We pass a roundabout with colossal pear statues the size of small elephants. On my hotel's gatepost there's another huge carved pear.

It doesn't take more than a couple of minutes' drive into the countryside to see where the reverence comes from. If the perry pear tree has a true modern heartland, it's here. Centuries-old goliaths, gnarled, knotted and heavy-boughed, tearing at the sky and straddling the landscape wherever you look. Unlike the Domfrontais, where they tend to be found in little clusters, the trees here grow most prominently in single straight lines along the boundaries of fields; an ancient way of delineating individual farms.

This is the Moststraße, the longest unbroken stretch of pear trees in Europe; a 200-km long 'Perry Road' slaloming through the fertile, clay-rich swathe of meadowland south of the Danube, linking farms and producers, and erupting into an unparalleled display of floral fireworks in April as blossom bursts and tourists come from across Austria to drink in the view and the freshly fermented perry.

Orchards back onto mountains

Estimates of how many trees there are range between 150,000 and 300,000, which makes the Mostviertel home to the greatest concentration of perry pears in the world. What's truly staggering, however, is that these represent only a fraction of how many there once were.

Pears and perry have ancient roots in the Mostviertel. The Romans were here, and certainly made wine, raising the tantalising (if unprovable) possibility that 'pear wine' might also have featured. Unquestionably, by the 13th century, we find the first written evidence that perry was not only being made as a small side concern, but, as it was in neighbouring Bavaria, was a central part of rural drinking culture.

Neidhart von Reuenthal, a Bavarian minstrel at the Austrian court, composed songs referencing perry as a key character as early as 1240. In the 16th century Philipp Jakob Grünthaler installed a 'paumgarten' in his castle at Zeillern, near Amstetten, for the cultivation of specific fruits, collecting scions of specific pears – including varieties such as the Landlbirne that are still in use today – and grafting them in the Mostviertel region for the first time.

The 'modern' history of the Mostviertel's perry tradition begins in the 18th century, when the Habsburg Empress Maria Theresa ordered a package of agricultural reforms, including the planting of pear trees along all municipal roads in Mostviertel. This was supported by her son, Joseph II, who not only continued the programme but awarded a silver medal to anyone who planted over 100 trees.

Austrian pear orchards making a comeback

Although most most – this gets complicated in English! – was consumed in huge volumes locally, the economic boom really arrived for perrymakers midway through the 19th century. The emancipation of the peasantry in 1848, allowing farmers greater land ownership rights, coincided with the construction of a railway line that joined the Mostviertel to Vienna, capital city of the Austro-Hungarian Empire. For the first time, perry could quickly reach major cities across the empire, and makers capitalised, producing more than ever before, and planting trees accordingly. Today, it's common to find trees of around 150 years old that were planted during this most boom.

This period was so lucrative that farmers built grand houses for themselves with the proceeds. These farmhouses still stud the landscape; huge, square, red-roofed affairs with open courtyards at their centre. Their distinctive shape gave them the name 'Vierkanters' – 'four corners' – and is commemorated in the iconic square-cornered base of most bottles of most today. Attend any tour in the area and you'll hear the phrase 'the Vierkanters were built by the Most'. By 1938 the collective orchard in the Amstetten district alone reached over a million pear trees – rivalling the Domfrontais, but without the need for illegal distillation.

Fall from grace, and stopped rot

Following the collapse of the Austro-Hungarian Empire and the increase in mechanised agriculture, most fell away dramatically. Pear trees were removed, fields were planted over with corn, and most became a far smaller concern, mainly made by farmers for personal consumption; a few barrels kept in the farmhouse; tired, unfashionable and of the past, as beer, wine and soft drinks claimed almost all of most's historic customers.

No longer a great commercial concern or source of income, quality fell as sharply as scale of production. Left to sit and slowly empty, barrels would oxidise and their perries would gradually turn more and more vinegary with acetic acid – a trait that became almost synonymous with most in the national psyche, if it was remembered at all. Outside of Austria, the perry of the Mostviertel might as well not have existed.

At the start of the 1990s, devastated by destruction of pear trees and dismayed at the reputational damage that had been done, a group of makers began pooling knowledge and experience with a view to stopping the rot.

Their model was clear. Austria is home to some of the world's most delicious white wines, in particular Rieslings and Grüner Veltliners

*The classic
Mostbaron outfit*

packed with bright citrus, stone fruit, florals and slatey minerality. Taste one next to a modern Mostviertel Birnenmost and the influence is unmistakable. Just as it's fair to make certain generalisations about French poiré, so Austrian perries often share a particular profile. Far paler than most British and French counterparts, it's also far more common to find bottled still perry here than anywhere else. And although there is, of course, a natural inflection of pear, with touches of melon and honey entirely their own, many Mostviertel Birnenmosts show the same green citrus, white flower and wet slate as the local wines, with a comparable seam of racy acidity. Always low in tannin, often dry, they are some of the most refreshing, food-friendly perries in the world.

In the drive to learn from wine and increase standards of production, cleanliness in the cellar was paramount. Anaerobic fermentations in temperature-controlled, stainless-steel vessels became the norm; pitched wine yeasts were favoured for a more reliable and even ferment, while maceration and filtration were practised to combat perry's tendency to throw sediment.

Some producers in other countries and regions see some of these practices as a little heavy-handed, suggesting that a little intensity and individuality of character is lost along the way. And today it is increasingly common to find producers starting to reduce levels of intervention. But in taking this scrupulous approach, the producers of the Mostviertel effectively eliminated faults such as acetic acid, ethyl acetate and mouse from all commercially bottled perry, to a degree beyond any other country, thus establishing arguably the world's highest minimum level of quality in the process.

Fermentation in the cool of a cellar

Mostbarons and the broad gastronomic picture

With quality improving, and with trees once again being planted, producers had built a platform from which most could once again kick on. Yet it still lagged far behind wine and beer in even the most local consciousness.

In 2003, seeking to raise its profile, two makers – Toni Distelberger and Sepp Zeiner – came up with the idea for an organisation: a co-operative of champions specifically intended to preserve traditions, improve quality and provide a hivemind for tackling marketing, distribution and exchange of knowledge. 'Mostkaiser' (Perry Emperor) and 'Mostkönig' (Perry King) were considered before they settled on something that Toni and Sepp felt linked sovereign quality to a more rural and down-to-earth atmosphere: Mostbarons.

Eyebrows were raised when they pitched the idea, but with the backing of a significant local politician, as well as several of their peers, the Mostbarons were officially formed, with a starting intake of 12 members.

With their crimson waistcoats or dirndls and black hats decorated with the white down from juvenile golden eagles, the Mostbarons are an iconic bunch. Now numbering 15, with a new elected 'Primus' every year (who sports a special chain and an elegant, sword-shaped glass pipette with a pear in its handle) they have been the driving force for most culture since their inception. Many of the region's best makers are numbered in their ranks, and their spirit of cooperation is embodied by the trio of 'gourmet mosts' – Brous, Preh and Exibatur – which they collaboratively produce from their best pears and perries every vintage.

Leo Reikersdorfer with the Mostbaron Primus chain and pipette

Yet, although many Mostbarons are makers, a vital aspect of the organisation is that they are also drawn from other sectors of the industry. There are sommeliers, restaurateurs and retailers – people who might not make perry themselves, but who understand how to talk about it and whose expertise links perry indelibly to a broader gastronomic culture.

That link is more tangible here than in any other perry culture on earth. Throughout the region perry can be bought by the jug or bottle at rural restaurants and inns, almost always with the option to 'spritz' it with sparkling water, as is the traditional serve.

It's when you marry Austrian perry with the local food that it rises to the apex of its potential. That bright zing of citrusy acidity, along with an almost wine-like body and a vibrancy of pure, clear, green-fruit flavour is tailor-made for hissing through the fat of local hams and cheeses, or skewering richer, heartier fare like schnitzel or goulash.

Producers, too, tap into this interwoven fabric of gastronomy, often via the Austrian tradition of the heuriger: a sort of 'pop-up tavern' system first installed by Joseph II in 1784, allowing wine and perrymakers to open for a few weeks a year to sell their own wine and juices on the premises. Though food was not initially permitted, it soon became part of the system, and today you'll find several Mostbarons running their own heuriger, exclusively selling produce grown and made on their own farms.

Perry pears are far more than merely a means to a drink here. Besides the broad use to which its dried fruit is also put, 'perry pear soup' is a delicious, spicy, savoury starter on local menus, usually accompanied by perry pear dumplings.

The tradition of the heuriger is what brings many local families to perry in these parts. My interpreter, Nicolina, a Mostviertel native, tells me it was only at the heuriger that she would ever drink perry. Like most from a younger Austrian generation, Nicolina tends towards beers and wines. Perry is still mainly seen as slightly quirky and dated; a rural drink for grandparents.

Perry by the jug = happy author

The modernisers

Critical to the work of the Mostbarons, then, is a reimagining of perry's image. Once again, wine is the primary guiding light. Increasingly, 750ml bottles in classic wine shapes, rather than the chunky, square-cornered, 1l bottles, are presented by the best, most forward-looking producers. Makers are taking pains to move beyond merely basic descriptors like 'sweet', 'semi-sweet' and 'sparkling' on their labels; varieties are almost always namechecked.

Particular pears are championed; varieties like aromatic Speckbirne and Stieglbirne, fruity, rounded Rote Pichlbirne, zesty Dorschbirne and – perhaps grandest of all – full-bodied, thrilling, structured Grüne Pichelbirne. Peter and Bernadette Haselberger even bottle a 'single tree' perry from this variety, picked from a tree over 160 years old. Late-ripening Grüne Pichelbirne has the particularly handy ability of clearing up perry that has gone cloudy, so there was a long tradition of making sure one was planted near the farmhouse. Today, it is as celebrated for its flavour and character as it is for its practical utility.

Though much Austrian perry cleaves to a particular stylistic framework, beneath this surface, just as in the Domfrontais scene, innovation bubbles in every direction you look. Toni Distelberger and the Haselbergers are just two producers to have bottled traditional method perry, while ice perry can be found from Toni and from Sepp Zeiner, and Distillerie Farthofer's mostellos are the only examples I've yet found of true fortified perry.

Makers are experimenting with oak barriques, and while there is a general trend towards a drier, more sophisticated style, there are also an increasing number of full-juice, flavoured perries aimed at an adventurous younger market. (Lilo, from Pirinum, features elderflowers, hops and butterfly pea flowers, giving it a vivid, naturally purple hue, and an unforgettable firework of flavour.) Labels are becoming smarter and more eye-catching, and some of the fustiness of yesteryear is being given an instagram-friendly lick of paint, without losing sight of the traditions that brought birnenmost to its modern point.

Traditional Mostviertel 'vierkanter' farmhouse

The drive for better-tasting, better-presented products has been spurred by the introduction of a 'mostsommelier' course, providing training not only in history, culture and making, but in the serving of most, its pairing with food, and the education of consumers in its complexities and characters. Every year, producers compete for the 'Golden Pear', awarded to the best perry of all, as well as the Most Trophy, presented as part of prestigious wine magazine *Falstaff*'s annual competition – an opportunity for most producers to serve their perries alongside Austria's best winemakers.

As Austrian perry regains its old standing and quality, eyes are once again on the capital city. 'The market isn't in the Mostviertel,' Bernadette Haselberger tells me. 'We sell to gourmet restaurants in Vienna – that's the group we're targeting.'

Centurion survivors, still bearing fruit

'We have achieved a lot here,' Toni Distelberger adds, 'but there is still a lot to do. We have succeeded in making the Mostbirne and its products the focus of tourism and many people in the Mostviertel are proud of this special treasure.'

The aims are ambitious, but Mostviertel perry deserves, and requires, ambition. This ancient, fiercely regional perry, inextricably linked with gastronomy, deserves a place on the list of any restaurant in the world. Perry's best-kept secret isn't likely to stay under the radar much longer.

SELECTED AUSTRIAN PRODUCERS

Distelberger

Every region needs its torch-bearer – someone who understands the potential of the place and its perry and strives to lift both up. England has Tom Oliver, France Jérôme Forget, and Austria has Toni Distelberger. Not only noted for the innovation and quality of his products – delicate traditional method perry, single varieties and blends across a range of sweetnesses, the best ice perry I can remember, and even a selection of spiced and flavoured perries – Toni simply wants the Mostviertel to succeed. Instrumental in founding the Mostbarons, and in reshaping perceptions of birnenmost, Toni has to be one of the world's most significant perry champions.

Distillerie Farthofer

To my mind, the crowning glories of the Mostviertel might just be the mostellos made by Joseph and Doris Farthofer. Unlike mistelles – blends of juice and spirit – these are true fortified perries; drinks to which spirit is added during fermentation, like Port, for a sweeter style, or after fermentation has completed, like sherry, for dry. Almost all are aged in oak for at least four years – though they also make a young, fruit-driven, unoaked expression – then in bottle for many years afterwards. Some of the finest, longest-lived drinks I'm lucky enough to have tried; deep, tawny evocations of dried fruit and spice, a crackling red-gold glow of autumn hearthfire in perry form.

Haselberger

Peter and Bernadette Haselberger are two makers who understand most's potential as an elegant, fine-dining rival to white wine. Focused on still, dry, thrilling single varieties, coursing with fresh fruit and often marked by a seam of cleansing acidity, their attention to hygiene is impeccable, and increasingly they are pushing the Mostviertel envelope on reduced intervention. Some of my favourites have been their grapefruit-scented Landlbirne, a flinty, toasty, traditional method blend, and, best of all, their mineral, green-fruited Grüne Pichelbirne from a single 161-year-old tree. These are long-lived, grown-up perries, comfortably at home on the table of any serious restaurant.

The Haselberger family

Mostbarons

I can't tell you how much I love this initiative; perhaps the ultimate collaboration in the world of perry. Comprising some of the best fruits from across the collective orchards of the Mostbarons, this range has its sights set on two distinct categories of drinker and occasions of drinking. 'Cider: Birne', their basic, low-alcohol 330ml bottling, is one of the happiest, juiciest – literally, it tastes like pure, fresh pear juice – and most downright crushable perries in the world, while their 'gourmetmosts' – in ascending order of weight and stateliness, Brous (Speckbirne and Stieglbirne), Preh (the same, plus Dorschbirne and Grüne Pichelbirne) and Exibatur (Dorschbirne and Grüne Pichelbirne) – fly a proud and prominent flag for birnenmost's potential elegance, ageability, seriousness, and, above all, place on the dining table.

Most'gwölb (Zeiner)

Sepp Zeiner is one of the elder statesmen of the Mostviertel's modern resurgence. Like Toni Distelberger, he crafts a range of 'modern classic' mosts, often off-dry single varieties or blends of early or late-harvest pears, just the thing for spritzing over a long, traditional Mostviertel lunch. And, like Toni, he enjoys pushing boundaries. His Fortissimo is an extra-dry, barrel-aged blockbuster that confounds the generalisation of perry as a delicate, wispy drink, while his Eis Birne (ice perry) sits on the fragrant, ethereal and nectar-tinted end of dessert perries – challenging conventions again.

Pirinum

Perry should be fun as much as anything else, otherwise what's the point? And Lilo, from Pirinum, is certainly that. It's bright purple, for goodness' sake. But this is no artificial colouring – it's the remarkable hue of the butterfly pea flower with which this perry is flavoured. (Its local, colloquial name is rather ruder and less printable.) Along with elderflowers and hops, it gives this perry an irresistible, floral, citrusy, perfumed brightness that complements its juicy fruitiness to perfection. I think of it as the Beaujolais of the perry world for its pure joie de vivre. It's no flimsy gimmick – a gold medal at Frankfurt's competitive CiderWorld underscores its quality. A drink that simply puts a smile on my face – for all sorts of reasons.

Reikersdorfer

An excellent example of the gastronomic ecosystem of the heuriger is
Mostheuriger Reikersdorfer, run by Leopold and Michaela. Like most
in these parts, they run a mixed farm, with a small herd of cattle and
orchards boasting plums and apples as well as pears. Leopold – a former
car salesman and professional footballer – crafts not only a beautiful
range of perries but a bewildering array of perry vinegars; from aged,
treacley balsamic to light, fragrant, garden herb-flavoured dressings.
Meanwhile, Michaela is responsible for huge quantities of dried fruit, a
staple of the Mostvierteler diet, for snacking on its own as well as baking
into a range of dishes, cakes and even chocolate bars.

Seppelbauer

The Datzberger family make their most just outside the town of
Amstetten, in the heart of the Mostviertel. And their range is classic
Mostviertel from top to bottom – dry and semi-dry still blends and single
varieties in the classic four-cornered litre bottles, a selection of sparkling
frizzantes, and a bewildering array of distilled eaux-de-vie. To my taste,
Seppelbauer perries embrace an acidic, food-friendly direction – even by
Mostviertel standards – with their Speckbirne expressing green, citrusy
tones. Very much rooted within their community, in addition to the
classic Mostbaron trio of Brous, Preh and Exibatur they've collaborated
with two other Mostbarons, Hans Hiebl and Michael Oberaigner-Binder,
on an additional 'gourmetmost', M3, as well as crafting a special cuvée in
collaboration with the people of Amstetten itself.

REST OF CENTRAL EUROPE

> '*The people of the West of Rhineland have another drink that some could almost not live without: it is the Beerewein (local dialect for perry). You only have to go to the right source and taste it, and you will be amazed at what Bacchus has given the people of the Hinterpfalz.*'
>
> (Ludwig Rösinger, 1926)

When I think of Central European perry – the perries of Germany, Switzerland, Luxembourg – I have come to think of a decommissioned harbour. The people and machinery have departed, the hubbub replaced with the eerie shrieking of gulls and the hollow slapping of waves. But the boats, though fewer in number, unused, skeletal and seemingly lifeless, are still there; not quite dead, not quite dormant, but waiting.

And then I think of an Irishman walking his dog.

A Schefflenz tree

Germany

It is almost absurdly improbable to imagine a world in which the dominant drink of Bavaria was not beer, but perry – yet once upon a time that was the case. Heinrich L. Werneck writes in 1963 that at the end of the 13th century most – perry, as in Austria – was 'the popular drink with Bavarians'. Indeed, an Austrian minstrel of the time wrote a song remarking on the quantity of perry drunk across the border.

Nor was this an isolated perry pocket. The *Kaiserslauterer Reichsspruch* of 1357 not only records the growing of pears and making of perry in the Western Palatinate, near the border with Alsace, but provides us with the earliest named perry pear variety I've yet encountered (besides Pliny's Falernian Pear) in the magnificently evocative Wolffes Birnbaum – Wolf's Pear Tree. Wolves seem to have been aligned with perry pears all the way through subsequent history. To this day there is a Wolfsbirne in Germany, as well as a Poire de Loup in France.

The Western Palatinate continued to be steeped in perry for the next 600 years, as reported by Dieter Zenglein in the *Westricher Heimatsblätter* journal, to whom I am indebted for much of this chapter's content. If the Domfrontais and May Hill emerged as prime pear country because the terroir didn't suit apples, this corner of Germany became perry-land at the point where grapes started struggling. The Rhine runs north along the Palatinate's eastern flank, then takes a sharp turn westwards along its northern border. Some of Germany's great wine producers are clustered

Remnants of an ancient landscape

along its banks – Nahe and Reinhessen to the north, Pfalz to the east. Head south into France and the great whites of Alsace cling to the slopes of the Vosges mountains. If vines could be grown, they were. But further from the river, where the land became rougher and heavier, the aspect less suited to Riesling, pear trees reigned.

Commenting on the improved agricultural practice of selecting the best fruits and grafting them, the 17th-century theologian and writer Johann Friedrich Mayer remarked, 'the perry pear, which is gradually becoming so famous, and whose goodness recommends it to everyone, is excellently suited for this purpose [...] the pears are very good for most, and quite without equal; for two or three years the perry is of excellent quality, equal to wine.'

Towards the end of the 18th century, writers were not only advocating perry itself but were suggesting that particular varieties of pear could be added to cider to improve it – the same suggestions made by John Beale in 17th-century England.

Even in Trier, on the western border, where perry was allegedly viewed as inferior, authorities had to take meaningful steps to protect the precious wine industry. So much perry was made that in 1594 a statute book decreed that there should always be at least two supervisors at the wine commission to make sure wine hadn't been 'adulterated with perry'. But even in unadulterated form, wine wasn't safe. So much perry was being drunk at its expense that, in order to safeguard vintners, the city of Trier rationed how much perry could be brought into the city, and taxed imports. There was so much of a backlash, however, that within two years a new decree had been passed, permitting 320l a year per person, tax free, 'for personal consumption'.

As recently as the early 20th century, perry was still a major drink across large areas of southern Germany. Ludwig Rösinger remarked on its primacy in the Western Rhineland, on the particular varieties of pear used, on its closeness to wine in flavours and quality, and on the ancient trees harvested in its making. One, the Frankelbacher tree, was reputed to be over 350 years old and so vast that 'two men can stand in the centre of it, and three men can barely grasp the massive giant'. Tragically, just ten years later, the landowner had the Frankelbacher hacked down for firewood, though its grafted descendants can still be found.

Within living memory, the south of Germany was comparable to the Domfrontais or the Mostviertel in the proliferation of pear trees and perrymaking. It was commonplace in certain regions for farms to have

lines of their own trees, and perrymaking was a community activity, with men, women and children all partaking (though blending and tasting would often be ring-fenced by a patriarch grandfather). Perry was not only drunk in these rural communities but would be carted into large towns like Kaiserslautern and sold at market directly from the cask. As elsewhere, however, mechanised agriculture and a general move towards urban living sounded a death knell for German perry. And unlike the Domfrontais, the Three Counties and the Mostviertel, no unified group emerged to prevent the culture diminishing almost entirely.

Switzerland

Of all the heart-aching falls from grace that perry has endured around the world, Switzerland's might be the saddest.

In the mid-1600s, when perry was being discussed in serious, reverential terms by British intellectuals for the first time, leading advocates were united in their belief that one pear stood above all others: Switzerland's so-called Turgovian pear, described by Worlidge as yielding 'the most superlative perry the world produces'.

John Pell wrote that it could be either simply fermented, or boiled 'so that it becomes almost as thick & as sweet as honey'. Writing to Samuel Hartlib, Pell added: 'Not long since, one sent me a bottle of liquor whose colour, smell & taste enticed me to pronounce it to be as good a muscatel as ever I had tasted. But he that sent it told me it was nothing but Turgo [Turgovian] wine ten years old. That is to say it was the juice of the small, ill-tasted pears of Turgo.'

The Turgovian pear so interested English perry pioneers that it was mentioned in John Evelyn's *Pomona*. Maddeningly, 'Turgovian pear' was as specific as any of the contemporary writers chose to be, inspiring Barry Masterson to undertake a personal quest 350 years later to uncover its true identity – finding it to almost certainly be the Bergbirne, about which Vadian had written so glowingly in 1529.

One of the challenges Barry faced was the sheer number of varieties of Turgovian origin. Thurgauer Mostbirne, for instance, was a synonym for the Sülibirne, a pear with which he was already familiar. 'Thurgauerbirne' (simply 'Turgovian pear') and 'Thurgauer Weinbirne' (Turgovian wine pear) were two more distinct varieties that proved to be red herrings. Schweizer Wasserbirne, later to catch the eye of Babycham's Francis Showering, was another that grew in Austrian and German orchards. So prolific were Swiss pears that gastronomy magazine *Das Pauli* describes 850 different varieties, and although no DNA records point to trees still existing in the UK, contemporary letters show that the mighty Bergbirne was certainly grafted in English orchards in 1666.

Just as in Germany, Austria, Normandy, and the Anglo-Welsh border-lands, perry was a central part of rural Swiss culture for hundreds of years. In 1863 Gustav Pfau-Schellenberg was still singing the praises of the Bergbirne's 'excellent flavour'. At around the same time, in 1855, German pomologist Eduard Lucas toured Thurgau and noted: 'It would be difficult to find another region in the north or south that surpasses the Thurgau in terms of magnificent and well-maintained fruit plantations. These rows of trees [...] which we encounter everywhere in numerous specimens, certainly amaze every connoisseur and friend of fruit culture who visits this region for the first time [...] the predominantly planted varieties are mostly used only for making Most [perry].'

Lucas's visit was predominantly to attend an exhibition of fruit, especially pears, during which he describes the varieties as too numerous to list in their entirety, simply name-checking the 11 most common; 'Bergler' (another synonym for Bergbirne) among them. His telling comment, 'I do not need to assure you of the great value of this exhibition and the beneficial effects it had on the improvement and perfection of fruit growing,' under-scores that perry was not only ubiquitous across the region, and country,

Swiss landscape before...

but supported at a federal agricultural level. As recently as the mid-20th century, Switzerland could claim the densest fruit tree population per sq km of any country in the world.

Yet when Swiss perry finally came crashing down, in sudden and violent fashion, it was the actions of government that were the major reason. In his brilliant book *Baummord* ('Tree Murder'), Franco Ruault describes how a scarcely believable 11 million fruit trees were wiped out in the space of just 25 years between 1950 and 1975.

Why? For 50 years prior to the 1930s, by a quirk of law, potato spirits had been taxed while fruit spirits had not. In a country which, at this point, was drinking a third as much again per person as France and four times as much as their counterparts in Germany, alcohol abuse became rife. Distillers of fruit spirits made hay. Understandably, the government corrected the original law and began taxing fruit spirits as well. But, committed to buying surplus fruit and spirits from the farmers at established minimum prices, found itself losing up to 15 million Swiss Francs a year.

What's more, though Swiss table fruit had been renowned across Central Europe, its big export markets of Germany and Austria, impoverished by the Second World War, stopped doing business and the Swiss home market was saturated. Still paying the farmers their guaranteed minimum prices, the government began describing fruit trees as 'parasites' and 'loss carriers'.

Three state officials offered a 'solution': Hans Spreng, the 'Obstbau-Papst' (fruit growing pope); Gustav Schmidt, 'Obstbau-Stratege' (strategist); and Ernst Lüthi, Obstbau-General. Spreng hated traditionally grown and pruned old trees. He wanted absolute order and yield over all other considerations and developed a new pruning system – the Oeschbergschnitt (Oeschberg cut) – to achieve this. Irrespective of variety and tree, this cut limited the trees to only four main branches and was utterly against nature. Not only did the Federal Alcohol Administration adopt his ideas in law, but as the head of the Swiss Fruit Growing Centre, Spreng could roll out his new system nationwide.

Schmidt, the strategist, was the radical who planned the destruction of the tall trees and the savage repruning of remnants, while Lüthi, the general, enforced the campaign, using alleged blackmail, threats and even violence towards farmers. Even his successor described

Dynamited tree

him as 'dictatorial,' while one of Lüthi's own sons admitted 'it was like a rape of the farmers, he put the knife on them'.

Gangs of fellers, often fuelled by vast quantities of spirit ('without a big schnapps we didn't look at a chainsaw,' Ruault records one saying), went in with chainsaws, petrol and even plastic explosives. Farmers were paid around 20 Francs a tree (less than the fellers got) and often given no choice. There were violent clashes between farmers and fellers – one feller interviewed by Ruault describes it as having been 'like a battlefield' – and farmers' sons were often turned against their parents, sometimes with tragic consequences. In the first winter, 400,000 trees came down. In the European Year of Conservation (1970) the Federal Alcohol Administration demanded the destruction of 500,000 more pear trees over the next five years.

The upshot was visually horrific. A landscape once defined by agroforestry turned into tillage desert. A rural way of life blown up, hacked down and burned away. In 1951, 16.6 million fruit trees were recorded in Switzerland. By 1980 it was 5 million. A country in which perrymakers numbered

*Swiss landscape
after...*

thousands today features barely any, and perhaps the most famous –
Jacques Perritaz of Cidrerie du Vulcain – finds pears so hard to come by
that he has begun making perry in France's Domfrontais region instead.

The Modern Picture

Modern German or Swiss perry, or the still-smaller scene in Luxembourg,
is no more than a tiny fraction of what it once was. Those cultures, recent
enough to be touched by living memory, are gone. But handfuls of perry
pear trees still cling on, and there are those in each country who trumpet
'perry' loudly. In fact, I might as well admit I would likely have had almost
nothing to write in this section on the historic perries of Central Europe
had it not been for the next-level perry obsession of Barry Masterson.

An Irish immigrant renovating an old farmhouse in southern Germany's
Schefflenz, Barry had been a homebrewer and key figure in the early days
of Ireland's craft beer movement. The farmhouse came with a small apple
orchard attached, but it was when he adopted a Border Collie, Anu, and set
out on daily dog walks, that he truly came to appreciate the historic
importance of the perry pear in his region.

Everywhere he went he saw remnants of a lost landscape of pear trees; along fields, in hedges, tucked into woods – even behind the local archery club. He had already started making cider, and some of the older residents in the village would wander over and ask if he tipped a few pears into the press, as they had once done.

It sent Barry down a rabbit hole of research, ultimately making him and his brand, Kertelreiter, a leading exponent of Central European perry, as well as an expert in the history and culture of the drink (and to whom this book owes so much). If anyone in the world is going to carry you along on a wave of perry enthusiasm, it'll be Barry. His morning walk photos are enough to restore your faith in the artist formerly known as Twitter.

Trees behind the German perry revival

But Barry is only one of a growing band of exceptional Central European perrymakers determined to protect an ancient heritage and a vital, irreplaceable environmental resource, and to make world-class perries that rival anything from the big three remaining cultures. There's 1785 Cider in the Black Forest, run by Patrick Mann and Wendy LeBlanc, who brought expertise learned in America's Seattle to Patrick's old homestead and the perry pears of Germany. There's Jörg Geiger, whose traditional method perries – blends, single varieties and especially his favourite pear, the Champagner Bratbirne – are considered standouts by no less a maker than Herefordshire's Tom Oliver.

In the north of Germany, Florian Profitlich makes delicious, wine-like perries in a region where there is little history, charting a path all of his own.

And across the border, Ramborn is reviving an ancient Luxembourgish tradition, working with over 100 farmers and picking pears from trees up to 300 years old.

With producers so few and far between, each with their own ethos, fruits and favoured styles, defining the flavours of Central Europe is as hopeless a task as summarising English and Welsh perry in a sentence. But although the weight of culture may have slipped away across the last century, the passion, skill and determination of those who keep the perry fire kindled may well be what ultimately saves it in this region. If the makers of Germany, Switzerland and Luxembourg can come together as those of Austria and France have, this once-central tenet of rural Central European life may not be confined to history after all.

Still standing, for now

SELECTED CENTRAL EUROPEAN PRODUCERS

Germany

1785

Patrick Mann and Wendy LeBlanc met in Wendy's native Seattle, Patrick having moved over from the Black Forest, where as a boy he'd helped his father press fruit for most. The pair became part of a small group of dedicated cidermaking amateurs who'd meet together to swap samples, develop palates and offer tips. The timing was perfect: craft cider had begun to boom in Washington State, just as craft beer had before it, and when they moved to the Black Forest, they brought with them a wealth of experience and new-found know-how. Their perries are always meticulously crafted, always faultless and always absolute in their expression of the pear, or pears. A maker whose wares I constantly wish I could access more easily.

Andreas Schneider

Based just outside of Frankfurt, in the heart of German cider production, Andreas Schneider is 'Mr Apfelwein', arguably the most famous and respected German cidermaker of all. Hand-picking all his fruit, he makes a bewildering number of expressions every year, revelling in the natural inconsistency of harvest-based fruit drinks. Unusually for this part of Germany, though, his head is also turned by the pear, bottling supremely elegant examples from organic, unsprayed orchards, mainly made from the Karcherbirne variety. Given Andreas' love of all things new and different, it's usually wise to snap up any of his perries as soon as you see them – it's unlikely they'll come round again.

Gutshof Kraatz

Soon after beginning his cidermaking journey, Florian Profitlisch began noticing handfuls of abandoned pear trees around his home in north-eastern Germany. One thing led to another, and despite having no prior knowledge of what perry should taste like, he began to make some. His fruits are wildings that have grown out of rootstocks, so varieties are often unnamed and unknown, forcing him to create his own mental map of flavours.

That hasn't stopped him from determinedly crafting a range of still, carbonated, bottle-conditioned and traditional method perry, or 'birnenwein'. North-east Germany may not have had much of a perry-making past, but with Florian around it could have an interesting future.

Gutshov Kraatz's Florian Profitlisch

Jörg Geiger

Perry is compared a little too often to Champagne for my liking, and the comparison doesn't always fly. But one of the exceptions I'll make is for Jörg Geiger. Working with Swabian meadow fruit, Jörg makes a broad range of perries, and his specialty is traditional method. He applies this to a range of varieties, but stateliest of all is the Champagner Bratbirne, which he offers with various levels of lees ageing. Whistle-clean, immensely refined, perfectly marrying the toasty, lightly smoky effects of autolysis with the variety's natural minerality, mouthwatering acidity and vivid green and tropical fruit, it is one of the most compelling Champagne alternatives in the world of cider and perry.

Kertelreiter

Despite his protests to the contrary, without Barry Masterson this book wouldn't exist. In the last few years there can be no one who has devoted themselves so completely to perry and perry pear trees: whether he's uncovering the lost history of Central European perry, mapping the ancient orchards of Schefflenz, tending the International Perry Pear Project, or

Kertelreiter pear tree, with a Barry for scale

making some of the most exciting perry in the world. Almost always dry, often made from the fruits of just a handful of trees – sometimes only one – his Kertelreiters are some of the most vivid and arresting perries I have tasted. Originally a home brewer, Barry brings the curiosity of a historian and the playfulness of craft beer along with the sensitivity to fruit of the best perrymakers. Whether it's a recreation of a historic spiced perry, a showcase of a variety or single tree, or his annual ripe, melony Levitation blend, opening a Kertelreiter is one of perry's ultimate special occasions.

Luxembourg

Ramborn

Ramborn are Luxembourg's perry revivers. Though fruit has likely been pressed and fermented in this tiny country since it formed part of the northern border of the Roman Empire, cider and perry culture had disappeared, just as it almost had in south-west Germany, across the border. But like its neighbour, Luxembourg still boasted ancient perry pear trees, many indigenous (such as Luxemburger Mostbirne) and reaching deep into their fourth century. Step forward Ramborn, whose founders shared memories of their grandparents pressing fruit for 'viez', the local term for most. In addition to orchard conservation, they make award-winning perries with a winemaker's sensibility towards fruit – from light, fresh, supremely juicy summer thirst-quenchers to weighty, tannic, barrel-aged, stately affairs, and even pear eau-de-vie and ultra-honeyed ice perry.

The Ramborn team

THE REST OF WEST AND EAST EUROPE

As cider continues its gradual worldwide revolution so perry follows slowly but steadily behind it. Almost all of the countries in which the fermented pear has found a home have well-established cider cultures. Ireland has been prime apple-growing country for centuries, and some of its best makers have proven themselves every bit as good at perry as their UK counterparts – generally planting traditional perry pears to boot. The orchards tended by David Watson and his cousin, Barry Walsh, at Killahora, near Cork, boast amongst the widest variety of perry pears I've ever encountered – from Britain, France, Germany, Austria and beyond.

As Europe gradually remembers its perry pedigree, and international enthusiasm for aspirational cider and perry continues to grow, so makers across disparate countries, particularly countries where vines can struggle, have turned their hands to the pear. Some of these countries have access to wild seedling pears, some with all the tannin and acidity of the propagated perry pears of the UK, France and Austria, while others, like Elegast in The Netherlands, embrace the perfume and softness of fruit that comes through culinary varieties.

One of the most exciting emerging perry countries in Europe might be Italy. Though given its borders with Switzerland and Austria, perhaps that shouldn't be surprising. As you might expect, cider and perry are concentrated in the north of the country, where a growing cluster of makers – armed with Italy's rich body of winemaking knowhow – are applying themselves to apples and pears. Two leading advocates of this Italian renaissance are Andrea Bedini of Torino Cider Club and Marco Manfrini, Italy's first pommelier, who together have formed Associazione Pommelier e Assaggiatori di Sidro. Though acknowledging that the Italian perry scene is both tiny and fledgling, Andrea eagerly tells me about eight producers who have set themselves to the task. Using a wide range of pears – (Madernassa and Spadone seem particularly popular) – these makers have explored single varieties and blends in styles ranging from still to traditional method. Unsurprisingly, in the homeland of prosecco, there are at least a few Charmat method bottlings too. In a country world-famous for cool, fresh, fruity white wines, perry feels like a perfect fit.

SELECTED WEST AND EAST EUROPEAN PRODUCERS

Eastern Europe

Berryland (Ukraine)

Until 2022 Vitalii Krvayha made a bewildering array of stunning natural drinks, including perries from indigenous fruits picked in the Kyiv and Bukovina regions, in his Berryland Cidery in Ukraine. Using varieties such as Noyabska, Bukovinka and Bera, many of them picked from wilding trees, his perries were fragrant, zesty, citrusy drinks, distinct in flavour from any others I've tried. Devastatingly, towards the start of Russia's illegal invasion, Vitalii's cidery was destroyed. Ukraine's cider and perry scene is remarkably dynamic and engaged, led by people like Vitalii and the family merchants, Cider Enthusiasts. This entry is written in support and solidarity, and in the hope that the resilient people of Ukraine will prevail, and that Vitalii will be able to build his business anew.

Jaanihanso (Estonia)

If I was compiling a wishlist of producers I'd like to see imported to the UK, Jaanihanso would be near the top. Having learned their craft under the venerable auspices of Somerset's Burrow Hill, they make the most graceful, ethereal traditional method drinks from their local Estonian fruit in an 18th-century farmhouse. Besides their supremely aromatic perry, wild fermented for primary fermentation before at least eight months' ageing on lees, they make a rounded, fruity, double-distilled eau-de-vie. One day I won't have to daydream anymore. One day.

Jaanihanso ferment all sorts of fruit

Mr Plūme (Latvia)

Māris Plūme and Dace Smilniece-Plūme picked a good place for their perry education, working on the Distelberger family farm in the Mostviertel for the 2010 and 2011 harvest. So it's no surprise that many of the trees they grafted in their native Latvia are Austrian varieties. They've since combined this with local wildings and even a couple of British pears, with plans to graft a few hundred more trees in the next few years. Inspired by the clean, fruity, high-acid style of the Mostviertel, and the finesse of Champagne, since 2020 they've released vivacious traditional method perry aged a year on its lees.

Mr Plūme

Ireland

The Cider Mill, Slane

'There is no tradition of pear growing or perry in Ireland,' Mark Jenkinson of the Cider Mill, Slane, tells me bluntly. 'The climate is too cold and damp except in sheltered or coastal spots.' That hasn't stopped Mark, who is an expert on Irish cider history and apple varieties, from turning his attention to the pear. He has harvesting rights to an orchard of French varieties – mainly Plant de Blanc, de Cloche, and Fausset – and in 2016 planted his own orchard of 120 English varieties on pyrodwarf rootstock, farmed with biodynamic practices for the last 10 years. Past their usual northern limits his pears might be, but his French varieties 'Piorraí' is a floral, aromatic treat. Only made in small quantities, it's one well worth hunting out.

Killahora Orchards

Following David Watson around his astonishing self-planted orchards on Ireland's south coast left my puny waif of a palate begging for mercy. David has collected as many different varieties of pear (and apple) as he possibly can, and we seemed to try every one of them – each, it seemed, more mouth-grindingly tannic than the last. The result is one of the best libraries of pear varieties anywhere in Europe: Swabian, Austrian, British, French, and more besides. Having planted them all within the last 15 years, most have only recently begun bearing fruit, but Killahora's Fine Perry – made with his wife, Kate, and cousin Barry Walsh, previously modelled on the style of AOP Domfront, now increasingly drier vintage on vintage – showcases this fruit diversity with a swathe of elegant minerality and beautifully ripe fruit. Already superb, expect even more excitement as that wondrous orchard matures.

Llewellyns Orchard

Ireland may not have the same perry heritage as its neighbours, but can anyone else boast that their perry has been drunk by the president of the United States of America, as David Llewellyn can? Having grafted his own pioneering, unsprayed orchard of over 40 different pear varieties, including one he discovered and propagated himself, David set himself to making traditional method perry that could rival Champagne. It's testament to his success that his 2014 was served to Joe Biden at a Dublin banquet. Let's hope the White House stocked up.

Kate, Dave and Barry, Killahora Orchards

Italy

Apple Blood

Inspired by the ancient varieties around them in their Alpine
home of Trentino, Francesco, Federico and Davide began
experimenting with local pears in 2020. Initially highlighting
the Spadone del Curato pear as a single variety (*spadone* means
'sword', which gives a clue as to the perry's acidity!) they've
since bottled blends of Spadone and table pears, further single
varieties and even piders. As experimental with yeasts and
styles as they are with varieties, they've played with single
yeast strains and multiple strains, maturation in French oak
barriques and stainless steel, Charmat method and bottle
fermentation. Expect further investigations in the near future.

Cascina Danesa

This third-generation grower-maker tending an organic 2-ha
orchard was one of Italy's earlier modern adopters of perry, having
made it for the last 10 years. Based in Bibiana, Torino, they adhere
to the Slow Food Foundation, placing a huge emphasis on their
land – their terroir – and in selecting pear varieties accordingly.
Their elegant Sidro de Pere is a blend of Madernassa, Kaiser and
Abbot, fermented in stainless steel before a secondary fermentation
in bottle with the addition of fresh juice for a natural sparkle.

Crocizia

The first of the makers recommended to me by Marco Manfrini
and Andrea Bedini. Based in the Parma Apennines, Crocizia, like
many new European perrymakers, are also natural winemakers,
tending organically certified vineyards and orchards and making
drinks without the use of additives, clarifiers, stabilizers, yeasts
or enzymes. They turned their attention to perry in 2017 and were
singled out by Andrea for the elegance and peculiarity of their
blend of Nobile pears and table varieties. Spontaneously fermented,
unusually, in open-topped fermenters, it's bottled pét nat-style
before fermentation concludes. 'An iconic bottle', Andrea tells me.

The Netherlands

Elegast

It was drinking this Dutch producer's sparkling perries that showed me how ignorant I had formerly been about the potential for perries from dessert fruit. There aren't many, if any, perry pears growing in The Netherlands, but that hasn't stopped Arjen Meeuwesen and Teun Durlinger making vibrant pét nat and traditional method perries from old local orchards. Arjen tells me that tree age is key to aromatic and flavour intensity, and that the natural acidity he finds is critical to producing a balanced drink. Using varieties like St Remy, Gieser Wildeman, Lucas and Legipont, his perries are green-scented, with citrus, fresh flowers and a unique touch of mint that I've never come across on another perry but found unforgettably alluring.

UWE Cider

Appropriately for a book about perry published by the Campaign for Real Ale, here's a producer who makes both. And why not? Though very different drinks, we've seen that beer and perry can be unlikely friends, and curious makers and drinkers these days are increasingly interested in cross-category exploration. UWE – the name comes from the last three letters of their home, the Betuwe, and underlines their interest in reflecting place in their drinks – have been doing so since 2007 using fruit from their own unsprayed orchards and from their food forest in Park Lingezegen in Elst. They ferment with ambient yeast and have played with styles ranging from hybrids to distillation to traditional methods, always with that distinctive UWE stamp.

Poland

Cydr Chyliczki

Right now, outside the biggest European cider nations, Poland currently rivals Norway, in my opinion, as the continent's most exciting cider destination. Well-documented by Rita Krawczyk in her excellent 'Cider from Poland' blog, the country is seeing a renaissance. This has come to my attention through the astonishing ice ciders I've tasted in competitions, and one of the very best producers is Cydr Chyliczki, founded in 2014, who, I was delighted to discover, also make delicious sparkling and dessert perries from old, organic Mazovian orchards, including the country's first ice perry. If the rest of Poland's corps of superb cidermakers catch on to the qualities of the pear, Europe had better watch out.

Filomelos

Another Rita recommendation, and the first Polish perry I was lucky enough to try after she kindly passed on a bottle. Adam Droździel planted an orchard of apples and pears in 2013 on land inherited from his grandfather. Specifically choosing varieties bred only for perry (including England's ancient Barland), he and his team make blended sparkling perry in a range of styles, with production set to increase as the orchard gradually matures. As ever, perry is a waiting game.

NORTH AMERICA

'O, cheap American Perry!
Most pleasant American Perry!
We need only all bear down, knock, and call,
And we'll have the American Perry.'

('American Perry', 1813)

Perry's presence in the annals of American history is limited, especially when compared to the genuinely nation-shaping roles that whiskey (and, indeed, cider) have played. Researching this book, I was told on more than one occasion that it hadn't been a feature. Yet, when one listens carefully, there are whispers that drift across the centuries from as far back as the likes of Beale and Hartlib in England. Seldom distinct, these are tantalising glimpses rather than a full picture. The suggestion of a presence.

It was certainly brought to Virginia by early European settlers in the 17th century. Alcohol production was a central feature of colonial life and settlers were keen to plant all the familiar crops of their home countries, especially those that facilitated wine, beer and cider. Amidst all this the pear found its first American home, and perry, along with pear brandy, was made in reasonable quantities. Around the late 17th century, one Richard Kingsmill made 40 or 50 butts of perry a year from the trees that grew in his orchard.

For most evidence of early American perry, though, we head north-east, to New England and New York State. 'Here in the Finger Lakes perry occupies a similar space as cider,' Autumn Stoscheck, maker and owner at Eve's Cidery, tells me. 'Except maybe with less colonial nostalgia. A beverage with origins in the UK and temperate parts of Europe whose production was brought to this continent by colonial settlers.'

The oldest living fruit tree in the United States is a pear tree, the Endicott Pear, planted by John Endicott, governor of the Massachusetts Bay colony around 1629. Still standing today, it was probably used mainly for cooking. But did it ever make perry? While we can't know for sure, we do know that cuttings from the tree were taken (President John Adams took a few) and that 'Government Endicot' and 'Endicot of Salem' were advertised as suitable for perry in the north-east.

*Wild pears can b[e]
hard to reach*

Even if Endicott's original wasn't harvested for perry, other trees in the area certainly were. Stephen Nissenbaum's *The Battle for Christmas* tells the story of four men from Salem bursting into 72-year-old John Rowden's house on Christmas night, 1679, drunkenly singing and stating that 'they came to be merry and drink perry, and perry they would have before they went'. On John's refusal (they attempted to pay him with lead pieces), they looted and smashed part of his house, throwing stones and bones at his adopted son.

Though the original plantings had been brought over from Europe, the pears that went on to be propagated in America were, like many other fruits, according to U.P. Hedrick's *The Pears of New York*, 'for the most part seedlings until as late as 1830'. These wild, tough and bitter pears would have made poor eating. Cooking would have softened them, but Hedrick's suggestion is that 'the great object of growing pears was for making perry'.

By the early 19th century, when Thomas Knight was undertaking his own pomological research in Herefordshire, catalogues issued by fruit nurseries near both New York and Boston were advertising not only propagated varieties but specifically chosen perry pears from Britain and Europe. An example from Prince and Mills names, over the span of around a decade across the 1820s and 1830s, 'Alduira, Besberry, Barland, New Holmar, Taunton Squash [sic], Huffcap – for Perry, said to afford a liquor equal to Champaign.' Perry pears from France, Germany and Austria also featured, alongside those intriguing Government Endicots, 'good and in use for perry'.

When Commodore Oliver Perry defeated the British at the battle of Lake Eyrie, the commemorative song, an extract of which is at the start of this chapter, made it clear that the drink certainly registered in the national psyche. In the years leading up to the civil war, perry was still cited as 'annually made in considerable quantities [...] in several places in our Eastern States,' by *The Fruits and Fruit Trees of America*.

So what happened? Frustratingly, its exit from the stage seems even less notable than was its presence upon it. By the time Hedrick was penning *Pears of New York* in 1921, he was bemoaning that 'although perry, the expressed juice of pears, is quite as refreshing as cider, this by-product of the fruit is little known in America'.

Small fruits, big flavours

While there doesn't appear to be a single definite answer, a perfect storm of troubles may offer some clues. By the late 19th century cider itself, from its position as a central feature of early colonial life, was being edged out – in part by the huge popularity of German-inspired lager. By the early 20th the temperance movement had led to prohibition, a disastrous experiment that decimated orchards whose fruits had been used for alcoholic drinks. Even following prohibition, the relative speed of repropagating trees compared to growing cereals and brewing beer meant cider didn't make a comeback.

For pears and perry though, there was an additional, perhaps even more violent, antagonist. While they may have found a happy climate, especially in the north-eastern states, pear trees were foreign to American soil, pests and diseases. In the 1780s an epidemic ripped through orchards along the Hudson. Though apples and other fruits were affected, it was pear trees that seemed by far the most susceptible, so much so that this new blight took the name 'Pear blight,' or, because of the blackened, scorched appearance that affected trees took on, 'fireblight'.

As early as 1805, orchardists were questioning the suitability of pears to the United States, such was the virulence with which fireblight was decimating the trees. As modern growers in both America and England know, there is no cure for fireblight, and the bacteria can't be seen until the tree is already heavily infected. Easily transmitted by humans walking from orchard to orchard, it's no wonder that pear trees suffered such devastation, or that producers and orchardists concluded that, ultimately, there were easier – and more popular – drinks to make.

Seedlings of revival

Around 15 years ago – a little earlier for a few visionaries – a movement began. American cider, which had fallen so far from prominence, started to gather traction again; crucially, also in cities. Fast forward to 2023 and the country has arguably the most dynamic, joined-up, innovative, vocal and enthusiastic cider scene in the world, spearheaded by the American Cider Association and world-leading producers, and celebrated at CiderCon, the world's biggest cider convention.

Taking inspiration from the biggest cider nations in the world – grafting English and French varieties where possible – while adding a distinct homegrown flavour with indigenous American varieties, it's no surprise that increasing numbers of the most inquisitive producers have turned their attention to cider's perennial sidekick.

Though few and far between, the great modern American perries are more than worth the search. Eve's, in the Finger Lakes, tell me of a surprising plethora of local, now-wild, tannic pears which exist thanks to the expert agriculturalists of the Haudenosaunee Confederacy, who lived on this land and maintained enormous orchards of apples, pears and peaches until they were forced out by government troops in a genocidal campaign of the late 18th century.

Eve's certainly aren't the only north-eastern maker reviving the drink. Black Duck, on the banks of Lake Cayuga, are perhaps the Finger Lakes' most enthusiastic perry champions, maintaining their own orchards as well as harvesting wilding pears. Steve Selin, at nearby South Hill, has also made stunning examples. All three have experimented with planting English varieties in these rugged hills, but just as the early perry pioneers found, life isn't easy for European perry pears here.

'It's a very disease-rich area', Autumn tells me. Fireblight has wreaked havoc with the English varieties she grafted, leading her to experiment with pears that show greater resistance. In the meantime, those wildings are doing sterling service.

The beautiful colours of harvest time

On the other side of the country, perry is also carving out a foothold in the more-protected region west of the Rocky Mountains – in Oregon, where the pear is the state fruit, and across the borders in Washington and even California. Fireblight is less of a problem here, so orchards have established themselves well, but, for the most part, these are eating pears, destined for the culinary market.

Many American producers have embraced this, choosing to make delicate, crisp, floral styles of perry from this abundance of culinary pears. Blossom Barn is one such Oregon producer – one of the few American makers for whom perry is the primary product, via bright, dry creations reminiscent of some Italian white wines, and joyful, fruity treats flavoured with natural juices. EZ Orchards, one of America's most revered cider-makers, also utilised Oregon's bounty of culinary pears, growing their own Forelle, Comisc and Bosc in the cool Willamette Valley.

There are tannic perry pears to be found, too, with French and English varieties being used by makers including Dragon's Head and the small-but-perfectly-formed Empyrical. I remember with special fondness a bold, structural, complex French pear bottling from Seattle Cider Company.

American makers are impossible to generalise, being as disparate geographically as they are in pear varieties and ethos. And it would be a gross exaggeration to suggest perry is more than a minority concern. Fireblight remains a menace, though researchers are working on disease management and breeding suitable varieties to cope with American conditions – work that will be globally crucial as the blight spreads internationally. It's also worth noting that, here, 'pear cider' doesn't have the same legal definition as elsewhere, often referring instead to an apple base to which pear juice or flavouring has been added.

But in this cauldron of creativity, home to an increasing number of world-class cidermakers, a long-established, world-leading wine industry, a relentless spirit of innovation allied to scrupulous attention to best-practice in production, and an association dedicated to unifying makers and pooling knowledge, it would take a brave soul to bet against American perry's presence growing in significance. Some of the world's best perries will likely come to be pressed from American fruit – a few already are. Make no mistake: from the forest-clad Finger Lakes hills to Oregon and Washington's Pacific valleys, and the sun-ripened Californian south, an American perry revival has begun.

SELECTED NORTH AMERICAN PRODUCERS

In the spirit of full disclosure, having had limited opportunity to travel around the perrymakers of the USA, one or two makers listed below are recommendations from other enthusiasts. While I hope to taste their wares myself someday, you may rest assured that those who made these recommendations are people whose opinions on perry I trust implicitly.

Pacific Northwest

Art and Science

A sporadically popular debate in cider and perry circles seems to be 'is the making of it an art or a science?' This Oregonian maker would seem to suggest both – and I'd agree! Working with their own and local orchards, using foraged, organic and even biodynamic fruit, and opting for wild fermentation, they seek to make perry that truly expresses its pears and its place. Using perry pears, dessert pears and varieties from wild seedling trees, they make six different perries, including single varieties, blends, pét nats, barrel-aged – even amphora-fermented, following the Georgian-inspired qvevri techniques that are now popular in natural wine.

Blossom Barn

It's perry or bust at Jeremy Hall and Erin Chaparro's Blossom Barn in south Oregon. Inspired by the perries of Herefordshire and Normandy, but surrounded by Oregon's orchards of culinary fruit, they tread their own path to make light, easy-drinking, delightful perries from local eating pears, while also planting English, French and Romanian varieties (Erin tells me Romanian pears do particularly well). Ranging from oak-aged, serious drinks to refreshing, dry, stainless steel-fermented expressions and sweeter, fruit-flavoured crowd-pleasers, this perry barn is a thumping celebration of Oregon's state fruit.

Dragon's Head

Another maker who comes with a glowing recommendation from none other than Mr Tom Oliver. 'Always Wes and Laura Cherry at Dragon's Head – with any of their perry,' he tells me, when I ask for his favourite makers. In their own orchards in Washington State's Vashon Island, just across the Puget Sound from Seattle, they make perry in a variety of ways from local fruit and their own graftings of English and French perry pears. Their Methode Traditionnelle, if you can find it, blended across varieties and vintages before secondary fermentation and on-lees maturation, is one of the true wonders of the perry world.

Empyrical

Beginning with feral seedling pears foraged around the Puget Sound Islands, Adam Wargacki and Elizabeth Lockhart researched old heirloom varieties for over a decade as they planted their Empyrical orchard in Washington's Snohomish River Valley. In 2021 they went commercial and by 2023 had already won Best Traditional Perry and Micro Producer of the Year at GLINTCAP, as well as New Cidery of the Year at the NW Cider Cup. Already an award-winning winemaker, it is the structure and aromatic intensity of fine wine that Adam looks to as his guiding star, with European pears like Winnal's Longdon, Hendre Huffcap, Yellow Huffcap, Barland and Thielersbirne inspiring Empyrical's cuvées.

Nashi Orchards

The pear didn't only travel west from its original home in the mountains of modern Western China. On its journey east it mutated into species entirely distinct from the *Pyrus communis* that ended up in Europe, and it is these fruits – so-called 'Asian' or 'Nashi' pears –that are celebrated by Vashon Island's Nashi Orchards. Marvellously describing their produce as 'Perry and Cider' (the order is important with these drinks), Jim Gerlach and Cheryl Lubbert began their journey when they fell in love with a house designed in the 17th-century Japanese tradition and boasting a 300-tree Nashi pear orchard. Though also making perry from European pears and wildings, their Nashi Pear perries are the stars, revelling in lithe brightness and crisp acidity.

Nashi Orchards' Jim Gerlach

Snowdrift

Peter Ringsrud fell in love with cider around 2003. Trained by England's meticulous Peter Mitchell, he makes supremely clean, expressive ciders and perries from his own and local fruit in Washington State. When I raise the question of 'best American perries', Snowdrift's Perry Reserve is, more often than not, the first answer I get back. A traditional method, made with European perry pear varieties, clocking in at a mighty (by perry standards) 10% ABV, it is one of the richest, fullest perries made anywhere on the continent – and indeed the world.

The Finger Lakes

Blackduck
'Perry is the noblest of the pome fruit beverages,' states the Blackduck website. Their own examples take advantage of both the Finger Lakes' bounty of wildings as well as extensive plantings of European varieties in their orchards on the shores of Lake Cayuga. Also taking graftwood from the wild trees, their plantings are now a diverse blend of native Finger Lake fruit and such varieties as Yellow Huffcap, Butt, Gin and Brandy. Dedicated to 'hands off' minimum intervention, with ambient yeasts and nothing added besides the fruit, they proudly continue the centuries-old perry tradition of the north-eastern states.

Eve's
My American perry revelation came with a wild-fermented, aromatic, textural wilding perry made by the team at Eve's. A 2020 vintage which, the description rather wonderfully explained, had taken 150 miles of walking from perrymaker Matt Moser-Miller to harvest. Autumn Stoscheck, founder and head maker, tells me that, in many years, foragers in the Finger Lakes are more likely to find an abundance of wild pears than wild apples – a legacy of the Haudenosaunee, whose efforts at land and seed rematriation Eve's are committed to supporting. It's largely thanks to these wild trees that Eve's are able to make perry at all, since their own plantings of English varieties have struggled immensely with fireblight. Undoubtedly one of the world's greatest makers.

Ezra and Autumn, Eve's

Grisamore

Simon Ingall and his brother founded Grisamore Ciderworks in 2015 on their family farm. Formerly a U-Pick operation, their father and grandfather had planted table fruit trees in the 1980s – Seckel, Bartlett, and Flemish Beauty. Though Simon has made perry from these varieties, he has since planted perry pears, including Barland, Butt, and Hendre Huffcap, still less than a decade old at the time of writing and only just starting to fruit. Experimenting with both pitched yeast and wild fermentation, Simon has been irretrievably taken by this most pernicious of drinks. 'I hope to have a similar pear crop to our apples in my lifetime,' he tells me.

South Hill

Like most Finger Lakes makers, Steve Selin began his journey foraging wild apples and pears from the surrounding forests. Today, he tends his own organic and biodynamic orchards of American and European varieties. One of the friendliest makers I've ever met, and one of my favourite American producers, it was the connection he felt between Champagne and perry that inspired Steve's investigations of the pear. Accordingly, he makes his perry in the traditional method, with no dosage, to promote the natural flavours of the fruit itself. Intriguingly, as well as pears from a huge wilding, and Seckel pears from nearby orchards, he uses Gelbmöstler pears planted around 100 years ago, pointing to perry still being made in the area around 1900.

Steve Selin at
South Hill

California

Hemly

Another Californian maker, using fresh-pressed, estate-grown Bartlett and Bosc. Preferring the term 'pear cider', the Hemly team, led by Sarah, make both all-pear creations and perries flavoured with other local, fresh-pressed fruits, herbs and spices. Leaning more towards pears than apples – their flagship pear cider was the drink that began their story – everything they do is about crisp, fresh, enormously accessible flavours, from their oak-aged Brut to their Strawberry Lavender blend and even their spicy Sloughhouse Jalepeño.

Raging Cider and Mead Co

You just never know where you'll find perry, but sunny California was a place that certainly took me by surprise. Yet pears have been planted at high altitude (up to 5,000ft) in the diverse granitic soils of the San Diego Mountains since the late 1800s. Dave Carr, whose parents (like all the

Dave Carr and family at Raging

275

best people) originate in Merseyside, was captivated by perries such as Ross-on-Wye's Flakey Bark, which he encountered when visiting family in England, and decided to make his own at his family cidery. They make a fresh and fruity style with the Lincoln Pear variety, but Dave's favourite is the 'Perry Feral', so-named for the wild trees from which he harvests high-tannin fruit. Fermented with ambient yeasts, it's reminiscent of the legendary Ross-on-Wye bottling that inspired him.

Midwest

Æpeltreow

Æpeltreow, in south-east Wisconsin, nicely encapsulate the spectrum of American perry. They have used European perry pears, including Thorn, Winnal's Longdon, Butt and Gin, to make bold, tannic, mouth-filling styles while also leaning into the American tradition of utilising culinary pears for something lighter, crisper and more approachable. Keen to emphasise where they believe perry (and cider) align with other drinks, they describe themselves as a 'winery', but in this instance their wines are of apples and pears, and have picked up awards aplenty at GLINTCAP, one of cider and perry's most important competitions. They're also distillers, and have played with pear spirit and mistelle to boot. A proper American all-rounder.

Canada

Domaine des Salamandres

You'd hope the country that invented ice cider would have applied the method to pears too. Domaine des Salamandres, named for the local amphibians of Hemmingford, Québec, and boasting ten species in their orchards, is happy to oblige. Using Flemish Beauty, Bosc, D'Anjou and Bartlett pears, they are one of the ultimate rebuttals to the suggestion that only traditional perry pears make good perry. This is the place to head for those with a sweet tooth. Besides decadent ice perries made in both methods – cryo-concentrated and tree-frozen cryo-extracted, swimming with tropical fruit, honeys and beautifully balanced acidity – they also make rich, gastronomic, barrel-aged ice perry mistelles matured for five and even ten years. Not to mention still, dry 'pear wine' as well.

AUSTRALIA, NEW ZEALAND AND ASIA

Australia

Tannic perry pears can be even harder to come by in other parts of the world; the time they take to grow mean most makers are still in the waiting phase. For the time being, many are exploring the undersung possibilities of culinary fruits, and exploiting the different flavours and textures found not only through these varieties but the unique terroirs of their various homes.

Australia, increasingly, could be perry's most enthusiastic next home outside the countries and regions already highlighted. Like America, it already boasts world-class wine and a craft cider culture that has come on leaps and bounds in the last decade, as a corps of talented producers spearheaded by an ambitious and well-organised association – Cider Australia – have raised the bar of quality, availability and education.

'There is some debate about the word perry,' Warwick Billings, current President of Cider Australia tells me. 'Some say it should be the only description, but the reality is that recognition of the word is poor.' The most common perry by far is Somersby's Pear Cider, a reflection that – as in the UK – the market is dominated by big commercial brands of relatively low juice content. Similarly, as Nick Geoghegan of Small Acres Cyder tells me, 'perry tends to be an add-on'.

It could, perhaps, have been a different story. In 1803 the third governor of Australia, Philip Gidley King, ordered apple and pear trees 'suitable for cider and perry'. Those trees never arrived, and shortly thereafter brewers cornered the Australian drinks market.

For the most part, Australian perry is built on culinary pears. Warwick himself, through his LOBO Cider company, is still selling a 2014 'Dry Pear' made with the 'monster' Pound Pear and appropriately fragrant Lemon Bergamot Pear. He cites Small Acres and CORE as his picks for modern Australian perry, giving special mention to Paracombe for having taken the brave step of specialising.

'There are some brave souls starting out on the perry pear road,' he says. 'It will be interesting to see the outcomes as trees come into bearing decent fruit quantities.' Some varieties have already been grafted, the most common being Yellow Huffcap, Gin, Moorcroft and Green Horse.

Like Australia's cider, most domestic perry production is based around cooler climate regions. 'While the main pear growing area is Victoria's Goulburn Valley, perry makers seem more likely to be based in the traditional apple growing areas like Tasmania and Orange, or wine regions like South Australia,' says Nick.

With Australia's array of superb terroirs, meticulous hygiene in the cellar, and track record with both wine and cider, Philip Gidley King's ambition might, 200 years later, be realised.

New Zealand

Neighbouring New Zealand, whose combination of seemingly limitless sunshine and relatively cool climate facilitated a wine phenomenon in their Sauvignon Blanc, as well as a host of aromatic whites, fresh, elegant reds and an increasingly admired hop industry, have similarly discovered a talent and fondness for fermented apple, with pear, naturally, following behind.

At present most of their perries are light, easy-drinking, lower-alcohol drinks from culinary fruit, generally labelled 'pear cider'. But in Wairarapa's TeePee, headed by Trevor and Frances FitzJohn, they have a superb maker dedicated to tannic perry pears; proof that these varieties could have a future in the orchards of New Zealand and the talented hands of the country's makers.

Intriguingly, Gabe Cook tells me that when in New Zealand, he unexpectedly came across a perry pear tree. Grafted, so entirely deliberate, he estimated it at around 150 years old – ancient by New Zealand standards. The current owners hadn't known what it was, or even that it was there. Who grafted it? What was made from it? As ever, the world of perry throws up more questions than answers.

Asia

While much of this book has been dedicated to the results of the pear's western migration from its origins in modern Western China, the fruit also travelled east, producing new varieties and species as it went. China, today, is the world's largest grower of pears, and although I've yet to encounter Chinese perry, the possibilities – especially in light of the country's flourishing wine scene – are tantalising.

Perry is certainly made in Japan, as Lee Reeve – one of the country's most important cider personalities – eagerly informs me. At present, producers are predominantly deploying dessert fruit, principally Bartlett and D'Anjou, mainly in the mountainous, high-altitude region of the Nagano Prefecture, where hot days and cool nights offer perfect fruit-growing temperatures. Lee is yet to be convinced by perries made with Asian 'Nashi' pears, but the results achieved with these fruits by Nashi Orchards in the USA suggest wonderful potential for pure, aromatic, thirst-quenching, aperitif-style perries. Japan's cider and perry scene, while still fledgling, is increasingly vocal and confident. Another exciting space to watch.

Perrymakers outside Western Europe and the USA are few and far between, and the difficulty in tracking them down means I will certainly have missed out not only talented producers, but countries, and conceivably even whole continents, in which perry is being quietly produced. But the tenacity of those who have dedicated themselves to this most mischievous yet magical of fruits and fermentations, and the ever-increasing quality being achieved, gives me great optimism. If perrymakers around the world can join themselves up to share knowledge and experience, we are in for a bright and exciting future.

SELECTED PRODUCERS FROM AUSTRALIA, NEW ZEALAND AND ASIA

Australia and New Zealand

Small Acres Cyder

The Kendell Family founded Small Acres in Orange, New South Wales, in 2006. Quickly gaining a reputation, their poiré and traditional method sparkling perry caught the eye (and palate) of Nick Geoghegan and Jannene, who moved to the area in 2018. When the owners moved on in 2020, Nick and Jannene took the risky mid-COVID plunge of buying the cidery and have continued its legacy with some of Australia's most lauded perries. With a handful of perry pear trees, as well as culinary varieties like Beurrie Bosch, Packhams, Howells and Red Anjou, the medium-sweet Poiré and Methode Traditionelle Perry, aged 12 months on lees before disgorgement, are two of the most highly rated drinks in Australia's cider and perry scene.

CORE

You must be doing something right if you're winning Best Traditional Perry at the prestigious Australian Cider Awards, and that's exactly what CORE have done for the last two years, defending the 2021 award they won with their traditional method 'Perilous' at the 2022 competition. While Perilous represents the high end for this 80-year-old, biodynamically managed producer in Western Australia's Pickering Brook, they also make easier-drinking, refreshing examples, as well as fruit-flavoured perries, best enjoyed overlooking the orchards from their beautiful estate. You can even book to go and do some of the picking, perhaps claiming a little of that award-winning credit for yourself.

Paracombe Premium Perry

Fourth-generation pear orchardist Damian McArdle taught himself to make perry in 2012 as a way to use fruit from his Adelaide Hills orchards that would have been rejected on aesthetic grounds by the supermarkets. Initially self-taught, he made a UK study trip in 2013, visiting Oliver's, Ross-on-Wye, Skyborry and others. He's since become the only maker in Australia to put primary focus on perry, making mainly crisp, low-tannin, elegant perries from single varieties such as Lemon Bergamot, Packham,

*Paracombe's
Amelia and Damian*

Beurre Bosc and Josephine. Fermenting with a wine yeast in stainless steel heightens the refreshing, pristine, aromatic, cool-climate style; the perfect perries for sunshine sipping at their Shed Door, looking out across the orchards.

TeePee Cider

Trevor and Frances started TeePee Cider at the turn of the millennium as a hobby. Being from the UK originally, and a keen student of the golden age of cider and perry in the 17th century, Trevor was keen to track down

cider apples and perry pears in his adopted home of Aotearoa, New Zealand. No easy feat, but he did find two old trees, including one sent by the head gardener of Crystal Palace in 1880. Their award-winning perry is wild fermented, traditional method, and aged on its lees for two years before disgorging. Having taken scions from the old pear trees, Trevor and Frances have grafted four trees in their own orchard which have recently begun bearing.

Frances and Trevor at TeePee

Japan

VinVie

The Takemura family have been farming apples in Nagano Prefecture for three generations. Inspired to make cider in 2014, and now producing a range of ciders and wines, they've recently – naturally – turned their hands to perry as well. 'VinVie's Pear Cider is probably the one I recommend the most when people ask,' Lee Reeve tells me. 'It's easy to drink, well-balanced and affordable.' VinVie ferment it in stainless steel, with a white wine yeast, to make the most of the Bartlett variety's natural, floral crispness: a perfect afternoon perry.

The VinVie team

Kamoshika

From their elegant, spotlessly clean cidery in the spectacular green hills of Nagano's Southern Alps, Kamoshika have made ciders influenced by the naturally sparkling, off-dry creations of Normandy and Brittany since 2016. When it comes to perry, inspired by AOP Domfront, they have crafted an elegant, pét nat, French-style poiré, again made from the Bartlett pear, that Lee hails as his favourite Japanese perry of all. He's not the only one: at the time of writing, it is the reigning champion for domestic creations at the Japan Cider Cup.

Kamoshika

EPILOGUE

I write this in the beer garden of the Yew Tree Inn at Ross-on-Wye Cider & Perry Company. It is the day of their annual cider and perry trials, and I've had the privilege of guest-judging. As you'd expect, I began with the perries and tasted all 20. Life is good.

Perry suffuses this place. At my right hand is a glass of Ross-on-Wye's winning medium blend – of Thorn, Flakey Bark and Moorcroft. Showing the best of all three varieties – Thorn's citrus, Flakey's weight and Moorcroft's joyous tropicality – it is everything I look for in great still perry. Makers and drinkers are all around me; perries on draught, on keg, in 750s; single varieties and blends; perries in pint and half pint pots, in craft beer two-thirds and wine glasses. To the south is May Hill, with its pine-barnacled crest. Just a few yards from where I sit are three stone pear statues – Gin, Blakeney Red and Flakey Bark – carved by Max Nowell, son of Jean, who did so much to revive Three Counties perry.

I can't see pear trees from this spot, but I am amongst them nonetheless, in the beating heart of perry country. They have been here for millennia; planted by Romans, abandoned, scorned, written off as fodder for the desperate and deprived. They have seen both triumph and disaster and along the way have etched themselves indelibly into the story of rural Britain.

Perry, against all the odds, has endured in this tucked-away place. And not only in the Three Counties and Monmouthshire, but in the undulations of the Domfrontais and the Alpine foothills of the Mostviertel. Its ghosts still whisper in Germany, Switzerland and Luxembourg, and echo across oceans to America, Australia, New Zealand, Japan.

There is no room for complacency. In living memory, perry has been diminished almost to nothing. The ravages of fireblight and human cynicism may yet, in our lifetimes, finish the job. Too few people have even heard of perry, much less discovered the treasures beneath its little-scratched surface.

There is much to be done. This book is only a starting point; a fragment of the full, global conversation with which perry needs to engage new and existing drinkers. But in this hallowed seat of British perry, glass in hand, surrounded by the people who care most about this rare, fragile, glorious drink, it is impossible not to feel the tangible breath of a soul. A soul of ancient trees with cathedral branches; of fruit that transforms, with care, into magic; of a miracle drink from the hand-me-down past whose best years may yet be ahead of it.

A Pear-Shaped Glossary

Acetic acid (see Faults section) Common perry fault caused by the conversion of alcohol to acetic acid by acetobacter in the presence of oxygen. Also by malolactic fermentation converting citric acid to acetic acid. Both result in flavours of vinegar.

Acidity A key element of the tasting experience, promoting crispness and freshness in a perry. Levels vary depending on varieties and ripeness, but all pears contain malic and citric acid.

Aromas The fragrances given off by a perry. These are caused predominantly by natural compounds in the fruit but can be enhanced by styles and maturation choices. Levels of natural aroma vary between varieties.

Astringency The sensation of drying or bitterness given off by a perry, especially by tannins. Some astringency can add wonderful freshness, texture, and ability to pair with food, but too much can be unpleasant.

Balanced A perry whose attributes of acidity, tannin, body, and flavour feel especially harmonious, with none standing out as excessive.

Bletting A natural softening process that occurs in pears after ripening, reducing acidity and tannin, heightening sugars and altering flavour. Too much can cause issues at pressing or progress to rottenness, but can add lovely depth and richness if well managed.

Body The perception of a perry's weight in the mouth – full-bodied being weightier, like oil, and light-bodied seeming lighter, like water.

Brettanomyces A naturally occurring wild yeast strain that can add flavours to a perry ranging from cloves and spice to animal, leather, sweatiness, and even dung.

Carbonation The level of fizziness in a perry, whether naturally induced or directly carbonated by the addition of carbon dioxide.

Clear A perry that shows no sediment to the extent that it is completely transparent. (These will often, though not always, be fined or filtered.)

Co-fermentation (often abbreviated to 'co-ferment'). The result of fermentation between pears and other fruits such as apples or grapes.

Complex A perry that seems to have a particularly wide range of flavours or aromas.

Conditioned When a natural carbonation process (see 'Styles of Perry') has concluded in a perry, either in bottle or keg.

Cut The interaction of acidity in perry with food, particularly fatty food.

Dry A perry with little or no perception of sweetness.

Faulty A perry that has been affected by a biological or chemical fault (see 'Faults').

Finish The flavours remaining in the taster's mouth after a perry has been swallowed or spat.

Floral A perry giving off aromas or flavours such as blossom or flower petals.

Fresh A perry that presents bright, vivid, fruity and often zesty characteristics. Often a young perry.

Fruity A perry whose characteristics are primarily driven by primary flavours and which reminds the taster mainly of various fruits, be they stone fruit, pome fruit or citrus.

Funky A wholly subjective and completely undefined term often used euphemistically to describe faults such as acetic acid or sulphides. (Can you tell I don't much care for it?)

Grafting The act of cloning a tree by attaching wood or buds from the desired variety to rootstock of a different variety.

Green A perry with flavours of leaves, grass or sharp fruits like limes or green apples. This can sometimes indicate an underripe perry or it could be a variety that naturally inclines towards those flavour characteristics.

Hazy (also 'cloudy'). A perry, usually unfiltered, in which tiny particles of sediment have thrown a natural haze.

Mature A perry that has aged for a few years and developed pleasant tertiary flavours. Crucially, a mature perry should not be over-aged or oxidised.

Medium A perry showing a certain level of sweetness. 'Medium-dry' and 'medium-sweet' can also be used to distinguish drier or sweeter examples in this otherwise very broad bracket.

Mineral A rather subjective term used to describe aromas that remind the taster of such things as petrichor, or wet rocks such as slate.

Mouse An unpleasant fault caused by certain lactic bacteria, especially in perries with low acidity to which no sulphites have been added. Presents as a retronasal mustiness, though many drinkers are genetically unable to detect it.

Oaky A perry with pronounced flavours derived from casks or oak additives. While some oak flavour can be wonderful, 'oaky' is often used when the fruit has been overwhelmed by oak.

Oxidised A perry that has been over-exposed to oxygen and taken on flavours of acetic acid, cardboard or sherry.

Pét Nat Commonly used abbreviation of pétillant naturel. (See 'Styles of Perry')

Phenolics Heavy flavour compounds, such as tannin, that often add weight, depth and texture to a perry.

Primary flavours Flavours derived from the initial fermentation of the pears themselves.

Ripe A perry showing pronounced juicy, fruity flavours indicative of full ripeness.

Secondary flavours Flavours derived from stylistic processes chosen by the maker, including the use of oak barrels, or autolytic flavours from secondary fermentation.

Sediment Particles of dead yeast or fruit solids left in the liquid. Can actively add positively to flavour but can be removed by fining or filtration. Some perries reform a sediment in their container even after being filtered.

Simple A perry with a limited number of flavours and aromas and perhaps a shorter finish.

Sorbitol An unfermentable sugar that naturally occurs at varying levels in all pears.

Spicy A perry with flavours of sweet or savoury spices, either derived from the fruit, from oak, or from other additives.

Sulphides The result of 'stressed' yeast. These give off unpleasant smells of sulphur, cabbages and even excrement.

Sulphites Sulphur dioxide. Naturally occurs in tiny traces in perry but can also be added deliberately as a preservative and to protect against bacterial faults like mouse. Virtually undetectable in small doses, but highly-sulphited perries (generally from the biggest brands) present an alkaline soapiness.

Sweet A perry showing a high level of sweetness, whether natural or added.

Sweetness The perception level of sugar left in or added to a perry.

Tannin A polyphenol occurring in some plants, and which contributes a marvellous texture to a drink. Certain perry pears are very rich in tannin. Excessive tannin can feel astringent and may need time to soften.

Tertiary flavours Flavours that have developed through maturation. Usually derived from the fresh primary compounds breaking down or 'evolving'.

Texture The characteristics imparted by a drink in the mouth besides flavours. Tannin, acidity, and body all contribute.

Unctuous A particularly full-bodied and often sweet perry such as a mistelle or ice perry.

Varietal A perry giving off distinct characteristics of the pear from which it was made.

Variety The particular sort of pear (or pears) from which a perry has been made.

Vintage The year in which a given perry's fruit was harvested or pressed.

Wilding A tree that has grown from a randomly distributed seed rather than been specifically grafted from another variety.

Youthful A perry defined by primary flavour characteristics. Sometimes a perry whose acidity or tannin ideally wants more time to soften.

Zesty A perry that gives off bright, citrusy flavours, usually with medium to high acidity.

Thank you to all of the following who pledged support for this publication

Aaron MJ Gore – *I love you, Nellie and Cassie!*

Adam Morgan

Alison Taffs & the team *at The Hop Inn, Hornchurch*

Barry Masterson. *Well done Adam for getting this out. Perry has deserved a dedicated book for a long time! Here's to the perry makers, and the dreamers of dreams.*

Cath Potter – *Foxwhelpians love Perry too!*

Cazza *(Caroline)*

Chris Lovelace *of Mitcham (though sometimes perrypatetic).*

Chris Mansfield. *The Cider Vault at Fram Ferment – Perry & cider delivered to your door, reviews & recommendations.*

Andrew Williams. *Seven Trees Cider, Reading, UK. Congratulations Adam, all hail the humble pear!*

Damin Sawyer. *Bone & Bottle Reviews*

Dave Lloyd. *Power to the Pears!*
Love to all the orchards. Good health to one and all. Love, Dave & Vanessa.

David Lindgren of Bushel+Peck *is pleased to support this first ever book dedicated to exploring the wonders of perry and the skill, craft and creativity of all perry-makers who seek to shine a light on the oft forgotten and misunderstood delights of the fermented pear.*

David O'Malley

Dick Withecombe. *Manchester Cider Club.*

Dr Clayton Slaugther. *With Love to Ellis and Calvin. We plant our trees for you. May all your days be filled with love, family, and friends.*

Edd Codrington & Flavia Rowse

Gillian Hough *has been campaigning, supporting, advocating for and enjoying real perry since 1984!*

Jack Benjamin Toye – *Viva La Perry!*

Hogan's Cider

Justin Patrick Wells

Kevin Ellis. *Dear Haylie, a little present for you, love from Daddy xxx*

Martin Hibbard. *To my wonderful wife who likes a drop of perry.*

Michelle McGrath

Mo Moseley. *Real life: real ale, real bread, real cheese, real chocolate, real coffee, real cider, and, last but not least, real perry.*

N.R. Jenzen-Jones

Nicky Kong

Paul Morris. *To Paul. Regards, Adam*

Peter Crawford

Peter Elderton – *ciderpoint.org*

Philip Scott

Rob Laidler. *A perry pear tree is a feature of the landscape. By broadening knowledge these great sentinels can be brought back into public awareness with the production of perry.*

Stuart Hassal

Susannah Mansfield. *The Station House, Durham: multiple winners of CAMRA Cider & Perry Regional Pub of the Year – for a reason.*

Lee Reeve. *Thank you, Adam, for a book as beautiful and delicious as the drink.*

Tom Oliver, Yarys, Siarl, Val *and all at Oliver's Cider and Perry.*